ADVANCE PRAISE FOR
HUSTLE & FLOAT

"In *Hustle & Float*, Rahaf Harfoush takes on a critical question for the decade ahead: How do I get lots of important things done without burning out? If we as human achievers are to compete with machines, we need to become productively creative and creatively productive. *Hustle & Float* brings a wealth of stories, examples and practical exercises to let us bring out our best."

—BRIAN FETHERSTONHAUGH,
Worldwide Chief Talent Officer for The Ogilvy Group
and author of *The Long View: Career Strategies to
Start Strong, Reach High and Go Far*

"*Hustle & Float* explores how our values and vision of work are colliding with the disruptive force of the fourth industrial revolution. It's an essential companion for business leaders who want to navigate this new economy, and build organizations that are aligned with the needs of 'Productive Creatives'—those responsible for ensuring our new technologies create a future we all want to live in."

—KLAUS SCHWAB,
Executive Chairman of the World Economic Forum

"Rahaf Harfoush's engaging book is an encouragement for all of us whose job is to be creative in environments that seem designed for cookie-cutter production. It will make you smile. It will make you think. It may make you cry. Don't miss out on a word."

—RITA GUNTER MCGRATH,
author of *The End of Competitive Advantage: How to
Keep Your Strategy Moving as Fast as Your Business*;
Professor at Columbia Business School; Top Ten
Global Management Thinker, Thinkers50

"Disruptive technology and new business models are constantly changing the rules of business. But many people and organizations are unaware that the systems they are using are relics from a bygone era. *Hustle & Float* reveals some profound changes that can enable creative-centric, forward-looking businesses."

—DON TAPSCOTT,
best-selling author of sixteen books

"Finally a book that debunks the gap between the quality of the work that you do and how much time/effort/energy and hustle that you put into it. There's this 'hustle and grind' myth that is both unhealthy and unproven, yet everyone is buying into it. I'm so happy that Rahaf wrote *Hustle & Float*. If you're grinding yourself into dust, are you really doing your best work or just working tirelessly? Please let this amazing book guide and define you. Want to thrive? Want a healthy relationship with your work? Here you go."

—**MITCH JOEL**,
author of *Six Pixels of Separation* and *CTRL ALT Delete*

"I've interviewed hundreds of leaders about the challenges they face balancing their productivity and creativity. *Hustle & Float* perfectly balances the personal intimacy of unraveling the hidden blocks of individual performance with an impressive broad analysis of the macro-trends that have reshaped the way we work, and the type of work we do. This is a book that speaks to the pain points all creatives face in their jobs, but offers a hopeful and optimistic outlook of a more human future."

—**SRINIVAS RAO**,
host of *The Unmistakable Creative Podcast*
and author of *Audience of One*

"To succeed today, companies must balance executing incredibly fast while relentlessly innovating. Rahaf deconstructs how antiquated thinking about productivity result in demands that are counterproductive, while also highlighting what the creative outliers are doing differently in order to enable their talent to realize exceptional results!"

—**LEEROM SEGAL**,
CEO of Klick and author of *The Decoded Company*

HUSTLE

& FLOAT

Reclaim Your Creativity
and Thrive in a World Obsessed with Work

RAHAF HARFOUSH

DIVERSION
BOOKS

Diversion Books
A Division of Diversion Publishing Corp.
443 Park Avenue South, Suite 1004
New York, New York 10016
www.DiversionBooks.com

For more information, email info@diversionbooks.com

Book design by Elyse J. Strongin, Neuwirth & Associates.

First Diversion Books edition February 2019.

Paperback ISBN: 978-1-63576-578-6
eBook ISBN: 978-1-63576-577-9

Printed in the U.S.A.
SDB/1902

1 3 5 7 9 10 8 6 4 2

To my husband Jesse.
My heart. My anchor. My Home.

CONTENTS

INTRODUCTION

MAKE IT HURT SO GOOD

Craigslist has developed a well-deserved reputation for being a marketplace where no request is too bizarre. Looking for someone with Jedi powers to help induce your labor? A person with a fantastic beard who can mentor you while you grow your own? What about a personal waiter who will serve you for two hours at your local McDonald's? In 2012, Maneesh Sethi added his own quirky request: he was looking to hire someone who would literally slap him in the face whenever he was being unproductive.[1]

You see, Sethi had been using a program to measure his productivity while working and wanted to see if he could improve his performance. Naturally, he turned to Craigslist and hired a young woman who, for $8 an hour, would sit next to him and slap him if he dared to check social media or lost focus by browsing the web.

The hack worked: Sethi claims to have quadrupled his productivity during his sadomasochistic, if not amusing, work experiment. Sethi, the editor of Hackingthesystem.com, a website designed to help readers find "unconventional solutions to live better, travel further, earn more money and be more productive," is also working on a new wearable device product that lets your Facebook friends zap you if you're not following through on your goals, a technological version of having an accountability buddy.

While Sethi's slapping solution was a little unique, his determination to increase his creative output (writing blog posts, drafting proposals, etc.) has become a standard part of being a professional creative in today's hyperconnected knowledge economy, and people everywhere are coming up with new (and bizarre) ways to accomplish this goal.

I was surprised to learn that face slapping wouldn't be the strangest proposed solution. In 2013, Rob Rinehart raised more than $3 million dollars in crowdfunding for his product, Soylent. Rinehart invented the "universally applicable" nutritionally complete, beige, smoothie-like meal replacement after he noticed that making healthy meals was a task that was taking up too much time. In Silicon Valley, the popularity of protein-packed liquid meals like Soylent (and other oddly named competitors like Schmilk, Schmoylent, and People Chow) is rising, promising to remove the pesky decisions around what to eat and get busy people back to work quicker than they can chew.[2] In 2017, Soylent further expanded into the retail market, becoming available in 2,500 7-Eleven stores across the country, followed by a 2018 expansion into 450 Walmart stores. Meal replacement extreme goes mainstream.

Following the same train of thought, at a recent SXSW panel on "Life Automation for Entrepreneurs," Dave Asprey, CEO of Bulletproof, a company that helps people "enter a system of high performance every day," recommended blending the contents of your dinner to be able to "drink it while you're doing something else."[3]

Lately, it seems like every corner of the Internet is seething with tips, tricks, and hacks to help us *do more*. Want the creativity-inducing, stress-relieving benefits of meditation but don't have time to meditate? Pop-guru Deepak Chopra has a one-minute meditation that can help—it has been downloaded ten million times. Need to inspire your work ethic but don't have the right inner motivation? Lifehack.org suggests faking adversity so you have an inner incentive to "prove them wrong."[4] Schools of thought, such as David Allen's Getting Things Done, Inbox Zero, and even the Covey Quadrant have developed cult-like followings all in the name of fitting more tasks into every hour of our day.

And herein lies one of the more interesting facets of our cultural psyche: the desire for more is one of the underpinnings of our intense focus on productivity. We want to be better, faster, stronger, richer. However, by constantly striving to do more, we are highlighting that on some level we believe that what we are doing is not enough, an attitude that is reflected back at us in the host of new services and tools aimed at helping us squeeze in as much as we can into each second.

This scarcity-focused mindset has implications on our self-worth, our mental health, and our happiness. After all, on the surface, productivity is billed as a way to free up more time. We operate under the assumption that by streamlining our tasks and obligations we will be rewarded more time we can use for other, more meaningful pursuits. Instead, many of us are filling up this free time with more work.

Overwork has become a hallmark of leadership behavior. In the tech industry, Marissa Mayer admitted to 130-hour workweeks at Google and sleeping under her desk.[5] Twitter and Square co-founder Jack Dorsey claims to work sixteen-hour days[6] while sleeping only four hours a night. Elon Musk is rumored to have worked one hundred-hour workweeks for the past fifteen years! And in this way, the values trickle down-wards, galvanized by recent stories like Goldman Sachs imple-menting a new rule that interns must leave the office between midnight and 7:00 a.m., which they implemented after a young analyst committed suicide from the top-down pressure of over-working. From art to politics, it's a theme that repeats itself across industries: the continuous obsession with output that is attained at all costs, where sacrifices like lack of sleep and personal time are worn like a badge of honor.

This is particularly disturbing for knowledge-work profes-sionals who must shoehorn their creativity into these mechan-ical, often rigid methodologies that add a constant pressure to produce, produce, produce. Write faster. Draw more. Ideate con-stantly. But where did this imperative to do more come from? What has shaped our collective obsession with productivity?

SHE GRINDS FROM MONDAY TO FRIDAY, WORKS FROM FRIDAY TO SUNDAY[7]

The idea for *Hustle & Float* was born in the midst of an epic meltdown.

It was April 2014, and I had just returned home to Paris after launching my book, *The Decoded Company*. I was feeling rest-less and anxious. I didn't know what to do with the sudden increase of free time, and for some reason I felt guilty looking at the empty slots in my calendar. With each passing day, I felt a mounting pressure to find the next deliverable, book, project, client—to do something useful. Something productive.

As I surfed the web in search of inspiration, I stumbled upon a post on Tumblr that had been shared hundreds of thousands of times. It was an image of a white ceramic mug with the cap-tion, "You have the same number of hours in a day as Beyoncé." The post helpfully mentioned that this quote was also available printed on a variety of merchandise ranging from hoodies and mugs to pillows and tote bags.

There, dressed in sweatpants and surfing Tumblr on a Tuesday afternoon, the discrepancies between myself and Beyoncé, in both achievement and performance, were perfectly clear. I snapped. I FaceTimed my younger sister Riwa immediately. "Beyoncé has already done so much," I told her. "I've wasted so much time being unproductive. My life is a failure."

Now, Riwa is a practical sort of person and a firm believer that if you couldn't beat them, you should join them. "Beyoncé is amazing," she agreed. "Let's learn everything we can about her to see how she does it."

And so, two sisters became Beyoncéologists, searching the web endlessly for all articles, interviews, and videos about the woman who was voted by *Time* magazine as one of the most influential people of 2014, is considered to be the world's greatest living entertainer, and who, at thirty-five, had already transcended fame to become a bona fide cultural icon. (And who could forget her endless other accomplishments, including several Super Bowl halftime shows, singing at both the 2008 and 2012 Presidential Inaugurations, being the first woman to reach Number 1 on the Billboard 200 with five albums, and having sold over 178 million records? Don't even ask me about Beychella, Lemonade, OTRII, or that legendary music video filmed at the Louvre.)

At first, our plan backfired. Being faced with such a high level of achievement was demoralizing, but we pressed on, determined to leave no link unclicked. The majority of Beyoncé's media coverage focused on two distinct themes: her obvious creative genius, and her unrelenting work ethic. "Let's hear it for Beyoncé, the hardest-working woman in showbusiness," declared one *Guardian* headline.[8] Beyoncé's sister, Solange Knowles, commented about her sister's nonstop pace in an *ASOS* magazine cover story saying, "I have never seen anything like it my life, from anyone. It's absolutely insane."

She added that motherhood hadn't slowed Beyoncé down in the least. "Now that she's become a mother, and the way that she's able to balance that, is so inspiring. If I am ever feeling like I want to open my mouth and complain about how hard I am working, I think, 'Uhh! Sit down!'"[9] We even discovered that Beyoncé's "legendary work ethic" had become the subject of a Harvard Business School case study, the ultimate example of the Productive Creative: a woman who had managed to successfully combine her creative pursuits into a lucrative, sprawling business empire.

Hours later (Days? Weeks? Time lost all meaning as we delved deeper into our search.), we stumbled on a newspaper article so brief we almost missed it. A short quote referenced the year-long hiatus the singer took between tours in 2011. "Things were starting to get fuzzy," Beyoncé was quoted as saying. "I couldn't even tell which day or which city I was at. I would sit there at ceremonies and they would give me an award and I was just thinking about the next performance. My mother was very persistent, and she kept saying that I had to take care of my mental health."

We were stunned. Even Beyoncé, with her reputation of never-ending hard work (the singer reportedly reviews video footage after every performance and circulates notes to her team about what needs to be improved or fixed), was not immune to the perils of hyperproductivity and had battled with burnout. The woman who was the Internet's gold standard of productive time management still felt like *she* wasn't doing enough. And if Beyoncé, the platonic ideal of creative success, feels the pressure of constant creative productivity, how are the rest of us mere mortals supposed to survive? As Productive Creatives we can certainly relate to feeling the pressure that you're only as good as your last good idea.

If Beyoncé could also fall victim to this work culture epidemic, then clearly this was something worth investigating. After all, based on our society's standards, the singer represented the pinnacle of creative and financial success: recognized by her industry as the most Grammy-nominated artist of all time, Beyoncé has released several critically acclaimed albums and launched a multimillion dollar business that spans clothes, fragrances, and sponsorship deals. What more could she want?

HOW DO YOU WRITE LIKE YOU'RE RUNNING OUT OF TIME?[10]

We didn't have to look far for other signs of the effects of hyperproductivity.

The symptoms of this dysfunction are all around us. According to a Glassdoor 2014 Employment Confidence survey, the average US employee only takes half of their allocated paid vacation leave.[11] More depressingly, when they do manage to take some time off, 61 percent of respondents admitted to feeling pressured to do some work anyway. In 2004, a study published by the Families and Work Institute estimated that one third of all American workers could be categorized as chronically over-worked—a condition that has been linked to an increased risk of clinical depression and a drop in performance.[12] In fact, sleep deprivation has been labelled a public epidemic by the Center for Disease Control. If that seems overly dramatic, consider that in 2016 sleep deprivation cost American companies a staggering $411 billion in lost productivity.[13]

Riwa and I are both guilty of getting caught up in the pressure to do and accomplish more and have personally experienced this craziness first hand. We have tried everything from waking up extra early (as recommended by Hal Elrod in his book, *The Miracle Morning*) to dividing up our week into certain types of days (Dan Sullivan's Strategic Coach Entrepreneurial Time System[14]). We have downloaded software like OmniFocus (which embraces David Allen's methodology of getting things done) and have looked to endless resources to help us resolve this particular pain point.[15]

The scramble to keep up with the expectation of a never-ending stream of creative output has resulted in a culture that is obsessed with hustling. Currently, Google lists 188,000,000 results when you type "productivity" into their search box. Amazon's productivity category boasts nearly 79,000 books designed to help us work better and faster so that we can "worry less" and "achieve more." Funnily enough, the first sub-category in the Kindle store is "stress management"—Amazon knows what's up. Apple's App Store has a dedicated productivity category with over 3,500 apps. In the rush to boost performance, we have become overworked, overscheduled, and overwhelmed. And is "productivity" a worthwhile goal in itself? Have we become so focused on working hard that we've lost sight of why we're doing all of this in the first place?

And thus, the conundrum: As creative professionals, we have come to believe that we can be simultaneously highly productive and highly creative in equal measures. We come to work armed with to-do lists, life hacks, and Inbox-Zero mentalities. We are trained to respond at a moment's notice, manage competing priorities, and rapidly jump from task to task.

We focus on attaining maximum efficiency while trying to generate creative solutions with the same rigor as completing our tasks. And when it doesn't work as planned, we force ourselves to push through, to work longer and harder to chase down the ideas that seem to elude us. We have evolved into an unsustainable hybrid state, trying to be both productive and creative, when that might not be effective—or possible.

In relationships, we define the experiences we've had with our exes as baggage—events that mold our behaviors in our present relationships. If your ex-partner cheated on you, then it's normal for you to carry that lack of trust into your next relationship. It's clear to us that we are in the same situation culturally with productivity. We wanted to understand why, to figure out and trace back the history that has created a nation of people who are overworked and overstressed. Instead of better managing our time, our energy, or our food, I wanted to dig deeper and examine our beliefs and attitudes—our operating system (OS) if you will, that runs in the background, influencing every decision we make.

Productivity alone isn't the issue. Things really get interesting when you add creativity into the mix. As we've shifted from a manufacturing-based economy to a knowledge work economy, we've brought with us a ton of our own baggage—behaviors that were supposed to help us but that instead hinder our creativity. For us, it is this tension between creativity and productivity that inspired us to explore the world of *Hustle & Float*.

To understand the tensions that exist within our contemporary work culture, we must understand how (and why) productivity and creativity changed from being completely unrelated to inexorably intertwined. The answer is that both of these concepts have undergone a fundamental shift in terms of scale.

Productivity started as a management practice developed by governments and militaries to manage large groups of people performing standardized tasks. It was adapted by businesses during the Industrial Revolution to improve the quality and output of manufactured goods as a way to ensure a consistency in speed, quality, and overall production. Today, productivity has shrunk. It has moved away from its group-oriented roots to become a deeply personal practice. As individuals, we are now responsible for our own productivity. From Inbox Zero to GTD systems, we are accountable for our own output in both our personal and professional lives. Productivity, which started out as a collective metric, has now become an individual obsession and is a recognized marker of success.

Creativity is moving in the opposite direction. During the Enlightenment, the Romantics defined creativity as a state of being, an inalienable part of human nature, while the social psychologists in the 1950s measured it as a cognitive strength. In both cases, the focus was on the smallest unit possible: the individual. The knowledge economy has forced creativity to expand, to become big enough to encompass organizations that now value this trait in their employees and are determined to measure it.

THE PLIGHT OF THE PRODUCTIVE CREATIVE

Hustle & Float started as a hobby project driven by my curiosity to investigate our "productivity" origins, to track and understand the events that have shaped our understanding of modern-day work, and to establish a context around how our attitudes, beliefs, and behaviors are impacting our ability as creatives to produce the type of work many of us feel called to do.

I started my research by speaking to people Riwa and I defined as Productive Creatives: anyone whose work involves unstandardized tasks and high cognitive ability: marketers, strategists, communication & PR professionals, managers, lawyers, accountants—the list is endless. If you're thinking this seems like a pretty broad umbrella, you'd be right—the majority of people today who are engaged in some type of knowledge work are facing high levels of pressure to produce. What we heard was consistent across the board: It was imperative to focus on honing one's performance in order to increase production.

For too long, creativity and productivity have been considered equally essential but unconnected. Thousands of books have been written about each of these concepts as separate entities. In fact, nearly every business book tackles achievement and performance through one of these two lenses. In reading the multitude of suggestions, solutions, and frameworks about work proposed by gurus, experts, and celebrities, three things became abundantly clear.

First, the rising popularity of content that focuses on issues such as mindful leadership, habits, creativity, productivity, and cultivating focus, signals a need that there is large population of people who are seeking to improve their working life status quo. Second, despite the varied approaches, the promise to the reader remains consistent across these genres: Follow the advice herein and achieve the holy grail of contemporary culture—that elusive work-life balance. Third, when you set aside branding and buzzwords, the majority of the advice is grounded in what can only be described as common sense:

- In her book *Thrive*, Arianna Huffington advocates the need for sleeping and eating regularly.
- In *Deep Work*, Cal Newport encourages readers to carve out periods of uninterrupted work time to improve creativity.
- Brigid Schulte, author of *Overwhelmed: Work, Love, and Play When No One Has the Time*, rails against our overscheduled culture and suggests to simply start "doing less."
- In *Essentialism: The Disciplined Pursuit of Less*, Greg McKeown urges us to narrow down our priorities to the two or three things that truly matter.
- According to Charles Duhigg, author of *The Habit Factor*, the solution lies in creating new behaviors that become routine.
- Tony Schwartz believes we should treat our energy as a resource that becomes depleted and needs constant replenishing.

Clearly, we are not alone in searching for some relief.

These books all provide sound, logical advice, and with so many resources available through a variety of channels including apps, podcasts, videos, books, and more, the real question isn't "What should I do to work better," but "Why *AREN'T* I doing it?"

In talking to over one hundred professionals including entrepreneurs, executives, artists, authors, and small business owners, we heard the same refrain: they know what they should be doing to work better. They know the virtues of taking breaks and meditating but couldn't seem to apply the advice to their daily lives. They were constantly busy. We wanted to know why. After all, these were smart, successful, motivated people. There clearly was a disconnect between what they should be doing and what they were actually doing.

Once again, Beyoncé came to the rescue, talking about how challenging she finds it to stop and take a rest. "It will be the hardest thing in the world for me to make myself not do an album and shoot a video and turn it in and say 'I'm ready [to relax]!'," the singer said. "I already have all these melodies and ideas in my head. I have to tell myself, 'Sit down! Sit Down!'"

That's when we figured it out: The importance of creativity in the modern workforce has resulted in a culture that idolizes creativity but worships productivity. Our modern-day heroes include entrepreneurs, CEOs, and celebrities who have turned their talents into financial success, usually through highly mythologized accounts of hard work. These stories share common themes including putting in long days, a lack of sleep, and a pride in outperforming competitors through sheer endurance and strength.

It is our reinforcement of the American Dream, a deeply powerful belief embedded in our cultural psyche that promises equal opportunities and prosperity to anyone willing to work hard. Our belief in the dream continues to be strengthened as we culturally internalize productivity metrics as a tangible way to quantify our effort, a way to actively measure our deservingness of a better life.

We treat our work as an extreme sport, where our struggles and sacrifices in the name of our job are glorified. No wonder we feel guilty when we turn off our phones. All of the above-mentioned tactical solutions and frameworks only ever addressed the surface symptoms of something much deeper: an entrenched yet subconscious worldview that fuses our self-identity to our profession, within a culture that values nonstop momentum as a validator of skill and strength.

In other words, we have a society where individuals are under extreme pressure to apply the tenets of productivity (inherited from the Industrial Revolution) in jobs which demand creativity. As we force creativity and productivity together, we can see the incompatibilities that so many of us experience on a daily basis at work.

For one thing, productivity is based on a model of continuous output, a need to account for every minute of the day, to prove that we are indeed contributing. Creativity, on the other hand, is a messy and disjointed process that often requires large chunks of unstructured time. One cannot corral our creativity through sheer willpower and endurance, but that hasn't stopped us from trying. We continue to favor models of work that reward sustained performance and falsely believe that doubling (or tripling) our efforts will result in a proportional increase in creative output.

Ironically, our frantic actions are sucking our creative juices dry. As we strive to eke out the most of every single second, the processes that we have implemented to make us more productive are actually depleting our creative resources. Our belief systems are leading us away from what we actually need: creativity in balance with productivity. It is only by recognizing and openly addressing our subconscious prejudices about work that we can shift toward a more balanced state of working and being.

Or, to use Beyoncé's words: we really just need to force ourselves to sit down.

A POST-WORK SOCIETY

As if competing against each other isn't hard enough, we're now also competing against machines, and it's a contest we're going to lose. Automation, artificial intelligence, and algorithms are all developing at an exponential rate and unbalancing decades of models and best practices.

When thinking about the future of work, especially within today's disruptive technological context, it's easy for us Productive Creatives to breathe a sigh of relief. After all, many of the labor upheavals that are looming on the horizon at first glance appear to be focused on industries that require a certain level of menial work: manufacturing, automotive (taxi drivers, delivery trucks), or other tasks that fall firmly within the realm of blue-collar work. This sense of security is false—a deeper look reveals that while creative automation is not as advanced as its manufacturing counterpart, it is being developed and deployed in decidedly creative jobs: from lawyers and doctors, to writers and artists, the technological revolution will spare no one, and it's time we started truly preparing for it.

Consider that an AI is already being used as a creative director for an ad agency and that Google's AI started creating original works of art mere hours after it was programmed. In Japan, a novel written by an AI was a finalist in a prestigious literary competition (more on them later). Companies like Goldman Sachs are using algorithm software that can do the work of ten analysts in seconds, while sophisticated chatbots are being used to help citizens navigate the legal system. This disruption will impact all of us: both Productive Creatives and non-creatives alike.

What happens when our society realizes that this isn't a problem that can be solved by working smarter or harder? What happens when the foundation of using work as a societal symbol of individual value and status symbol begins to crumble?

It is clear to us that in the peak of our contemporary obsession with work, we are nowhere near ready to face this upcoming change. We'll never be ready to embrace the dramatic work upheaval coming our way if we can't break free of our past. We need to start asking these difficult questions now.

A COMPLEX ISSUE

There is no single culprit to point to.

The culture of work spans nearly every field you can think of and then some. We saw relevant conversations happening across an array of diverse fields, and we believe *Hustle & Float* is unique in not shying away from this complexity, instead embracing the interconnectedness of who we are and what we do. We've focused on a cross-disciplinary approach that includes research insights from neuroscientists, historians, media critics, sociologists, artists, managers, CEOs, dancers, artists, philosophers, celebrities, entrepreneurs, and more.

What started out as our trying to answer some questions about our own behavior has evolved into an exploration of the increasing tensions between productivity and creativity as contextualized by our social, historical, and biological constructs. We've strived to unpack how our ideas of contemporary work have evolved, and pinpoint the moments, people, and ideologies that have shaped our current outlook of work to paint a holistic and deeply human view of the challenges we face in being Productive Creatives.

From the origins of the American Dream and the worship of Silicon Valley Bros Culture, to entrenched legacy systems and outdated performance metrics, we'll never shift toward a more balanced state of working and being if we don't acknowledge the imprints these cultural legacies left behind on our contemporary work culture. We'll delve into the hidden forces that are influencing our work behaviors by exposing how our history has created a set of cultural narratives, archetypes, myths, and symbols that subtly reinforce specific attitudes about the values of work in our modern society.

This book is broken down into four sections. The first three sections each focus on one hidden force that we believe underpins our modern behaviors and beliefs: our systems, our stories, and ourselves. These three forces combined create the foundation for our work belief systems, a powerful mix of history, learned behavior, and genetics that influence our behavior in ways we're not aware of. *Hustle & Float* is the first book to approach this subject from a holistic perspective that looks at how these forces interact within a broader cultural and psychological ecosystem. The fourth section takes all of these forces and extrapolates them into the future, exploring how technology disruptions will play a part in shaping our worldview around work.

Let's dive into each section:

1. Our History [Systems]

Contemporary work culture is the product of hundreds of years of thinking about the role of creativity, productivity, and the value of work. Understanding its origins is key to revealing our biases and the basic assumptions we take for granted that are entrenched in the business systems governing our lives today.

In this section, we'll take a look at how the concepts of creativity and productivity evolved throughout our history to encapsulate our modern-day views. You'll read about Venetian merchants, who in the thirteenth century were the first to measure Return on Investment (ROI) of their sailing fleet. We'll look at how military and government institutions were the first to effectively deploy productivity metrics. You'll also see how creativity was once seen as a divine gift of the gods and how over the years it has transformed into a carefully honed and highly valued skill set for most of today's Productive Creatives.

2. Our Media Culture [Stories]

The second section will focus on the cultural aspect of work, or how we as a society use media, journalism, and the arts to transmit and validate specific ideas about success. We'll take a look at the American Dream, one of the most powerful and enduring ideas in our history, and reveal how it still resonates deeply with people from around the world on a visceral level. Its inception, evolution, and representations in pop culture is a fascinating exploration of how we have translated our understanding of the centrality of work into representation of morality, success, and achievement wrapped in our hopefulness and optimism of a brighter future.

We'll dive into our cultural obsession with entrepreneurship and examine the influence that major cultural figures like Steve Jobs, Bill Gates, Mark Zuckerberg, and Elon Musk have had on how we think about our work and our self-worth. We would be remiss not to mention the social media revolution and the unimaginable amount of terabytes created by regular people sharing pieces of their lives online. We'll track how the rise of certain hashtags (#soblessed, #hustle) have created a subset of digital culture that dictates how we talk about our work and share our successes (or not) within our society today. We'll trace how the merging of self-help, work culture, and New Age spirituality have created a new era where financial success must also be matched by a spiritual fulfillment in the shape of a calling or greater purpose.

3. Our Identity and Biology [Self]

In the third section we turn our focus inward. We ourselves are a type of biological machine, programmed with inputs and impulses that are not altogether within our control. We'll look at some of the latest studies from fields like neuroscience to show how modern-day work culture has hijacked our primal instincts—once used by our ancestors to survive, we now use those same instincts to navigate our complex work hierarchies. We'll look at how the forces of nature and nurture play a part in our productivity and creativity. In this section, you'll read about how our egos and desire for hierarchical recognition are often triggers for a host of complicated hormones and neurochemicals that can impact our behavior at work, as well as arguments for and against the case of creativity being a genetically passed trait.

4. Scenarios

In this section we'll take a look at some of the changes that are looming on the horizon. We'll spend some time discussing the economic costs of overwork in countries around the world, including how countries like Germany and France are passing new laws to protect knowledge works from the physical and mental burdens of hustling too much without any float. We'll assess how beliefs are made and what we can do to begin recognizing and changing our own worldviews. You'll read about both the promise and perils of the technology-driven Gig Economy and see how Uber's premise of providing workers with autonomy and financial freedom comes with a dark side. And we'll end with a few case studies of countries that are exploring alternatives to modern-day work, including options like basic universal income, robotic taxation, and more.

Online Section: The Frameworks

We've added an online section that you can find at www.hustleandfloat.com. We researched so many different aspects of productivity and creativity over the past three years, and we couldn't include everything we wanted to. That's why we consolidated some of the work that we thought would be most helpful for you to enjoy as an added benefit. This includes book lists, summaries, frameworks, and more. We'll be regularly updating this with new resources we find, so be sure to check it out!

A TIME FOR REST

In white water rafting, riders battle waves, heavy rapids, and unpredictable drops. They have to hustle hard to avoid obstacles, respond quickly to changing river conditions, and paddle with all of their strength to safely reach their destination. These heart-pounding bursts of strenuous activity are punctuated by periods of rest, when the water becomes calm enough that riders can float and enjoy the scenery. As any experienced river guide will tell you, the ideal trip is comprised of both hustle and floating—a balance between focused exertion and intentional recovery. Too much hustle leads to exhaustion that can jeopardize the split-second decision-making that's needed to avoid injury. Too much float will result in a boring and aimless ride, devoid of challenge or purpose.

As it turns out, there are many similarities between the way we white water raft and the way we live our lives. The rise of the creative economy has engendered a work ethic among creatives that focuses exclusively on the hustle.

I wish I could tell you that the "Beyoncé Incident" was enough of a wake-up call to have us changing our habits. It wasn't. Over the course of the three years it took to research this book, we both suffered with the ramifications of overwork.

I suffered an episode of burnout so severe I was incapable of producing anything for several months, delaying this project and adding to my productivity shame. It felt as though my brain simply stopped working. Whenever I tried to reach for an idea or attempted to complete a cognitive task, it was as if I was reaching into blank space. It was one of the most petrifying experiences of my life. To make matters worse, I suffered physical symptoms including fatigue, insomnia, and hair loss. The hair loss was a particular rock-bottom for me, as I discovered it at the hair salon, where my stylist's gasp caught my attention. I looked up to see a fistful of my hair in his hands. I hid in the washroom and bawled my eyes out, certain I had ruined both my health and my mental well-being permanently. Through it all, I berated myself for not being able to get it together, for not writing enough, missing word count deadlines, not waking up at 5:00 a.m. to journal and drink kale smoothies.

The irony of undergoing these types of struggles while writing a book about the natural rhythms of creativity did not go unnoticed by me. The frustration of knowing better and yet not doing better was a sharp reminder of the gap that often exists between our beliefs and rational mind. The tools we've provided in this book have been created and used by us, and we hope they'll help you on your own journey.

It wasn't until we started digging deep, forcing ourselves to look at the entire ecosystem that creates and promotes these cultural values, that we started to unravel the beliefs that had wrapped themselves so tightly around our ideas of the importance of work.

I believe this is an essential message for all Productive Creatives and one of the major reasons I wanted to write this book. There isn't a single person who won't nod their head in agreement at the advice that they should take a break, work less, or take more vacation. And yet we don't.

This isn't a book about quick fixes. I hope this book will spark conversations that will help us to shed light on these interconnected forces in order to start making real, positive changes. If we don't start deconstructing our relationships with work, picking apart all the pieces that have been put into place by history, by our upbringing, by our experiences, by our media, we will continue to spiral deeper into a belief system that will actually hurt our ability to continue to produce creative work in a meaningful way.

As creatives, we have been at the front lines of new economies powered by innovative and disruptive technologies that are redefining the nature of work. The global economy continues to shift toward knowledge work, and the days of standardized work are long gone, replaced by the mounting pressure to come up with endless ideas to maintain our competitiveness. Where employers once prioritized productivity as the ideal employee trait, they now expect their workforce to be endlessly creative as well. Today's Productive Creatives must be constantly creative and constantly productive.

This is the first book specifically aimed at Productive Creatives to tackle the issue of the future of work. We wanted to share what we learned so that others in the same situations could apply this insight within their own lives.

If you are working in a job where unstandardized tasks and problem-solving are the norm, then this book is for you.

If you've struggled with burnout, held yourself to impossible standards, lamented your life in comparisons to others on social media, and woken up in the middle of the night with the fear that you're never going to get to that novel, that project, that business idea—this book is for you.

If you've ever felt suffocated by the pressure of producing, producing, producing—this book is for you.

If you're willing to challenge some of society's most closely held definitions of success and achievement—this book is for you.

If you're ready to accept that there is a better way and are prepared to ask yourself difficult and maybe painful questions—this book is for you.

Hustle & Float is both a record of our past and a call to action toward a better, more human, more balanced future. This is not just a book about work but an extensive overview about our own history, identities, and beliefs. This is our story and your story.

We are the Productive Creatives, and it's time to take back the world of work.

Happy Reading,

—Rahaf

OUR HISTORY [SYSTEMS]

1.

FIRST CLASS MEN

PROCESSING TO ZERO

In April of 2011, Merlin Mann, founder of the website 43folders .com, issued a long-awaited update on the status of the book he had been working on since 2009.[1] The book had been billed as the last word on Inbox Zero, the personal productivity system he'd developed that turned on ending one's day without any unanswered emails. All incoming emails were subjected to one of five actions: delete it, delegate it, respond to it, defer it, or do it. But if his fans were hoping to hear news of its upcoming release, they were sadly disappointed. Instead, Mann described the toll that overwork had taken on his personal life, mainly, spending time with his wife and young daughter. "I've unintentionally ignored my own counsel to never let your hard work fuck up the good things," he wrote. "So I'm done fucking that up. I'm done cranking. And, I'm ready to make a change." The book would never be published.

For us, this was a shocking development. Mann had been our gateway into the world of personal productivity. From his early writings at 43folders.com we had been introduced to

David Allen, the patron saint of "Getting Things Done" (GTD for acolytes), a time management system that he outlined in his 2001 best-selling book. *Getting Things Done* was a revelation. Following its advice, we upgraded our humble to-do lists into a sophisticated system for effectively processing tasks, and that was just the beginning. We developed an insatiable appetite for productivity literature (or as it is sometimes affectionately called, "productivity porn"), eager to absorb the tips, tricks, and frameworks that would help us work better, do better, and, ultimately, be better. Over the years we've read hundreds of books, including the seminal works of Stephen Covey (7 *Habits of Highly Effective People*), Peter Drucker (*The Effective Executive*), Cal Newport (*Deep Work*), Tom Rath (*Are You Fully Charged*), Tony Schwartz (*The Way We're Working Isn't Working*), Greg McKeown (*Essentialism*), Arianna Huffington (*Thrive*), Tim Ferriss (*4 Hour Workweek*), and many, many, more.

That wasn't all. Riwa and I installed a plethora of apps designed to help improve our performance on our computers and devices. There was OmniFocus, software based on Allen's GTD philosophy, that was as complicated as it was addictive. Freedom blocked our access to social media sites for a limited time so we could focus on real work. We used IFTT for automating boring tasks like saving pictures to the cloud, not to mention dozens of other apps for calendars, to-do lists, habit tracking, sleep tracking, exercise tracking, and more.

Yeah, you could say we were fully and happily immersed in this world. Listening to podcasts about various "productivity hacks?" Check. Watching videos of people filling out their bullet journals? Check. (Fun fact: YouTube features an entire sub-category of videos, entitled "Plan With Me," that shows various individuals filling out their planners, agendas, and other productivity paraphernalia.) Reading and implementing various methodologies? Check. Pinning pictures of our organized calendars on Pinterest? Check.

Never fully feeling like we were on top of anything? Double check.

In hindsight, that should have been our first giant red flag. We had become productivity scholars, and yet nothing seemed to stick. Our morning miracle routine, championed by Hal Elrod, fizzled after a few weeks. Stacks of empty notebooks, agendas, and planners collected dust on shelves in our respective homes. Apps were downloaded and forgotten. None of these systems had saved us from working ourselves sick. As Mann had pointed out, sometimes expertise wasn't enough to protect us from the darker aspects of productivity.

This obsession with measuring and optimizing productivity is not new. In the thirteenth century, Venetian merchants carefully calculated the difference between the costs of the sailing voyages they underwrote and the revenues they ultimately earned from the goods sold, one of the first iterations of the Return on Investment calculation (ROI). This practice gave birth to the double bill accounting system and the "Equity - Assets = Liability" equation that's still used today to determine the profitability of a business. During the Industrial Revolution, manufacturers used similar calculations to determine their factories' productivity: they divided the total amount of money paid out in salaries by the value of the goods their workers produced. At its core, productivity was a straightforward economic concept that was applied to large groups of people.

But somewhere along the way, the concept of productivity was co-opted by psychology, managerial sciences, self-help gurus, and entrepreneurs to become a measure of individual self-actualization, a national obsession, and a much-touted path to happiness, prosperity, and success. It has transcended its origins as a straightforward economic concept, applied to large enterprises and big groups of people, to become a deeply personal practice that impacts every aspect of our lives. Whether we know it or not, it has become tied to the cultural values and societal norms that drive our behaviors.

How did this happen?

That was our first major research question. We wanted to understand how productivity had mutated from an economic metric into a self-flagellating addiction.

MAN MEASURES ALL THINGS

Our smartphones seem to know more about us than we do. They know how many steps we've walked, the number of hours we've slept, and the number of calories in our afternoon snack. They help us track our moods, our behaviors, our habits, even our locations. It's easy to be dazzled by the constant supply of apps, wearables, software, and smart devices designed to help us to better understand ourselves.

It's easy to forget that while the tools themselves are shiny and new, the impulse to track and measure is a behavior deeply rooted in our primeval past. Humans have always been compulsive measurers. Farmers in ancient Egypt kept meticulous records of crops and yields, enabling them to learn the best times to plant and harvest. In the mountains bordering Swaziland and South Africa, scientists discovered a 43,000-year-old baboon fibula with markings that helped our ancestors track the phases of the moon.

This ingrained penchant for measuring extends to performance, too. One of the earliest examples of performance appraisals dates back to the Wei Dynasty during the third century, when emperors would rate officials on a variety of different metrics. We were amused to note that even back then, employee evaluations were a touchy subject. "The Imperial Rater seldom rates men according to their merits," grouched one historical document. "But always according to his likes and dislikes."

Similar systems were used during the Napoleonic Wars. The Royal Navy relied on peer reviews and other feedback to determine advancement and promotion. As you might imagine, the military was rife with internal politics, as evidenced by the testimony of Captain Anselm Griffiths in 1811, who complained about those who were promoted because of their social standing or influence.[2] "I am not only a strenuous advocate for correct discipline," he wrote, "but a decided enemy to that littleness of character, known by the appellation of courting popularity." It seems that even back then, some people were more interested in working the system than actually working.

If you've ever had an awkward performance evaluation meeting, consider yourself lucky you weren't working in Robert Owen's cotton mills in the early 1800s. Owen, a Scottish industrialist and social theorist, pioneered a quality-control system in which wooden cubes with different colors painted on each side were displayed above employee workstations. Each color was associated with a rating to (publicly) indicate an employee's quality of work for that day. White signified excellent, while black meant the output was "bad." Owen made a point of passing through all of the rooms of his factory on a daily basis. "The workers observed me always to look at these telegraphs," he wrote. "When black I merely looked at the person and then at the color." Ladies and gentlemen, the original giver of side-eye.

All of these systems shared a common trend: scale. For the most part, it was government organizations, businesses, and the military—groups with large workforces, hierarchical structures, and decentralized locations—who used these types of performance management systems. In 1813, the US military implemented its own system of performance appraisals, introducing forced-choice rankings (where raters are given a set of descriptor statements and must make a choice) and trait-rating (where behaviors are ranked on a numerical scale). Over the next several decades, the US Congress would also introduce appraisal systems into its operations, rating clerks on such attributes as efficiency, competence, attention, and even faithfulness. (With the seemingly endless parade of political scandals, we're not sure modern-day politicians would fare so well using some of these metrics!)

STANDARDIZED FIRST CLASS MEN

Despite the influence of naval officers and emperors, the person who would have the most lasting impact in the field of productivity would be a mild-mannered, bespectacled mechanical engineer, armed with a stopwatch that would forever change how we worked.

In the early 1900s, Charles Schwab, the president of Bethlehem Steel, hired a man named Frederick Winslow Taylor to improve operations and increase profits at his Pennsylvania mills. If machines could be optimized to better their performance, Taylor thought, then why not people? It was a radical notion that would launch the field of scientific management and become one of the most significant contributions in the field of productivity.

Instead of simply forcing people to work as hard and as long as they could, Taylor theorized that factories could produce better results if each worker focused on honing a specific skill that they could do over and over, like a machine. Using his stopwatch, he timed workers as they completed their individual tasks. He broke down each process into the smallest and most efficient microactions. The goal was to have each worker trained to perform one assigned task in a highly specific and standardized way.

Each worker was reduced to a specific functionality that could be tracked and measured. This was a shock to workers who were used to being left to their own devices without any incentive to improve their speed or efficiency since they depended on continued employment and worried that increasing speed could result in their own redundancy.

Taylor believed that workers were primarily motivated by money, so he introduced the concept of a "fair day's pay for a fair day's work," in which workers' compensation was directly related to their output. His focus on standardization yielded two important insights: first, that there was an optimal way to achieve each task, and second, that there were optimal types of people who were more suited to this type of work than others.

Peter Drucker, arguably one of the greatest management thinkers of the twenty-first century (and, as it happens, the man who coined the phrase "knowledge worker"), described Taylor's lasting impact as follows:

"Frederick W. Taylor was the first man in recorded history who deemed work deserving of systematic observation and study. On Taylor's 'scientific management' rests, above all, the tremendous surge of affluence in the last seventy-five years which has lifted the working masses in the developed countries well above any level recorded before, even for the well-to-do. Taylor, though the Isaac Newton (or perhaps the Archimedes) of the science of work, laid only first foundations, however. Not much has been added to them since—even though he has been dead all of sixty years." [Peter Drucker, *Management: tasks, responsibilities, practices.* p. 181]

The rigidity of the purest form of Taylorism rendered it obsolete by the 1930s, but Taylor's legacy lives on in management science today, especially around such concepts as efficiency, standardization of best practices, knowledge transfer between management and labor (and vice versa), and a focus on metric-based operational decision-making. Taylor's work would lead to the development of the Gantt chart (a way to visualize workflow and task components) and eventually gave rise to other fields such as industrial psychology.

In addition to absorbing Taylor's methods, we also inherited some of his *beliefs*. Taylor's language reflected a very specific worldview. Workers who were eager to implement his system and increase their output were described by him as "first class men," which attached a sense of elitism and morality to individual output-based job performance.[3] In Taylor's eyes, a person's ability to produce was reflective of their worthiness. He defined success as a state of "maximum prosperity," which could only be attained by maximizing productivity.[4]

Piggybacking on powerful cultural ideals such as the American Dream (which we will dive into in depth in a later chapter), Taylor inadvertently seeded the idea that maximum-measured output was a moral goal worth pursuing.

Despite the work of others, such as Australian psychologist Elton Mayo (the father of Human Resources and Organizational Psychology), who advocated for considering a worker's emotional and psychological fit for the task, the tenets of standardization and the use of productivity as a moral indicator became integral parts of corporate strategy. This link between self-worth and output will be a reoccurring theme that remains entrenched in our work behavior to this day.

After World War II, there was an underlying need within the United States to fill positions and to improve production as quickly as possible. Workers were seen as interchangeable cogs in a machine that was solely focused on output. Businesses would hire many of the men responsible for developing army officer appraisal and training systems to apply the same methodologies to blue-collar workers. Many of these systems were rudimentary, focusing on past performance, and were usually filled out by the managing supervisor with little input from the workers.

But whether it was the frontlines or an assembly line, these systems shared a philosophy of interchangeable labor and standardized output, two things that are out of place in today's creativity-oriented professional landscape. As many of the people we interviewed told us, their days are filled tackling big projects, finding solutions for clients, and other work that is decidedly unstandardized. Yet, we can't seem to shake our industrial production roots.

Additionally, early notions of productivity were based on benefitting a collective (the work force as a whole), compared to the individual lens contemporary creatives apply to their personal productivity approaches.

This history sheds light on why so many creatives often feel stifled by the rigidity of a system that doesn't reflect how they work. When you stop and think about it, is it logical for knowledge economies that prize innovation and originality to champion systems that reinforce standardization? You can't produce ideas on an assembly line, and so we scramble to fill our timesheets with busy work to justify our value and expense to our bosses, or worse—to ourselves.

This was our first clue of some of the deeper contradictions that govern the world of creative work, but we knew we'd barely scratched the surface. Over the next several months, we continued reading, interviewing, and asking lots of questions. Soon, a few clear macrotrends emerged that helped us understand how our opinion of productivity has shifted.

THE KNOWLEDGE ECONOMY: THE RISE OF CREATIVITY AS A SKILL

The first big shift we observed was that creativity went from being an unimportant skill to a necessary one in many businesses. The main tenets of management theory date back to a time when creativity wasn't required for most jobs. More than that, it wasn't something that employers wanted. If you worked on an assembly line, your best characteristic as an employee was your ability to conform, to produce goods at a standardized level of quality at a predetermined speed. The entire appeal of organizations was their ability to execute labor at a large scale, with a focus on efficiency. Management did not expect workers to be creative, and that is clearly reflected in the literature that outlined best practices: efficiency, cost reduction, and standardization were the best ways to manage risk and ensure a consistent output.

But what happens when the product or service we are providing becomes more intangible in nature? The economy's gradual shift to include more knowledge work meant that creativity was suddenly a highly desirable trait. That's where the Productive Creatives came in: to stay relevant and profitable in a rapidly evolving economy, companies desperately needed problem solvers, strategic thinkers, and idea generators. This new type of work created a ripple within traditional workplaces, which now struggled to apply the same clear-cut approach to the creative class. Organizations had to adapt the decades-old systems that developed standardized organizational capabilities to ones that cultivated individual experts who could respond to market conditions with agility.

Peter Drucker was one of the first people to recognize the tensions that arose when Productive Creatives were pressured to contribute quality work in a system designed to measure quantity. He identified six major factors that determine knowledge worker productivity:

1. The ability to define their task.
2. The autonomy to manage their own time.
3. The need for continuing innovation.
4. The need for constant teaching and learning.

5. An emphasis on the quality of the work produced over quantity.
6. The requirement that creative workers be recognized by the organization as assets rather than costs to be minimized.

Sounds pretty great, right? There's just one problem. As Drucker put it, "each of these requirements (except perhaps the last one) is almost the exact opposite of what is needed to increase the productivity of manual workers." Yikes. He's right. How can we, as creatives, excel in workplaces that equate performance with metrics like the numbers of hours worked?

Where Taylor was obsessed with breaking down and measuring repetitive tasks, Drucker understood that the twenty-first-century worker would be challenged by a work environment that required strategic problem-solving. Productive Creatives need to think and work at a high level that can't fit into the rigidity of a system designed for assembly lines. Drucker also recognized that these new kinds of employees had the upper hand: their ideas, experiences, and creative abilities were highly valuable skill sets that they could take with them to another job if they were unhappy. This led him to conclude that "the ability to attract and hold the best of the knowledge workers is the first and most fundamental precondition" of not just prosperity but civilization itself. The understanding and improvement of knowledge worker productivity, he wrote, was among the "first survival requirements" of developed nations. (We will talk about how these power dynamics changed in a subsequent chapter.)

And yet, despite his warnings, productivity and the outmoded performance metrics that are used to measure it still remained a top organizational priority. Decades of legacy system thinking are hard to change.

Instead of changing their systems, organizations simply passed along the responsibility for tracking productivity to the creatives themselves. Suddenly, it was up to us to justify how we were spending our time. To prove that we were adding value to the bottom line, we had to fit our unstandardized responsibilities into units that could be easily assessed, counted, and measured by management. This required us to equate coming up with new ideas to making widgets. If this seems nonsensical, that's because it is.

Simply put, the system that we all subscribe to, the one that has been embedded in corporate strategy since the Industrial Revolution, has been stacked against us from the beginning. No wonder we're struggling within its confines—it was never designed for creative work.

While our tasks keep getting increasingly complex, we're still trying to adapt outdated metrics that prioritize continuous output over expertise—or, as Drucker put it, quantity over quality. It is this foundational tension that has given rise to the modern dysfunction of today's creative workforce.

OUR LIFESTYLE CHANGED: THE MYTH OF THE IDEAL WORKER

We have clear expectations about how knowledge workers are expected to act in the workplace, a collection of best practices that sociologists referred to as the "Ideal Worker." But these are increasingly out of synch with the realities of our lives.

See if any of the following sounds familiar: The Ideal Worker arrives to work early and is able to complete his tasks with a high level of speed and focus. He is principled, punctual, moral. He doesn't bat an eye about needing to work late, secure in the knowledge that his wife is taking care of the kids and the household. Freed from these personal responsibilities, he has the liberty of being able to devote himself completely to his professional endeavors. *Mad Men*'s Don Draper could afford to be an advertising genius because his wife, Betty, was at home making sure the kids were looked after, the house was clean, and dinner was on the table. But can we?

While never explicitly stated in corporate strategy books, early stage white-collar productivity systems were created based on the assumption that an employee could be devoted to his work because his wife shouldered most of the personal labor at home. These unwritten standards created work ideologies that persist despite shifting socioeconomic conditions that make it nearly impossible for today's Productive Creatives to attain that same level of devotion.

Labor statistics show how far we've come from the conditions that made the Ideal Worker possible. According to the Bureau of Labor Statistics, almost half of married couples are dual-income families in which both partners are employed. The entry of women into the workforce has been one of the biggest shifts in employment trends in recent decades, with working mothers representing the biggest increase within the labor market.

Unsurprisingly, it is women who are bearing the brunt of this disconnect. Many of the male executives we interviewed reported low levels of work/life conflict, since women continue to shoulder most household burdens. A 2015 survey by the Working Mother Research Institute showed that 79 percent of working mothers were responsible for doing the laundry at home, 67 percent were responsible for cleaning the bathroom and dusting, 64 percent did general household chores, and 62 percent did the weekly grocery shopping. Reinforcing traditional gender norms, the majority of working fathers owned chores such as taking out the trash (63 percent), car maintenance (72 percent), and mowing the lawn (61 percent).

When it came to childcare, women were the predominant caregivers, even when they were the primary breadwinner.

Seventy percent of working mothers were solely responsible for kid-related shopping, 62 percent took time off work for a child's medical appointment, and 58 percent prepared breakfast in the morning. The American Bureau of Labor Statistics puts this in concrete terms[5]: according to its research, women spend 2.2 hours a day on household activities compared to 1.4 hours for men. Despite the empowered narratives around women in the workplace, the statistics show how much we are still clinging to outdated social norms.

The news is not all bad. The gap is slowly starting to shrink, especially with Millennial parents, who divide household chores more evenly. Millennial dads are more likely to be responsible for laundry or grocery shopping than Boomer or Gen X fathers.

But what's blindingly clear is that the Ideal Worker can no longer exist in today's uncertain economic climate. Even if he is male, his focus is divided by his increased domestic responsibilities, especially when it comes to raising children. And as Baby Boomers enter retirement, many Millennials are now feeling the additional burden of "eldercare." Today's creatives must also grapple with a far more complex socioeconomic landscape, in which the nuclear, one-income family has been replaced by many variations. The expectations that we continue to place on them are based on a socioeconomic model that is all but extinct. In other words, the world has changed, but the expectations that drive our standards at work have not. And so, we work ourselves to distraction trying to live up to outdated cultural norms that are neither realistic nor attainable.

WORK DEVOTION AND CORPORATE MANLINESS

You might be wondering how the myth of the Ideal Worker, a Don Draper-era artifact, applies to your work as a Productive Creative. According to the sociologist Mary Blair-Loy, author of *Competing Devotions: Career and Family Among Western Executives*, its influence can be discerned in a phenomenon she called Work Devotion, in which workers are compelled to perform acts of struggle and sacrifice to prove their commitment to their jobs, to their bosses, and to their colleagues. Behaviors like coming in early and leaving late, volunteering for extra tasks, and being accessible 24/7, not to mention telling your colleagues about how hard you've been working or how little sleep you've gotten, characterize this phenomenon.

If you're reading this and thinking that this behavior seems totally normal, then welcome to the world of subtle cultural influence. "Work Devotion defines the career as a calling or vocation that deserves single minded allegiance and gives meaning and purpose to life," writes Blair-Loy. Many of us take this mindset for granted, she adds, without even noticing its influence on our thought processes and our ability to make decisions. Her research also indicates that people who demonstrate a high level of Work Devotion are not only more likely to be promoted but to expect an increased level of Work Devotion from their own subordinates, further continuing the cycle of unreasonable expectations.

Work Devotion has become an ingrained part of our cultural ideology. It's why we don't think there is anything strange about the behaviors that we mentioned above. Many of the people Blair-Loy interviewed reported that work gave them a strong sense of identity, competence, belonging, and purpose. What's interesting to note here is that Work Devotion isn't about the work itself but the moral qualities of the person who is demonstrating these behaviors. It's less about the work and more about being a "good worker."

Some organizations are attempting to adapt to these changes by introducing more flexible work policies. It sounds like a reasonable solution, right? We thought that most people would jump at the opportunity to design a work schedule that was more accommodating, but we were surprised to discover that such efforts are often met with considerable resistance. The tensions between progressive policies like flextime and the pervasive and often deep-rooted beliefs that necessitate them are strong enough to prevent many people from taking advantage of them.

In *Reshaping the Work-Family Debate*, Joan Williams shows how Work Devotion beliefs and the realities of changing family dynamics clash. Many employees hesitate to avail themselves of their employer's adaptive work policies because of "flexibility stigma"—the fear that colleagues will consider you less committed and less hardworking than you should be and therefore not entitled to promotions, bonuses, or other rewards. Simply put, there is a political price to pay if you don't express the appropriate level of Work Devotion.

In a 2013 *Forbes* article entitled "Why Men Don't Take Paternity Leave," Jason Hall describes the ambivalence many fathers feel about paternity leave.[6] "The stigma of being the guy in the office who takes the maximum amount of leave haunts many dads," he writes. "It's not the fear of losing a job exactly, but the unspoken disapproval—and questions about dedication that can come with a long leave." Hall interviewed a corporate accountant in Kansas who took only two days off after the birth of his son, both because he didn't want to appear to not be working but also because he was afraid he'd make himself a target for future layoffs.

Research carried out in Britain in 2011 by the National Childbirth Trust revealed that 43 percent of mothers on maternity leave went back to work earlier than they liked, with job security cited as the major reason. Interestingly, when asked about sharing parental leave with their spouses, more than a third of the women surveyed indicated they wouldn't want to share parental leave because, as mothers, it was their responsibility to stay home and rear their children—another example of how certain historical norms such as the "stay at home mom" retain their cultural power, even when they no longer reflect reality for the majority of people. 30 percent of the respondents were afraid to take advantage of existing flexible work policies, lest they put their jobs in jeopardy.[7]

It's important to note that corporations aren't always the evil parties in these conversations. In 2015, Netflix announced that, following the example of such companies as Pocket, Prezi, Evernote, and Gusto, they would provide unlimited paid maternal and paternal leave for all full-time employees.[8]

"We want employees to have the flexibility and confidence to balance the needs of their growing families without worrying about work or finances. Parents can return part-time, full-time, or return and go back out as needed. We'll just keep paying them normally, eliminating the headache of switching to state or disability pay," wrote Tawni Cranz, Netflix's chief talent officer. "Each employee gets to figure out what's best for them and their family."

Sounds great! But while many praised the move, some remained unconvinced. *Bloomberg Business* columnist Megan McArdle wrote: "There's a reason that you tend to see this perk at places like Netflix, rather than places like Walmart: They're staffed with workaholics who probably don't take much of their vacation time anyway."[9] *Slate* Associate Editor L.V. Anderson argued that "Unlimited paid vacation, unlimited paid parental leave looks like a recipe for confused, resentful, and stressed-out employees. I don't have kids, but if I ever do, I don't want to be vulnerable to judgment and resentment because of my choices about maternity leave—I'd rather know exactly how much paid time off I (and my colleagues) are entitled to." The article even has a picture of an adorable baby with the caption "Mom, are your co-workers silently judging you?"

It's not the policy itself but the unspoken code of conduct around Work Devotion that is undermining its otherwise great and very generous goals. Tech writer Natt Garun echoed this unease. "Until paid parental leave is a mandated policy in America, there is always potential for guilt and fear that your workplace relationships will be strained if you decide to take an extended leave," he wrote. "The culture, unlike in Europe where parental leave is common and supportive, seems unforgiving."[10]

I spoke to Rony Zibara, partner and managing director at Fahrenheit 212, a New York–based innovation consulting firm, who confirmed the struggle of going on vacation is a real issue. "That's why we've come up with a solution," he told me during a coffee meeting in Paris. "We just make everyone take vacation at the same time. We shut down the email servers. That way, no one feels guilty, and everyone can enjoy themselves. It's been a great success."

In her 1992 book *Money, Morals, and Manners: The Culture of the French and the American Upper Middle Class*, sociologist Michele Lamont explores how the workplace feeds into our notions of self, identity, and worth. "We know that work occupies a central role in the life of upper-middle class men," she writes. "In contrast to blue-collar workers, these men rarely live for 'after-work': work is the means by which they develop, express, and evaluate themselves."[11] She concludes that the result is a belief system where being ambitious and a hard worker are "doubly sacred," since the two traits are viewed by the majority of respondents as "a central component of moral character." Lamont goes on to write that embodying these types of behaviors "signals a moral and socio-economic purity." In contrast, laziness was described as "one of the most despicable traits one could have." This finding is echoed in other studies, which show again and again how essential employment is to winning social respect.[12]

As if untangling that mix isn't complicated enough, yet more nuance is added when we consider how, for many men, work is also a kind of theater of masculinity. In 2000, leading sociologist Marianne Cooper suggested that our emerging transition to knowledge work had also resulted in a new way for men to express their masculinity and was directly linked to their identities as fathers, managers, and individuals.

Cooper's observations of a group of Silicon Valley fathers and knowledge workers showed how they advertised their Work Devotion through displays of strength and endurance. "Successful enactment of this masculinity," she wrote, "involves displaying one's exhaustion, physically and verbally, in order to convey the depth of one's commitment, stamina, and virility."

These displays further cement the notion of the Ideal Worker, which now excludes many working families, especially working mothers who must struggle to keep up without paid help or an extra twelve hours in the day.

In a 2013 Harvard Business Review article entitled "Why Men Work So Many Hours," Joan C. Williams wrote that "workplace norms cement felt truths that link long hours with manliness, moral stature, and elite status. If work-family advocates think they can dislodge these 'truths' with documentation of business benefits, they are sorely mistaken."[13]

By now, it should all be starting to make a weird kind of sense. The foundations of our workplace behaviors and expectations reflect a reality that was always partly mythical, and that is now sorely out of date.

DON'T MESS WITH MY BELIEVIES[14]

David Allen (of GTD fame) wrote that it should be "possible for a person to have an overwhelming number of things to do and still function productively with a clear head and a positive sense of relaxed control." We had to shake our heads at his choice of words. To overwhelm is to bury or drown beneath a huge mass of something—in this case, work. Even when faced with a huge wave of it, the priority is still to function "productively," instead of looking for the root of our overwhelm.

We found a fascinating paper by Adam Okulicz-Kozaryn of Harvard's Institute for Quantitative Social Science, entitled "Europeans Work to Live and Americans Live to Work (Who is Happy to Work More: Americans or Europeans?)" that compared the working hours and life satisfaction of Europeans and Americans.[15] It found that Americans were happier than their European counterparts to work more hours, in large part due to their perceived belief that a strong work ethic is a desirable trait and that working hard is an essential marker of success. We demonstrate our moral righteousness and the elite status it brings us through our displays of struggle and sacrifice, reinforcing these narratives as an important part of our contemporary work culture.

For us, the issue was never a lack of time but the erosion of boundaries that left us vulnerable to an infinite flow of requests, emails, meetings, and information, each providing a tempting opportunity to display our Work Devotion to our colleagues but also to ourselves. Our feelings about work run deep and are fundamentally tied up with our notions of self-worth, morality, and identity. For all the advances we've made in efficiencies and life-hacking and the forty-hour workweek, we haven't spent enough time examining our underlying beliefs.

FROM ALL TO ONE

The truth is, many of us Productive Creatives are guilty of becoming mini Frederick Taylors, obsessed with measuring our own performance. The stopwatch has been replaced with endless productivity apps, and we've become so obsessed with tracking our behavior in order to validate our Work Devotion that we don't even need a manager watching over us—we're more than happy to monitor ourselves in the name of optimization. Productivity has changed from a collective measure to an individual one. We've taken a methodology once used to manage large groups of people and internalized its principles on a personal level.

Even at the height of our overwork, when we knew that our productivity systems were failing, we blamed ourselves and kept searching for a new system that would optimize our performance and our output to a point where we could regain a sense of control. But productivity, at its core, is about predictability, and predictability doesn't fit well with creative professions like ours.

Our very obsession with personal productivity reveals how ineffective traditional productivity metrics actually are. Our attachment to time as a unit of effort highlights our futile attempt to reclaim a sense of certainty and safety in our work.

To add to the irony, one of the obvious drawbacks of productivity porn is the fact that the countless hours we wasted on it could have been spent accomplishing real work. But we can't seem to help Taylorizing ourselves, hoping to stumble upon that magical "best way" that will transform us into First Class Men (and Women).

But here's the biggest irony of all: Frederick Winslow Taylor was actually fired by Bethlehem Steel for failing to produce tangible results. It turned out that after a brief spike in performance, forcing workers to produce more in less time exhausted them to the point that their overall productivity was damaged in the long run. Taylorism isn't just stacked against creatives but against the very people it was originally designed for. Yet we remain trapped by it.

As if productivity isn't complicated enough, things get really crazy when we factor in how creativity has been evolving within the knowledge economy. As you'll see in the next chapter, creativity is undergoing its own big shift, but in the opposite direction: as organizations grow to value creativity as a strategic skill set, creativity is no longer regarded as an individual attribute but a factor of production that can be applied and managed by large corporations and other collectives. In the midst of all of this change, we begin to unravel the tension that lies at the heart of *Hustle & Float*.

Summary of Big Ideas

➡ Productivity is shrinking from big (organizational) to small (individual) accountability.

➡ Creativity has become a valued skill in the labor market.

➡ Productive performance appraisal systems remained in use even as the labor market shifted to hard-to-measure knowledge skills.

➡ Work Devotion is a sociological phenomenon where workers demonstrate their commitment to their jobs by expressing their struggle and sacrifice.

➡ The Ideal Worker introduced expectations and standards that were only possible because of spousal support at home, and those conditions no longer exist, yet the pressure to perform to those unrealistic standards still hold true.

2.

THE CREATIVITY BOOM

"I want to be a machine."   —Andy Warhol

One of the first things we did when we decided to start writing *Hustle & Float* was to talk to as many people as we could. We started by posting on our Facebook pages, which led to hours of Skype, FaceTime, phone, and in-person interviews with executives, entrepreneurs, designers, authors, artists, strategists, marketers, dancers, freelancers, and more. A couple of our rock star clients generously allowed us to host workshops and learning lunches with their teams to refine and develop our ideas.

It was immediately clear that despite the abundance of literature, resources, and tools to help us improve, build, hone, and develop our creativity, the concept of creativity itself was abstract and ambiguous, open to many different interpretations, even within similar industries.

We were surprised to learn that our friend, DJ Saul, CEO of iSL (iStrategy Labs, a WPP-owned digital marketing agency based in Washington, D.C.), considers himself to be creative but doesn't identify as "a creative." For him, that term is reserved for photographers, videographers, artists, graphic designers, and other people who directly contribute to the final client work. As strategic a marketing executive as he is, we thought he would fall under that definition for sure.

There were lots of other opinions. Kane Sarhan, the head of Global Brand for the Starwood Capital Group and co-founder of The Well, believes that while he doesn't contribute to the physical production, his vision, ideas, and strategy are all a part of what makes him a creative. This was echoed by Joel Halpert, creative director at Loaded for Bear in Paris, who told us that for him, the job entails being paid to think. "I believe the place of the creative is to connect the dots between idea and consumer," he said. "Or provide access to information to the consumer in a way that they can easily understand and be passionate about."

Laetitia Vitaud, a future of work researcher, shared her definition. "A creative is anyone who does anything that is not automatable, processed, or mapped out," she said. "It can involve manual work but not assembly line work. Craftsmanship is the broadest sense of the word."

Some people focused on specific artistic talents, such as drawing or painting. Others emphasized the professional aspect, as in, "a job that you are financially compensated for." (To be clear, the distinction we're drawing is between people who define themselves as A CREATIVE as opposed to simply being creative.)

Despite all the different opinions we heard, there was one strong commonality: regardless of how you define it, creativity is a valuable trait. In 2014, *Time* magazine published the results of a poll that found that 94 percent of Americans value creativity in others more than they value intelligence, compassion, humor, ambition, or beauty.[1] We should pause for a moment to let that sink in. More than intelligence, compassion, humor, ambition, or beauty. Creativity has become a true cultural obsession. More significantly, it has only *recently* become such an obsession. The words "creative" and "creativity" were used quite sparingly in American books until 1920 and 1940 respectively, and yet less than one hundred years later, creativity is its own literary category—almost 500,000 titles are listed in a Google Books search for those two words. Those titles range from business books that help you produce more ideas to neospiritual guides on how to find your divine "flow." Some of these books interpret creativity as a science, while others draw on the archetypal characteristics of the artist—and yet, the idea of creativity as either a science or a spiritual practice only dates back about two hundred years!

Today, there is an overabundance of resources to help you "unlock," "unleash," "channel," and "harness" your latent creative forces. Creativity is a trait that we consider fundamentally human while also being a virtue we place squarely on a pedestal.

So how exactly did our ideas about creativity evolve? Where do our references for creativity come from and what really drives our understanding of the concept?

As we mentioned in Chapter 1, as the productivity metric shrunk from one that measured the output of whole workforces to a measure of our individual time, creativity has been expanding in the opposite direction—from the individual to the collective. In this chapter, we'll trace how creativity has shifted from a little talked-about attribute to one of the most important cultural values of our time.

CREATIVE GODS

Creativity is a Gift from the Gods

Creativity as we know it today didn't really exist in Ancient Greece, China, or India. As a word and even as a concept, it wasn't present in a meaningful way because creativity was considered, at its core, an act of divine discovery or imitation. It wasn't an esteemed value or character trait, and great thinkers of the time, such as Plato, rejected the notion altogether. When asked whether or not a painter truly "makes" anything, he responded: "Certainly not, he merely imitates."[2]

While baffling, especially for those of us striving for some version of originality today, Plato argues that no human endeavor is truly creative because it is merely an imitation or combination of things that already exist. For Plato, only the gods were capable of creativity. Interestingly, in this polytheistic era, while the Greeks attributed their inspiration to the gods, they still took individual credit for what they produced. (For example, everyone knew who designed the Parthenon.)

For later Greek and Roman Judeo-Christian societies, creativity was rooted in the Biblical story of creation. If creativity was considered a human act, it came from outside the self and therefore wasn't valued as a character trait. Unlike the Parthenon, the cathedrals that were built during this era were often done so anonymously.

In short, over a long span of our history as a species, people didn't spend a lot of time thinking or worrying about creativity. Despite the incredible works of art, poetry, and literature that were produced since the beginning of mankind (consider that one of the earliest artworks discovered were a set of paintings on the walls of a limestone cave in Indonesia dating back 39,900 years[3]), creativity didn't hold the same status as the virtuous, desirable trait that we see it as today.

Creativity was a divine gift from the gods, a mysterious force that emanated from outside of ourselves. Even today, the influence of the Greek Muses, the goddesses of art and science, can be seen in the way we speak about finding artistic inspiration. The concept of an artistic muse is a familiar one, and its contemporary definition has expanded to include ordinary mortals. From Picasso's mistress, Marie-Thérése Walter, who was featured prominently during the artist's surrealist period, to John

Keats's unrequited love of Fanny Brawne that led to some of his best and most passionate poems, creatives have historically embraced the presence of an outside force that pushes them to bring their best work forward.

Being writers, we can't help but point out that the presence of the muses are also hidden in plain sight within our language. It's not surprising to learn that the word "museum" comes from the Greek word *mouseion*, which means seat of the muse (*mousa*). Even the idea of someone being "gifted" refers to this idea of divine grace and blessing. Even after thousands of years, our ancestors' views of creativity have trickled down into the words we use today, and some part of that core belief remains within our collective cultural awareness of creativity.

CREATIVE INDIVIDUALS

Creativity is Something Only Geniuses Have

It wasn't until the Renaissance, and eventually the Enlightenment, that creativity would begin to be linked to human performance. At first, creativity was seen as a rare talent found only in special geniuses, but eventually, over the course of several hundred years, our understanding shifted toward the categorization of creativity as an all-encompassing human trait.

The Italian Renaissance was a period (peaking in the fifteenth-sixteenth century) of renewed interest in classical (Greco-Roman) learning and culture. Prominent figures of the era include the great artist and inventor Leonardo da Vinci, the humanist philosopher Pico della Mirandola, the poet Dante Alighieri, the artist Michelangelo, and the political philosopher Niccolò Machiavelli, among many others.[4]

This was the era of humanism, when a strong bias toward human agency and critical thinking emerged. Renaissance thinkers felt a certain emancipation and intellectual freedom from the often dogmatic and superstitious era that preceded them. They were changing the game and wanted credit for their contributions to the world. After all, in many cases they were considered to be making something from nothing. Words like imagination, intuition, and originality replaced imitation when it came to describing creative processes. Previously, philosophers had been thought to "think up" concepts, painters to "shape" paintings, writers to "realize" ideas, and so on. Semantics aside, this phenomenon is historically significant because it marked the emergence of a new, very human-centric perspective on the world.

In the eighteenth century, two very different views of creativity emerged, laying the groundwork for some of the fundamental tensions we see in work today.

In one corner, you have the Rationalists. These are the proponents of the Age of Reason, who basked in the triumph of science (Newton, Leibniz, Bacon) and of philosophy (Descartes, Locke, Spinoza, Kant, Voltaire, Diderot, Montesquieu). The Age of Reason was defined by "restraint, order, logic, technical precision, balance, elegance of diction, an emphasis of form over content, clarity, dignity, and decorum."[5] Intellect trumped emotion, just as wit trumped imagination and man and his thinking were firmly in the spotlight.

For these great thinkers, the idea that creativity was something mystical was absurd. The development of the scientific method demanded an objective, analytical approach. It's no surprise that this frame of mind brought a new empirical lens to our understanding of creativity. The burgeoning discipline of psychology refuted the notion of mystery, seeing creativity as an act of intelligence, a product of the conscious mind—a big leap from divine inspiration.

Perhaps even more significantly, the Age of Reason coincides with the emergence of European capitalism and industrialism. As the feudal system collapsed, a couple of things happened.

First, many independent craftspeople went to work in factories and in cities, adopting new vocations, lifestyles, and pastimes to align with the changing economy. Secondly, the upper class began purchasing cultural commodities (paintings, sculptures, opera tickets, books of poetry, etc.) that underlined their differences from the commercial and working classes.

"Exclusivity" is the key word here because the one factor that drove up the market value of works of art was the signature of an "artist." This is the moment in history when the idea of the creative "genius" is born. In that light, creativity was valued because it was considered an individual trait—though at this point a trait that was attributed to only a few rare, talented men.

As the idea of creative scarcity took hold (that is, a limited supply provided by an exclusive few who were lucky enough to have been gifted with this special talent), a fundamental shift in the concept of creativity took place: it went from creating something from nothing to making *new* things. This idea of novelty continues to be a large part of our modern definition of creativity. From the collision of rationalism, capitalism, and industrialism evolved a creative pecking order, in which profitability › originality › imitation. Profit became a metric for creativity, just as the first copyright laws were born in Britain.

But at the same time, another school of thought was forming that had decidedly different views about creativity. In the late eighteenth and early nineteenth centuries, the Romantics took the idea of the "natural genius" and ran with it, electing imagination and freedom as its virtues. Romanticism pushed back against the idea that creativity was a rational, conscious choice, instead choosing to emphasize the superiority of imagination to reason.[6] Rejecting the rational concept of creativity, the Romantics believed it emerged from the unconscious mind. Imagination not only had the power to transform things, it was a way of experiencing and finding meaning in the world.

The Romantic poet and thinker Samuel Taylor Coleridge drew a cunning distinction between two different types of imagination: the first, "fancy," was practical—this is the imagination we use to understand the world or "recall memories, make plans, and solve problems." The second, more noble imagination is "an auxiliary light that changes everything it illuminates," fusing together the self and the world. The Romantics spiritualized creativity, and this still influences our expectations today, as creativity has assumed a transcendent role in our work and personal lives (more on that later). Many Romantics rejected the commercialization of art, decrying the development of modern economies (capitalism) and things produced en masse (industrialism) as signs of cultural decline.

Romantics like Coleridge and Matthew Arnold believed that the artistic elite and their art could have a powerful influence on society that was "untainted by commerce."[7] These are the early signs of a conflict that would only intensify in the years to come.

Our modern beliefs around creativity reflect this original tension between Rationalism and Romanticism: Rationalism gives credit to the conscious mind for creativity, while Romanticism accredits the unconscious mind and even the soul. Tracing subsequent movements in art, we can see that Romanticism prevailed throughout the nineteenth century. After that, the pendulum swings back and forth, from the detachment and coolness of twentieth-century Modernism (rationalism), to the wildly-inspired and spontaneous abstract Expressionism (romanticism), and eventually to the minimalistic and unemotional Postmodernism (rationalism).[8]

Whether or not creativity is a function of the conscious or unconscious mind, there was one thing that both sides agreed on: creativity was something that was firmly in the realm of humans and not the gods. This human-centric shift would represent the next big evolution in our thinking: creativity became something that we possess as humans instead of something that was gifted to us.

CREATIVITY AS SOMETHING YOU DO

At a high level, we've traced how creativity went from an extra-human characteristic to one that is highly associated with individual ability, in the form of geniuses and rare talents. This too would change. The late nineteenth century was a period of deeper investigation of creativity, inspired by the ongoing development of scientific methodologies but also in part by the innate differences in humans identified by Charles Darwin. In the post-WWI twentieth century, creativity expanded to include more than the artist—scientists, politicians, and technologists would all fall under the rubric of creators.[9] There was a new interest in understanding the "creative process" as a way of documenting how discoveries were made.

The study of the "process" of creativity evolved in tandem with developments in the discipline of psychology. In 1926, the social psychologist Graham Wallas developed one of the earliest mental models of creativity in his book, *The Art of Thought*. (If you're curious, the stages are preparation, incubation, intimation, illumination, and verification.[10]) Though Wallas was early, he wasn't alone for long.

Creativity Studies emerged formally in American psychology in the 1950s and '60s. Doctors like J.P. Guilford, Osborn, and Torrance had a difficult task: figuring out how to measure something as intangible as creativity.

Coleridge's romantic definition of creative imagination was impossible to measure. Instead, Guilford chose a more pragmatic definition as a proxy: idea generation. In 1967, Guilford released a standard test that we've all taken at one point or another: how many uses can you imagine for a paper clip (or a brick, a pencil, etc.)? This was an important milestone for contemporary creativity because it marked a very significant and subtle distinction: we began measuring creativity as something we *do*, rather than something we are.

So much of how we understand creativity today stems from this subtle distinction, which reflects a bias in the way we define it. Take, for example, the studies that relate work ethic and creativity. There is plenty of science that confirms that creativity in both the sciences and the arts is the result of deliberate, conscious, hard work. Simonston found in his research that "Nobel laureates publish twice as much on average as other scientists who are nonetheless good enough to make it into *American Men and Women*." Creativity is considered the result of time, effort, and hard work—that is, when creativity is measured by output.

In this way, creativity has become more accessible: we've rationalized and codified the process and rejected Romantic elitism in favor of something more democratic. In doing so, we've also accepted that creativity is no longer something we *are* but something we *do*. In this swing toward rational creativity, we also leave behind the Romantic disinterest toward what is created. (We'll dive into the genetic and biological research on this topic in a later chapter; for now, we just wanted to trace the shift in thinking.)

PRESENT: FROM DOING TO BEING

Fast-forward to the twenty-first century where any remnants of creative elitism have been decisively replaced by the idea that everyone is creative. The sociocultural approach to understanding creativity matured and now looks beyond the individual and his or her creative genius to social factors like education, support networks, and systems of collaboration. Creativity isn't individual, it is collective. It's not a fluke, it's a science. While Wallas's mental model wasn't disproven, countless other models emerged from this growing body of research and inquiry.

Despite trying to leave its philosophies behind, at a deep level, our beliefs and ideas around creativity are still rooted in Romanticism. What we have today is a slightly confusing understanding of creativity that is actually a mix of romantic and rational: we champion individuality and celebrate intuition, but we believe in the ten-step process for honing each of those things. We have writers like Elizabeth Gilbert telling us the compelling story of her creative muse moving through her as an external force and Ken Robinson telling us how schools systematically kill creativity.

Our mental models of creativity use outputs like idea generation, novelty, and effort to measure it. They tell us that if you aren't producing you're "blocked" (versus the Romantic concept that you can be creative without creating anything). The cult of creativity permeates both the personal and professional worlds. The conversation has become so prevalent that not only is everyone expected to be creative, we're confused when anyone questions or rejects that notion.

CREATIVE COMPANIES IN THE GLOBAL ECONOMY

It's hard to find a force outside of nature as strong as the open market. The development of creative organizations has eclipsed creative individuals, which in turn has led to a burgeoning of creativity in the literature of management science. Once the domain of the gods and then of man, creativity has emerged as an economic measure and a valuable corporate priority.

Market forces like globalization and competition present significant challenges to cities and organizations; the changes they produce demand responses. Economist and author Michael Porter has outlined two distinct responses related to this transformation: the first is to cut costs by mastering productivity (Taylorism). The second is to increase innovation (by heightening creativity).

The earlier part of the last century predominantly focused on the first response, with the pursuit of cheaper foreign labor and the introduction of processes and technologies to increase efficiency. However, as manufacturing industries are replaced by a more specialized, knowledge-based economy, productivity alone can no longer provide a competitive edge.

Hence the pursuit of creativity as a competitive advantage. It's no surprise that, like any other organizational asset that can increase competitiveness, governments and organizations want to maximize creativity within individuals, organizations, and the economy. Any number of new MBA programs offer degrees in individual and organizational creativity, as well as short courses like Harvard's Creative Thinking: Innovative Solutions to Complex Challenges. Alternative accelerator programs like THNK School of Creative Leadership or the Berlin School of Creative Leadership have arisen as well. Art schools across the world now commonly offer business and management degrees. Organization, governance, management, networking, expertise, and evidence have all come together to establish a strategic framework for enhancing and driving creativity. Romanticism may have championed the individual as the primary source of creativity, but this doesn't exactly provide a scalable model to grow the competency within organizations.

Annual lists of the most innovative companies reflect the cultural prestige that comes from being seen as a creative place to work. Books on managing creatives and building creative cultures have gained vast readerships. A few examples of these include:

- Ed Catmull's best-selling *Creativity, Inc.*, which explains how Pixar Animation Studios ensures that its employees remain inspired and motivated. It was named one of the best books on "Creative Leadership."

- Jon Gertner's *The Idea Factory: Bell Labs and the Great Age of American Innovation* traces the history of AT&T's famous research and development lab, one of the first places that consciously and deliberately sought to manage innovation.

- Adam M. Grant's *Originals: How Nonconformists Move the World* uses examples from different industries to teach people how to recognize and champion good ideas.

- The title of Tom and David Kelley's *Creative Confidence: Unleashing the Creative Potential Within Us All* pretty much says it all.

As you can see, creativity has become a big topic for organizations who recognize its competitive value and want to harness it in service of their productive goals. And lest we forget the importance of personal productivity, there are now many books targeted specifically at helping creatives manage their time:

- *Productivity for Creative People: How to Get Creative Work Done in an "Always On" World* by Mark McGuinness

- *Organizing for the Creative Person: Right-Brain Styles for Conquering Clutter, Mastering Time, and Reaching Your Goals* by Dorothy Lehmkuhl

> ◾ *Time Management for the Creative Person: Right Brain Strategies for Stopping Procrastination, Getting Control of the Clock and Freeing up Your Time and Your Life* by Lee Silber

As we mentioned in the last chapter, these books are perfect examples of how the practice of productivity has shrunk from an organizational priority to a highly personal one. Productive Creatives are expected to navigate these complex systems themselves in order to maximize their creative output. As you might have noticed, dealing with a lack of time is a regular theme within this category. Keep this in mind because we will explore the new time realities of Productive Creatives in a later chapter.

Looking at book categories as a whole allows us to step back and observe the overarching narratives that are being created around our evolving relationships with work. We couldn't believe how far our society has come in thinking about the role of creativity in our professional lives. We have inherited a concept that was once reserved for a small and exclusive group of artistic geniuses and have turned it into a foundation of our modern-day business models.

CREATIVE ECONOMIES (AND THE RISE OF CREATIVE CITIES)

This scaling of creativity didn't stop at the level of organizations but has expanded to include national economic priorities as well. In 2001, John Howkins developed the concept of the "creative economy," which shifts the paradigm for economic resources: instead of using land, labor, and capital to create value, the creative economy is a system that uses "novel imaginative qualities" to do so instead. This relatively recent idea is not exactly novel: as Howkins puts it, "Creativity is not new and neither is economics, but what is new is the nature of the relationship between them."

This growing relationship between creativity and the economy requires a shift in the way governments look at their national statistics. Conventional measurements such as GDP, annual economic growth, unemployment, cost of living, and foreign-exchange reserves fail to align with the changing nature of the economy and what is needed to stay competitive in the future. As such, creativity has become firmly ensconced on policy-making agendas. While some governments have been slow to respond, there are signals that indicate that this shift is already underway.

In 2004, the government of the Hong Kong Specialized Administration Region (HKSAR) commissioned the development of a Creativity Index to measure Hong Kong's creative capital, assess the city's competitiveness, and "compare its creative vitality with its neighbors." A reference point for policy-making and strategic planning, the Creativity Index was a response to a changing "new age economy" in which creativity is a key factor of production.

Hong Kong isn't alone; countless other developed economies have taken exactly the same approach to prioritizing creativity as an economic imperative. From 1997 to 2007, the New Labour Party in the United Kingdom hoped to revive national growth and competitiveness by expanding the definition of creative industries to include the financial and service sectors. The headline of their 2001 Green Paper boldly stated that "Everyone is Creative." Similarly, Australia published "Creative Industries—A Strategy for 21st Century Australia," in which the leading quote was, "A creative nation is a productive one."[11]

The element of "hype" around the creative industries is underscored by Monika Mokre, chairwoman of the European

Institute for Progressive Cultural Policies, who explains why it's in a country's best interests to promote creativity as an important driver of economic growth. The first is tactical and political: expanding the definition of creative industries means increasing the number of people who feel as if they are a part of them, resulting in a bigger base of constituents. The second is practical. When these broader definitions are used, the statistical data does in fact prove that creative industries are critical drivers of economic growth. Policy measures that benefit cultural and creative industries have positive effects on employment and international competition.[12]

The notion that creativity is an important economic force has matured across the globe, one study at a time. As the manufacturing bases of the developed economies have contracted, creative industries have more than made up for the difference. Art, culture, and creativity are ripe for capitalization. We've singled out creativity as the signal virtue of our time, and its election manifests itself in many subtle and surprising ways. As Elizabeth Wilson points out in her book *Bohemians: The Glamorous Outcasts*, the flexibility and mobility that characterizes the modern creative worker has its roots in "drop outs," a tradition established by artists rejecting the rules and discipline of modernism.[13] The creative loft and irregular working hours are no longer just for artists—they've become the prerogatives of the new creative working class as well. Adopting the symbols of bohemian artists and other "rejecters of the system" and incorporating them into the very systems and institutions that they rejected is ironic, of course, but it isn't inherently bad. As we "strive for better" within a flawed system, we are often in search of more ethical methods of living and working. Wilson's criticism, and ours, is that we should be aware of what is driving and inevitably shaping our deeply rooted beliefs about the role of creativity in our lives.

Just as our evolving understanding of productivity and work ethic has impacted our deeply held beliefs about the nature of work, so it is with creativity. Economics and cultural policies influence our lives in sneaky ways. Policies shift culture because we absorb their implicit values slowly and subtly, until we believe that our attitudes and behaviors are natural and inevitable, simply because they are so familiar.

But what's undeniable is how few of us now believe that creativity is just for the few. Adobe's global-benchmark study on how creativity is perceived and valued in different regions (the research was fielded in March and April of 2012, with 5,000 adults in the United States, United Kingdom, Germany, France, and Japan interviewed) found that only 25 percent of people believe that they are living up to their own creative potential.[14] More than 75 percent feel that their countries are lagging as well.

What's even more interesting to us is that the impact of bringing free market principles like competitiveness and entrepreneurship to the table goes beyond "industry"—it impacts the individual because the pace of production, creation, and value are all ways that we measure ourselves. But like the privileged classes of the eighteenth century, we have also fallen prey to the notion that we can differentiate and distinguish our creative selves merely by purchasing or participating in the fruits of commercialized creativity.

In his *New Yorker* essay "Creativity Creep," Joshua Rothman captured this phenomenon perfectly,[15] writing:

"We live in a consumer society premised on the idea of self-expression through novelty. We believe that we can find ourselves through the acquisition of new things. Perhaps inevitably, we have reconceived creativity as a kind of meta-consumption: a method of working your way toward the other side of the consumer-producer equation, of swimming, salmon-like, back to the origin of the workflow. Thus the rush, in my pile of creativity books, to reconceive every kind of lifestyle as essentially creative—to argue that you can 'unleash your creativity' as an investor, a writer, a chemist, a teacher, an athlete, or a coach. Even as this way of speaking aims to recast work as art, it suggests how much art has been recast as work: it's now difficult to speak about creativity without also invoking a profession of some kind."

And so, we fold "creativity" into a ferociously competitive economy.

A MATTER OF SCALE

On April 21, 2001, our hometown of Toronto introduced World Creativity and Innovation Day, an initiative spawned by the creativity expert Marci Segal to encourage citizens to use their creativity to make the world a better place. By 2006 the day had expanded to a full week, starting on April 15, Leonardo da Vinci's birthday. All around the world, communities get together to share ideas and participate in creativity and innovation courses, workshops, and lectures.[16]

The lone creative genius with a rare skill has been replaced by a community—a more accessible notion that encompasses the wide variety of new skills needed to power emerging knowledge economies. It's a relatively new idea, anchored by the rise of Productive Creatives who have expanded the definition of creativity to encompass new fields and skill sets that didn't exist before. No longer the realm of artists, we would argue that creatives can be found in every field: from data science to communications.

In the last two hundred years, we've managed to completely redefine what it means to be a creative in terms of individual characteristics, learned competencies, and, for many of us, a vocation. The term has become all-encompassing: an adjective to denote new topics of managerial interest (creative leadership, creative management) and economies (creative economies, creative class). Even the way we use this word changes: being creative, as an activity, versus being "a creative," as a self-identifier.

As a word, creativity has become imbued with cultural currency and relevance while it is inconclusive and ambiguous. It's a celebrated pillar of our contemporary work culture and value system, and while we all agree that we need more of it, we're not quite sure what "it" actually is.

The definition of creativity continues to expand. We're no longer artists praying for divine inspiration; we're Productive Creatives who are contributing to economies and markets that were built on the tenets of productivity. After thousands of years of separate development, creativity and productivity have collided spectacularly.

In the next chapter, we'll take a look at what it means to live and work in a world where creativity and productivity operate in direct competition, each vying for priority. For now, we'll end with a pithy quote which succinctly captures this conflict from the publishing sensation Nora Roberts, author of over two hundred best-selling books. "Every time I hear writers talking about 'the muse,'" she writes, "I just want to bitch-slap them. It's a job. Do your job."

Summary of Big Ideas

➡ Many of the ideas we have about creativity today are only a few hundred years old.
➡ Creativity is growing from small (individual) to big (organizational) priority.

- ➡ Historically, creativity has transformed from a blessing you were gifted from the gods, to a core part of your identity, to a skill that you have, and finally, a unit of economic output.
- ➡ Creativity is now driving new economies and is reflected in the creation of new government policies, showing its value on the global scale.

3.

THE GREAT STRETCH-OUT
AND SPEED-UP

"Never get high on yo' own supply."   —Notorious B.I.G.

THE GREAT LIE

The Japanese language is notorious for its concision and its
ability to articulate complex notions with profound specificity.
Boketto, for example, means to stare off blankly into the distance, while *fuubutsushi* refers to the feelings, scents, or images
that evoke memories of a season, causing one to anticipate its
return. One of our personal favorites is *tsundoku*, which is defined as not reading a book after buying it, usually leaving it
with other unread books.

In the 1970s, a new word emerged into Japanese conscious-
ness: *karōshi*. *Karōshi's* literal translation is "death from overwork." After multiple deaths of young, high-ranking business
executives at the peak of Japan's Bubble Economy in the
1980s, the socio-medical term defined an emerging epidemic
of exhaustion and extreme psychological stress, which was legally recognized as a cause of death.[1] Both the word and the

phenomenon it refers to are still quite current. According to recent studies, around 8,000 of Japan's 30,000 annual suicides are thought to be work-related. Another 10,000 deaths each year from things like heart attacks, strokes, or even cerebral hemorrhages are also attributed to *karōshi*.

The survivors of victims of *karōshi* are entitled to compensation. In November 2014, the Tokyo District Court found a restaurant chain liable for the suicide of a twenty-four-year-old manager who hung himself in 2010. The worker had logged an average of 190 hours of monthly overtime in the seven months before his death.[2]

As if that wasn't bad enough, research shows that productivity is actually dropping in Japan—along with the national birth rate. It seems that people are working so hard they don't have the time or the energy to start families. The Japanese Labor Board has introduced new legislation to tackle this issue. Parliament passed a law in 2015 that makes it mandatory for workers to take at least five days paid holiday a year. Interestingly, it lays the responsibility for compliance on employers rather than employees. Though Japanese workers are entitled to eighteen days of paid vacation and sixteen one-day national holidays, on average they take only nine days of paid leave a year, including sick days.

It takes more than legislation to change deeply rooted behavior and belief systems. "The Japanese work-life balance is horrible," notes Cary Cooper, a professor at Lancaster University and an expert on Japanese work culture, "because work is such an important part of their identity, especially for males."[3] Asking for time off is seen as being inconsiderate and even disloyal to colleagues left behind to pick up the slack. In a system that is ruled by complex conformist cultural norms around harmony, pride, honor, and duty, this can be a great cause of shame and anxiety.

To understand just how embedded these values are in modern Japanese society, consider the standard exchange when leaving work. The person who is leaving first says, *"Osakini shitsurei shi-masu"* (I'm sorry to leave while you're still here). Then the other person responds, *"Otsukarasama deshita"* (You've worked hard today, you must be tired). It's amazing when even routine verbal exchanges are infused with so much cultural baggage around work ethic!

Additionally, it's difficult to expect workers to take advantage of anti-*karoshi* legislation when Yuu Wakebe, the Health and Labor Ministry official responsible for setting those standards, himself works an average of one hundred hours of overtime each month and takes only five paid vacation days a year (one day was to nurse a cold). "It's actually a worker's right to take paid vacations," Wakebe has been quoted as saying. "But working in Japan involves a lot of volunteer spirit."[4] Volunteer spirit, in this case, translates into unpaid overtime, another norm in Japanese work culture, which isn't counted in productivity metrics—explaining why, on paper, Japanese employees work fewer hours per year than Americans.[5] It is estimated that Japanese workers work millions of hours a year of unpaid overtime.[6]

Karōshi as a phenomenon is linked to the regeneration of Japan's postwar economy, which was largely accomplished by the dedication of "salarymen"—the disciplined white-collar workers who selflessly committed themselves to the organizations they served, the Japanese version of the Ideal Worker we wrote about in Chapter 1. It should come as no surprise that this persona arose due in large part to the work of Scientific Management (it always goes back to Frederick Taylor, doesn't it?). Much of the groundwork for Japan's postwar economy was laid by W. Edward Deming, who was also influential in the creation of the Japanese Production Management System, with its emphasis on *kaizen,* or continuous improvement, which would revolutionize the manufacturing industry.

Kaizen seeks to improve productivity in part by minimizing waste. Unfortunately, in Japan, the definition of waste expanded from traditional cost-cutting measures to include any time spent not working: idle time, break time, even vacation time. Within many Japanese organizations, workers are encouraged to continuously make suggestions for improvement, even to their own detriment.

The result is a work culture where working crazy long hours is the norm, the only way to meet impossible demands that go hand in hand with the constant pressure to increase productivity, despite economic hardships such as the 2008 recession (that was a psychological doozy for everyone involved, more on that shortly).

Is it surprising that in the face of impossible sales expectations, lack of sleep, vacation time, or leisure, workers would suffer from anxiety, depression, and a slew of physical ailments?

Paralleling the American Ideal Worker, the Japanese division of labor during this period was based on the assumption of certain gender roles, with women taking the majority of household and child-rearing tasks. While this situation has changed drastically in the United States (remember that working mothers represent one of the biggest new entrants to the labor market), in Japan, women are having a much harder time. Only 64 percent of women participate in the workforce, one of the lowest rates among the OECD economies. Japan also ranks 104 out of 142 countries in the World Economic Forum's Global Gender Gap Index, with women earning only 70 percent of a man's salary for the same role.[7]

The pervasive influence of traditional gender roles is most apparent when looking at Japan's parental leave legislation. One of the most progressive countries when it comes to guaranteeing paid leave for new parents, Japan has been providing maternal leave since 1947 and parental leave since 1992, where the period of leave was extended to one full year for each parent.[8]

But in 2014, only 2.3 percent of eligible fathers took advantage of these generous conditions, in large part due to the social backlash that comes from acting against the social norms of masculinity. In 2016, when Kensuke Miyazaki, an MP from Japan's Liberal Democratic Party, announced that he would be taking one month of paternity leave, the only member out of seven hundred MPs to do so, he faced criticism from the secretary general of his own party, who told reporters that Miyazaki's absence could damage the party. "There will be a problem during an extremely tense situation," he said, "if one vote can make a difference in the outcome."[9]

Take a minute and let that sink in: a first-time father gets publicly shamed in the media for actually wanting to take advantage of a policy that his own party supports. Once again, we see the tensions between "do as we say, not as we do."

In the case of Japan, the unwavering dedication to work is rooted in what is known by industrial psychologists as the "three treasures." These "treasures" define the labor system and are made up of lifelong employment, wages driven by seniority, and company unions.[10] Together, these create both a moral imperative and an unwritten social norm that is responsible for an often-punishing work culture. Shinzo Abe, Japan's Prime Minister, recognizes the challenges he faces in making profound change to his country's work ethic, admitting that his "[is] a culture that falsely beautifies long hours."[11] There is an important interplay between the systems we enforce and the culture we create.

Japan illustrates how different cultural values can result in the same obsession with work. It's not unique to Americans, but it is a global phenomenon that is impacting people across industries and countries. It's fascinating that social drivers like duty to the collective can result in the same symptoms of overwork as the American focus on attaining individual success. On opposite sides of the world, two different belief sets have created eerily similar work conditions.

"Overwork" and "work stress" have become part of the popular public narrative all over the world. In Korea and China's rising economies, many people are also driven by the ethos that "any job worth doing, is worth doing excessively."[12] The Chinese, for example, also have a word for death from working: *guoalogi*. An estimated 600,000 Chinese die every year from work-related stress. The South Koreans, who only moved from a six-day workweek to a five-day workweek in 2001, also have a word for it: *gwarosa*. Before the shift to a five-day week, Korean employees worked on average 2,499 hours annually, the highest number of hours recorded by an OECD annual survey.[13] To give you a point of reference, during that same period, American workers logged 1,814 hours. Unfortunately, while the numbers of hours worked in Korea has declined slightly, in 2014 workers averaged an annual 2,124 hours.[14]

The Anglo-American system is in no better position. While the English language may not have a word like *karōshi,* the links between burnout as a work-related disorder and disease and depression are widely recognized. Extreme worker devotion and unyielding loyalty turned Japan into an economic superpower but at a terrible cost. Its declining population and low birthrate suggest that its labor force has little time to do much else.[15]

THE 2008 RECESSION: PESSIMISM AND A NEED TO WORK MORE HOURS

Japan's devastating recession during the early nineties would provide advanced economies with a sobering taste of what they would experience in the years following the 2008 collapse, as economic stagnation exacted a continuing toll. Originally called "the Lost Decade" (1991-2000), some economists also include 2001-2010 in the period, referring to it as the "Lost Score." In fact, consumer spending has yet to return to its precrash highs.

We've spent a lot of time outlining the underlying influences and beliefs that have shaped our own tendencies to overwork, and none have been as influential as our own Great Recession. The uncertainty it engendered about our job security—and the stability and viability of our whole economy—created big psychological effects that are still being felt today.

Much like the Japanese in the Lost Decade, we are still being impacted by events that unfolded a decade ago and more. It's an unexpected development, as economists used to believe in pretty well-defined cycles of economic dips, followed by clear recoveries. But that's not what happened in Japan, and it's not what happened in the West. Recessions have a longer reach than we thought, and the long-lasting damage they do on both an individual and a societal level has been identified as Economic Scarring.

John Irons, a researcher with the Economic Policy Institute, described these long-lasting repercussions in a prescient paper in 2009. "Falling incomes can force families to delay or forgo a college education for their children. Frozen credit markets and depressed consumer spending can stop the creation of otherwise vibrant small businesses," he wrote. "Larger companies may delay or reduce spending on R&D." Irons reported that increased credit rates and the decline of consumer demand was especially tough on new and small businesses. In 2008, 43,500 businesses filed for bankruptcy compared to 28,300 in 2007 and 19,700 in 2006.

Irons also noted that the effects of these types of events can be felt across generations. If your parents struggled to make ends meet, there is a high likelihood that you'll struggle, too. We found a study from 2005 (Oreopoulos et al.) showing that children whose fathers experienced a job loss earned 9 percent lower income than children from similar families where the father enjoyed stable employment.

OVERWORK AS A MEANS TO RECESSION-PROOF

Imagine the economy is held up by three pillars: the stock market, the housing market, and the labor market. If one of these markets suffers a downturn, the other two are there to keep everything else from crashing. In the 1981-1982 recession, for example, the labor market took a huge hit (unemployment rates rose from 7.2 percent to 10.8 percent), but housing prices stayed the same and the stock markets actually rose. The 2001 recession included a stock market crash and a slight increase in unemployment, but those were offset by an increase in housing prices. So, while it was a turbulent time, consumers were at least somewhat cushioned; it wasn't the perfect storm we would see in 2008, when all three markets collapsed.

In 2010, Michael D. Hurd and Susann Rohwedder from the National Bureau of Economic Research published the findings of a series of high frequency surveys, in which over 2,600 households were questioned monthly about the impact of the recession between November 2008 and April 2010.

Close to 40 percent of the households surveyed were behind in their house payments, experienced unemployment, foreclosure, or had negative equity in their homes. These troubles tended to cascade. Thanks to the popularity of adjustable rate mortgages and no down payment loans, many homeowners suddenly faced ballooning mortgage payments, even as the housing market crashed and their houses decreased in value. As unemployed workers blew through their unemployment benefits and their savings, many of them—even those who had borrowed responsibly and made all their payments—were in danger of losing their homes and all the equity in them.

Another factor that added to the impact of the 2008 recession was the gradual shift by employers from a Defined Benefit pension system, in which the employer provided a set monthly benefit to retired employees, to Defined Contribution pension plans, in which the individual employee is responsible for their own retirement planning through a mix of individual contributions, employer contributions, and various tax benefits. Many people who had retirement assets in the stock market saw those retirement assets wiped out. In November 2008, a quarter of the survey respondents between the ages of 50-59 had lost more than 35 percent of their retirement savings. Young workers weren't immune either—unemployment meant that their expected lifetime earnings may well fall short of what was expected, which could have a big impact on future generations' retirements.

The average respondent household reported feeling pessimistic about the future of the stock and housing markets, and fear of unemployment remained high, even after the recession was officially declared over in 2009. "Overall, the data suggest that households are not optimistic about their economic futures," the report concluded.

This particular quote jumped out at us: "Despite the public discussion of the necessity to work longer, expectations about working to age 62 among those not currently working declined by 10 percentage points," the authors wrote. "In our view this decline reflects long-term pessimism about the likelihood of a successful job search."

WORK MORE: STAY SAFE?

Earlier, we mentioned how some corporations were trying to offer more progressive policies for their employees, but many corporations took a less-than-altruistic approach in handling the 2008 recession and its subsequent impact. Many of those policies are still very much in evidence even eight years later.

Let's dig a little deeper into that quote we mentioned above about the "necessity to work longer." We wanted to find additional research that captured the mentality of how dire everything seemed when we were in the thick of it. After all, it's been nearly a decade since the recession, and it would be too easy to look back and underestimate the emotional and psychological toll exacted by this event on many people.

Before the recession, the job market was booming. According to Randstad's Future of Work reports issued between the years 2003-2007, employee confidence was at an all-time high, with many workers open to changing their jobs and negotiating robust benefit packages. As conditions started to change in the lead up to the recession in 2008, Randstad reported that that level of confidence was waning: instead, employees recognized that jobs weren't as plentiful as before and became more invested in ensuring their own job security as employers regained the upper hand. Interestingly, Hurd and Rohwedder's report stated that despite this new economic uncertainty, job satisfaction was at an all-time high since 2004, and this surge is attributed to the fact that with increased news of layoffs and stock market free-falls, workers felt grateful to have a job at all.

You can see from the survey results the difference that one year makes in psychological impact. While there was a decline in the 2008 compared to the 2007 survey in workers who thought it was a good time to look for a higher paying job, ask for better benefits, or negotiate a raise, one particular behavior caught our attention: only 35 percent of respondents said they would feel comfortable requesting additional help from their employer to "lighten the workload." In contrast, 68 percent of workers said that it was a good time to take on extra work. If we look at these two numbers, we can see that respondents didn't want to give the impression that they couldn't handle their workloads—an attitude that is almost certainly driven by anxiety about being replaced. In response to this stress, workers reacted by trying to prove their worth to their employers (the report describes this as an attempt to recession-proof their jobs) by actively seeking out extra work. Our coping mechanism was to work harder, faster, and longer, hoping to show our bosses that we should be kept on. Research also shows that the number of hours worked increased by twelve points compared to the previous year.

This sentiment was echoed in a psychological overview of workaholism in the twenty-first century by Online Psychology Degree, an organization profiling careers in the field. "Because the threat of downsizing and layoffs consistently plagues to-day's workers, many feel compelled to bury themselves in an avalanche of responsibilities. They want employers to think them valuable assets to the team and assume unrealistic work-loads as a sort of insurance policy; nobody wants to lay off a real go-getter, they think," the report reads. "An almost fanatical devotion to the office, in their minds, increases their chances of receiving validation in the form of raises and promotions."[16]

In addition to working more, the Randstad report indicated that workers appreciated their jobs so much that they were less likely to push for things like flexible work hours, promo-tion opportunities, or more paid time off. (47 percent said increased paid time off was important in 2008 compared to 53 percent in 2006.) They were also willing to work more for less money. When looking at expectations in the workplace in 2008 compared to 2006, the sharpest declines were in the area of competitive pay. Generation X (70 percent, down nine points) and Millennials (71 percent, down fifteen points) reg-istered sharp drops in the importance they placed on compen-sation, which aligns with the overall satisfaction with having a job at all.

Consider that America's productivity doubled each year be-tween 2008 and 2010. According to a report by the Economic Policy Institute, corporate profits have risen nearly 22 per-cent since 2007. Output increased while the number of people available to do the work went down. According to economist and California-Berkeley professor Brad DeLong, today's firms "take advantage of downturns in demand to rationalize operations and increase labor productivity, pleading business necessity in the face of the downturn to their workers."[17]

Basically, employers took advantage of the downturn to tighten budgets and increase workloads. Employees didn't push back because they felt lucky to have a job. Since companies were able to "make do" and in fact turn a profit, they didn't hire back laid off workers, leaving existing workers with bigger workloads, longer hours, and no additional pay. In short, they achieved their record-breaking profits on the backs of their overworked labor forces. Carl Van Horn, a political scientist at Rutgers, summed up this new reality succinctly: "Everything is tilted in favor of the employers...The employee has no leverage. If your boss says, 'I want you to come in the next two Saturdays,' what are you going to say—no?"[18]

THE GREAT SPEED-UP AND STRETCH-OUT

In 1941, the US Temporary National Economic Committee published a report entitled "Investigation of Concentration and Economic Power." Based on two years of testimonies and the insights of many economists, academics, and experts, the report evaluated the state of the American economy during the preceding two decades and summed up some of the work practices that were currently being used across various industries.

We were particularly fascinated by a chapter entitled "Technology in Our Economy," which with just a few tweaks could have easily been used to describe the situation we find ourselves in today: "Technology, a historical development without general plan or purpose, has come to dominate the pattern of modern living," it declared. "Benefits and disadvantages are consequently intermingled and interspersed within the complexities of the current situation and await analysis and evaluation from some central viewpoint grounded in considerations of economic health and human well-being."[19] This is also the premise of *Hustle & Float,* and it appears to be something that we've been struggling with since the earliest integration of technology into economic processes. The reason for this is the deep impact that our work has on the rest of our lives.

"What technology is or does depends upon the essential characteristics of the contemporary social order at any time and place," the report continued, listing a variety of factors that can influence how technology is adopted within a workforce, such as the "nature" of the economy, the characteristics of the available labor pool, the composition of the ruling classes, and the "prevailing popular habits of taste, ambition, and apprehension." All of these things will determine not only the way that technology, a neutral tool in and of itself, is deployed but also the reactions to it on a personal level.

The authors remind us that the primary driver for technological advancement in capitalist economies is the pursuit of profit, which creates a pressure for quick and continuous improvements. "The rapidity of its technical advances under capitalist stimulus has been so great that the controls necessary to their better social employment have often lagged behind, so that the machine is today still employed for medieval and even barbarous purposes," they wrote. "Any modern invention of consequences will be found exploited in some measure by those whose social conscience is relatively primitive."

This passage is particularly interesting as it forces us to consider not just the technology that is being used within the workspace, but the intentions, values, and *beliefs* of those who are leading the charge, as those also influence the subsequent rituals and cultures that evolve. Unfortunately for us, the majority of the attitudes toward labor during the early years of the

Industrial Revolution were combative. Workers were considered replaceable cogs by a management that had little interest in their emotional and physical well-being. Ultimately this gave rise to unions, as workers organized to protect themselves.

Two examples of unfair labor practices faced by workers during this time are "the speed-up" and "the stretch-out." The speed-up is when a worker has to perform his assigned tasks at a faster pace than usual, while the stretch-out is when a worker is assigned more tasks as a part of his or her job description. Neither included corresponding increases in pay, which led to increased profits for employers because less workers were needed to complete the same amount of work.

To make this even more unpleasant, management used these blatantly unethical practices in manipulative ways. Writing in *The Voice of Industry,* a New England newspaper, in 1848, Sarah Bagley, a leading critic of working conditions during this era, recounted an infuriating story about a cotton mill that managed to double the number of looms it used, and hence its output, without hiring any additional staff.[20] How? Well, first, management secretly altered the speed of the machines overnight, reducing their overall output. When workers reported this drop in production to their bosses, they were told that the material they were producing wasn't selling well and that they would have to either accept a lower piece rate or be laid off.

Then they were offered a seemingly generous option: if they would agree to manage additional looms, they could keep their jobs. Many workers were forced to comply or be unable to pay their room and board. That was the stretch-out. Then things got worse. No sooner were the workers operating twice the number of machines they had been, then once again, during the night, management snuck in and returned the machines to their original speeds, forcing the workers to keep up a grueling pace. Workers were now forced to produce more but at a lower rate per piece. That was the speed-up.

As if that wasn't bad enough, the workers were informed they were actually earning more than their managers, which was unacceptable. The solution? Give each worker still more responsibilities and tasks—more stretch-out—and reduce their wages. "In 1840," Bagley concluded, "a day's work was 120 yards [ed: of fabric], the wages for the same, 75 cents. Now [in 1848], a day's work is 140 yards, the wages—44 cents."

This was done repeatedly, with factories demanding increased output while whittling away piece rates, meaning workers could only maintain their income (or slightly raise it) once they met the new demand rate.[21] Some factories even had punitive measures, such as money fines or even corporal punishment for those who couldn't keep up or whose outputs were sloppy.[22]

"The companies do not pay more for the same amount of work," Bagley wrote, "but the operatives do more work than formerly. A few years ago, no girl was required to tend more than two looms. Now they tend four, and some five: and because they make a few cents more than they did on two, it is trumpeted all over the country that their wages have been raised."

As you can imagine, these practices resulted in bitter disputes, sometimes including violent riots, strikes, and walkouts, until after decades of struggle, negotiations between unions and management established clear guidelines and protections. In 1941, the House of Representatives launched an investigation into unfair labor practices. In its report, the US Temporary Committee blamed employers for "putting more work on the employees than they can do."[23] Foreshadowing what was to come in our time, the report added that while "a generalization for the entire economy is not possible...a fair inference is that for the period of 1919-1939, in a substantial portion of it, gains in productivity have not been paralleled by gains in worker earnings."

Does any of the above sound familiar? It should, and that's because the cycle repeated itself in 2008, this time targeting knowledge workers, who didn't have the benefits of collective bargaining or the protection of unions. Instead, we have technology that makes it possible for management to demand that workers be connected 24/7 and a work culture that positions sacrifice and struggle as badges of honor.

And that's where it gets a little sad: despite the mountain of external evidence that shows how we are being systematically overworked and under-resourced, there is an insidious psychological narrative at play that makes us believe our inability to keep up is our own fault—a consequence of our failure to not "work hard enough," which in itself is a product of our deeply held beliefs about our individual value in society.

SUPER-JOBS AND THE SUPER WORKER: THE DEATH OF THE FORTY-HOUR WEEK

As we mentioned earlier, taking on increased responsibilities was a stress response to unpredictable job markets in which layoffs were always looming on the horizon. Workers struggled to make themselves "valuable" through acts of sacrifice to signal their Work Devotion to their bosses and colleagues. Working hard is the only way to prove that you have what it takes, to survive the next round of downsizing. And so, the average week went from forty hours to fifty-five and above.

We don't use words like "speed-up" or "stretch-out" anymore; instead we've devised a new term that captures both of these concepts together: the super job. According to the *Wall Street Journal*, which coined the term in 2011, companies have taken advantage of the employment crisis by "asking employees to take on extra tasks that have little to do with their primary roles and expertise—with engineers going on sales calls, accountants pitching in on customer service, and chief financial officers running a division on the side."[24]

One thing that we found especially interesting was that while reviewing the many management theories that arose during the majority of the twentieth century, limiting the workweek to forty hours was considered a standard best practice in most of them. The introduction of the forty-hour workweek was largely made possible by the struggles of unions. But it should be emphasized here that while unions pushed for the change, business leaders agreed to implement it because of its measurable beneficial impact: a large body of evidence showed that when factories cut hours, profits and productivity rose. Even Frederick Taylor's experiments, which we outlined in Chapter 1, supported this conclusion. Taylor himself noted that reducing work times resulted in a remarkable increase of a worker's total output.

While the exact origin of the forty-hour workweek is somewhat disputed, the notion of a shortened workweek has been around for a long time. One of the first supporters of this idea is our old friend Robert Owen (the mill owner we mentioned in Chapter 1, who used colored wooden blocks to evaluate his workers' daily performance). In 1817, Owen launched his "Eight Hours Labor, Eight Hours Recreation, Eight Hours Rest" campaign.[25] Karl Marx pointed out the virtues of a shortened workweek in *Das Kapital* in 1866, and Sidney Webb and Harold Cox published *The Eight Hours Movement* in 1884.

The forty-hour workweek was famously popularized in America by Henry Ford in 1914, who made the (then) radical step of paying workers double what they had been earning while also reducing the numbers of hours they worked from nine to eight daily. Ford didn't invent this concept, as is often thought (indeed, many economists call it "Fordism"); he merely adopted the practices, which proved a massive success as his workers could afford to also be his consumers. Other competitors quickly followed suit, and eventually the forty-hour week became standard across industries, cemented through the New

Deal legislation. The Fair Labor Standards Act, introduced in 1938, officially established the five-day, forty-hour workweek as a national standard. And the virtues of a shortened work-week continued to be confirmed through studies conducted in the decades following, to the point that it became an unquestionable truism in most factories and offices across America during the '40s, '50s, and '60s.

Essentially, the bottom line (pun intended) was this: workers had the mental and physical capacity to work eight solid hours a day. As unions began to lobby for disability compensation and workplace safety, they drew on numerous studies that showed that an overworked labor force was more likely to cause disastrous accidents resulting in severe injuries, death, and, perhaps even more frightening for coldhearted managers and owners, the financial exposure to broken machines and stopped assembly lines.[26] Labor and management alike agreed: pushing people beyond their limits was not only cruel and useless but dangerous as well.[27]

In the 1980s, a report released by The Business Roundtable showed that there was one exception where organizations could increase their productivity by increasing weekly hours from 40 to 60, but only very briefly and at great risk.[28] There were two serious drawbacks.

The first was that these short-term gains did not follow a 1:1 ratio—meaning that increasing a worker's hours by 30 percent did not result in a 30 percent increase in output but in something much lower. Since eight hours is a person's natural limit, their ability to concentrate and perform their assigned tasks well diminish as they approach the final hour. Forcing them to push beyond that will further strain their performance, and the quality of their output will decline until they eventually become exhausted.

The second issue is that beyond the daily strain of over-work, research has shown that there are cumulative effects that need to be taken into account as well.[29] In addition to their diminishing productivity and quality after eight hours, workers' overall weekly productivity suffers as well. Without adequate rest, a workforce pushed to the brink will show rapidly declining productivity outputs with each successive week of overwork, as workers' ability to focus and react are severely compromised.

Here's the kicker: after eight weeks of sustained overtime (sixty hours per week), productivity is so impacted that it would have been better (and safer) to have adhered to the forty-hour a week schedule. When you push the number of hours worked a week up to eighty, that break-even happens even faster—in just three weeks. As if that wasn't bad enough, the impacts of working such punishing hours are felt long after things get back to normal. The Round Table study showed that it could take several weeks of reduced productivity at forty hours a week before your team is recovered sufficiently to resume its optimum activity levels. So, if you don't use a time crunch appropriately, you'll suffer both short-term and long-term impacts even after the pressure is lifted.

Workers need time to recover from the mental and physical strain of overwork. The study recommends one to two days of paid vacation for every week of overtime. (Knowing what we know about how likely we are to take vacations and rest days, take a guess as to how many companies offer this type of policy, and worse yet, how many of us would actually take advantage of it!)

Unfortunately, the bad news doesn't end there. As we've shown, we are always impacted by the legacy and baggage of our past. As we moved from assembly lines to desk jobs, we took the eight-hour day along with us, without ever questioning whether the same assumption about the number of hours held true. A body of evidence proves that manual workers achieve maximum productivity with eight hours, but what about knowledge workers?

As it turns out, we definitely should have asked that question sooner because the answer shocked us: knowledge workers actually have FEWER numbers of hours of peak productive work than factory workers do. Instead of eight, research shows that the real number is likely closer to six good working hours per day. After you spend six hours on a challenging mental task, your brain is basically done for the day. Staying later won't accomplish anything for you (or your boss), but it will push you toward your breaking point faster.

What does this mean? For one thing, our baseline of working hours is already suboptimal. As creatives, we should probably be working closer to thirty hours per week if we want to maintain peak performance. Did you read the number thirty and blink in disbelief? Does it sound too low to you?

Creative jobs—full-time, with benefits—are hard to come by. Forty-three percent of the creative industry is freelance in the United Kingdom, and that number is expected to tip into the majority by 2020.[30] Many freelancers need to take on secondary, side work to cover their costs or to make up for a lack of pensions and benefits. Built into our understanding of the work ethic that is required of "successful, productive" creatives is the additional, adjacent, and often unreported work that takes up bigger and bigger parts of our days and weeks—even for those of us who do have traditional jobs.

Isn't it funny that our anchor number (the one that helps us determine if something else is too high or too low) is already too high, based as it is on a system that was built for an entirely different type of work? After all, we can't come up with creative concepts or strategies at the same rate as someone manufacturing widgets on an assembly line. The metric of having an eight-hour day is already redundant by any logical, evidence-based standard. This is why the work of people like Tony Schwartz has been so important. Schwartz advocates measuring our energy instead of our time to maximize our creative outputs. If you're doing very intensive intellectual work, you might be exhausted after three hours—in which case you should probably take a break or even call it a day. It's a radical new approach that is redefining the way we work and which we will dive into in greater detail in a later chapter.

WORK DETACHMENT

The 2008 recession had a profound effect on our attitudes around not just work but specifically overwork. Living with the constant fear of unemployment was a scary reality for millions of people. With so much uncertainty, it's not surprising that we focused on practical things we could control: the hours we worked and the effort we put in to demonstrate our worth to our bosses. We were trained to not just expect long hours but to actually be happy and grateful for the opportunity to work them. It's clear how the stresses and anxieties of living through periods of economic turbulence seeped into our collective psyche.

To be clear, blue-collar workers suffered a crippling blow as they had to deal with increased redundancies due to outsourcing and technological innovations. In other words, as chronicled in the heartbreaking article "Mortality and Morbidity in the 21st Century," once those jobs disappeared, unlike jobs in other creative industries, they weren't ever going to come back.[31]

Productive Creatives fared slightly better. While many creative industries appeared to bounce back after the recession, the truth is that the celebrated recovery was achieved at the cost of wages and working conditions—this time for white-collar workers who were subjected to the same mistreatment as their blue-collar contemporaries, only decades apart.

Creative workers and blue-collar workers alike have internalized many of the work anxieties that were at their peak between

2007 and 2009. Fusing them with our culturally ingrained Work Devotion, creatives have constructed a toxic work environment for themselves that is typified by overwork, burnout, and a fanatical obsession with output.

In Adobe's global study on creativity, they cite a common refrain in knowledge worker industries called the "Workplace Creativity Gap," defined as "more pressure to be productive than creative at work."[32] We don't make time for creativity, despite it being a core value and a fundamental competitive advantage.

I know I've felt this way as well. I was recently at a fiction writing retreat where the discussion shifted to maintaining a competitive edge in publishing. I was told that the only way to stay relevant was to dramatically increase my writing output. Some writers brag about releasing four novel-length books a year. There's the speed-up. The other piece of advice I heard was to take on more of the marketing, promotion, and social media work that's required to build audiences. That's the stretch-out.

We're seeing this happen across industries. Everyone's trying to do more, with less, for less. And it's not working.

Over the course of the past decade, we have managed to reinforce a work culture that has turned continuous output into both a signal of personal validation and a professional survival imperative. That's a lot of complicated, intense emotion to attach to the jobs that we do. These emotional ties cloud our judgment, which is why we don't change or alter our behavior, even when we know that it is hurting us.

There are also some disturbing implications. For one thing, we now know that many people are doing the work of more than one person, and yet we're being told that failing to keep up is a reflection of our poor management of our own productivity. It's highly convenient for companies to take advantage of this notion, when in reality, it is simply not possible for us to fit the work of two or three people into a single eight (or even ten or twelve) hour day. And so, we try to keep up, we promise to do better, we read hacks, use frameworks, attack our inbox with vigor—all for a game in which the odds have been stacked against us from the start.

Summary of Big Ideas

➡ The 2008 financial crisis was psychologically devastating and underscored the importance of overwork as a means for survival—behaviors we've maintained despite the economic recovery.

➡ After the economic recovery, many employers utilized the great speed-up (requiring workers to increase their pace of production) and the great stretch-out (adding more responsibilities to a role) which added to the culture of overwork.

➡ The forty-hour workweek was a construct created for manual labor during the Industrial Revolution and is not reflective of the working conditions Productive Creatives face today.

OUR MEDIA CULTURE
[STORIES]

4.

THE SHADOW DREAM

EVEN JACK DORSEY WANTS TO BE STEVE JOBS

Steve Jobs is both man and myth. As the obsessive hero behind Apple's global ascendency, his story has been captured and spread through Silicon Valley lore, twice on Hollywood screens, and in the 592 pages of Walter Isaacson's best-selling biography. It's hard to ignore his influence and notoriety, nor the role he played in the modern rendition of the classic "something from nothing" tale. Jobs helped solidify the mythology of the garage start-up, which has become a recurring narrative in entrepreneurship: work hard enough and the world can be yours.

Not surprising, then, is that Jobs has sparked many fanatic followers, each seeking to adopt his personal characteristics, managerial methods, or minimalist lifestyle. Countless articles that promise to reveal the secrets of his success have been published. Even modern tycoons aren't exempt from the desire to emulate him.

Elizabeth Holmes, the founder of the embattled health care company Theranos, which at one point was valued at $9 billion USD, looked to Jobs as her idol. A 2016 article described her as someone who "comported herself in a distinctly Jobsian fashion. She adopted black turtlenecks, would boast of never taking a vacation, and would come to practice veganism."[1]

In *Hatching Twitter*, Nick Bilton describes Twitter CEO Jack Dorsey's obsession with Jobs:

> "During one discussion with a well-known Apple designer who had been hired at Square, Jack heard that Jobs didn't consider himself a CEO but rather an "editor." Soon Jack started referring to himself as "the editor," not "just the CEO" of Square. During one talk to employees, he announced: "I've often spoken to the editorial nature of what I think my job is. I think I'm just an editor."

The gravitational pull of a hero is strong—whether they intend it or not, people are driven to follow in their footsteps. As we struggle to make sense of these cultural icons, we reduce them to a set of quirks and characteristics. In his many portraits, Jobs is portrayed as an uncompromising perfectionist with an unyielding work ethic, who sacrifices everything for his vision, including close friendships and even his relationship with his daughter.

The patterns and themes that emerge from his and other archetypal hero stories are significant; they give us clues as to what is shaping our beliefs today. In his best-selling book *The Black Swan*, Nassim Taleb describes the narrative fallacy: the tendency that humans have to bind facts together to support their worldview, even when they may not be strictly true.

Taleb writes:

> "Once your mind is inhabited with a certain view of the world, you will tend to only consider instances proving you to be right. Paradoxically, the more information you have, the more justified you will feel in your views."

While this seems to impose a sense of order and meaning on tangential chaos, the narrative fallacy only gives us the illusion of understanding.

The characters and stories that define what we believe to be the "keys to success"—and the heroes we choose to champion in rhetoric, art, and media—are products of their time, and as such can be quite telling. For example, when we talk about our modern-day heroes, we tend to focus on one central theme: work. Whether it's Steve Jobs or Beyoncé, Bill Gates or Oprah, Mark Zuckerberg or Elon Musk, the narratives that we build around them almost always focus on their intense focus and seemingly endless capacity for labor. Hard work is the new marker of heroic deeds, and it is an essential part of how we see the world.

At the heart of our contemporary relationship with work is the American Dream, the ultimate ethos that has captured our collective yearning to realize our potential. One of the most culturally enduring and pervasive narratives, it dangles the promise of opportunity and prosperity to every individual who is willing to work hard for them. America's most influential export, this notion has become a myth, told and retold through every medium, from books and television shows to newspapers and politics.

Over 240 years old, the American Dream has been adapted, evolved, tweaked, and adjusted in response to a constantly changing world. In this chapter we'll deconstruct how various people and events shaped it: from the early European settlers who came to America looking for a better life, to the double inflation crisis of the '70s. Each piece of our history contributed something to the dream, making it what it has become today.

But where did this idea of "working hard" come from? When did filling our hours with toil become something praiseworthy?

In ancient Greece, the elite distinguished themselves by their ability to *not* work. Having leisure time—that is, time that they could spend on such lofty pursuits as philosophical debate and self-development—was seen as the ultimate marker of success. Work was considered an unpleasant necessity that should be delegated to slaves and members of the lower classes. Working more than was needed to create this time for self-reflection was frowned upon.

It must be noted, however, that the Greek definition of "work" emerged long before the notion of a knowledge economy existed and referred to manual labor. Developing a deeper understanding of the world through philosophy and science was understood to be the ultimate expression of human purpose. Looking at how knowledge work has evolved, one could argue that the Greeks would consider much of today's creative work to be the domain of the lower classes as well, as the current systems of overwork rarely allow sufficient time to sit and reflect.

During the Middle Ages, Christian dogma began to influence attitudes about work in a few ways. First, work was seen as divine punishment for man's original sin and hence as an act of penance. It wasn't until the Protestant Reformation in the sixteenth century that work came to be seen as good in and of itself. For John Calvin and Martin Luther, work was a form of worship, a direct opportunity to serve God. This idea would have an enormous influence on the way we view work today.

A DREAM WAS BORN

The phrase "The American Dream" was coined in 1931 by historian James Truslow Adams. In his popular book *Epic of America*, he described it as "a dream of social order in which each man and each woman shall be able to attain to the fullest stature of which they are innately capable and be recognized by others for what they are, regardless of the fortuitous circumstances of birth or position." Though Adams's book was published, ironically, at the height of the Great Depression, the sentiment itself was seeded in the allure of an unexplored frontier, the opportunity to go out into the great unknown and be rewarded with prosperity. For all its hardships, European pioneers enjoyed much more freedom in the New World than they had in the strictly hierarchical, aristocratic societies that they'd left behind in Europe. Coming to a new land gave them the opportunity to reinvent themselves. Tracing the evolution of the American Dream was one of our favorite parts of writing this book, as each generation has interpreted and built upon its ideals to create a vision for their own future. Let's take a look at foundations of the dream, and how they've changed over the past several decades.

A CITY UPON A HILL

The roots of the American Dream extend all the way back to the ideologies of the Puritans, reformed Protestants who fled to New England to escape religious persecution at the beginning of the seventeenth century. In fact, according to historian and Harvard professor Perry Miller, an authority on American Puritanism, "without some understanding of Puritanism, it may safely be said, there is no understanding of America." This view is echoed by the American studies scholar Andreea Mingiuc, who stated that "one might rightfully claim that the Puritans' power of vision built America and its mythology."[2]

John Winthrop, the spiritual leader of one of the Puritan factions that set sail in 1630, had a specific vision of what the New World could provide: a model society built upon Christian charity that would act as an example for the rest of the world, or, as Winthrop famously put it, that would be "a city upon a hill," an expression he borrowed from Jesus's Sermon on the Mount.[3] Those words would eventually become a metaphor for American ideals and would be quoted by John F. Kennedy, Ronald Reagan, and Barack Obama, who in a 2006 commencement speech proclaimed that "I see students that have come here from over one hundred different countries, believing like those first settlers that they too could find a home in this City on a Hill—that they too could find success in this unlikeliest of places."[4]

The Puritans believed that they were elect—chosen by God for a special purpose and led by Him to a promised land. This perspective would set the stage for the "doctrine of exceptionalism" that would become an integral part of the American Dream and a defining element of America's identity as a whole.[5]

Work as a Virtue

While we had heard the phrase "Puritan work ethic" hundreds of times, we never really understood what it was that drove the Puritans to work so tirelessly. We learned that they were driven by an unshakable belief in the doctrine of predetermination. Rejecting the Roman Catholic Church's notion of free will, the Puritans believed that on the day they were born, God already knew whether or not they would be going to heaven or hell. But while God might know if they were chosen or not, they didn't. All that they could do was look for signs of it in their lives.

Puritans constantly reflected about their actions, looking for clues about the fate of their souls. They believed that a person's way of life provided a good indication of their soul's status, since those who were chosen for heaven were not only thought to perform good works, pray, and attend church regularly but exhibit a strong work ethic, a sense of frugality, and, not incidentally, accumulate a significant amount of wealth.

And here's where the role of work really comes into play: Even if you were chosen, you still had to work hard and prepare for this act of grace by leading a righteous life. Those who were lazy were seen as exhibiting signs that demonstrated that they were *not* elect and had not been chosen for salvation. Thus, work became both an act and a proof of moral virtue, directly tied to the fate of their immortal souls, while idleness was seen as a vice.[6] Work, as noted above, was also a kind of worship; it glorified God and added a benefit to society. This also planted the seeds of the "rags to riches" narrative that would become such a familiar story. The rise from poverty wasn't just about material success but attested to a spiritual success as well.

This philosophy dovetailed neatly with the needs of the Industrial Revolution—it was convenient to characterize work as something moral and good, just as industries were expanding rapidly and factories had large numbers of manual labor slots that needed to be filled. The Protestant work ethic instilled a dignity in labor, regardless of the task.

The echoes of this work ethic were still reverberating in 1971, when President Richard Nixon addressed the nation on Labor Day and stated that "the work ethic holds that labor is good in itself; that a man or woman at work not only makes a contribution to his fellow man but becomes a better person by virtue of the act of working. That work ethic is ingrained in the American character. That is why most of us consider it immoral to be lazy or slothful—even if a person is well off enough not to have to work or deliberately avoids work by going on welfare."[7] The words he used are clear: being lazy is immoral. Working hard is virtuous. This has given us one of our most powerful beliefs, one that still complicates our relationships with ourselves (as we'll see later on).

He Who Suffers Conquers

The last thing that struck us when evaluating the influence of the Puritans on the American Dream (and what we've written here by no means exhausts the topic; please refer to our extended reading list online, should you wish to explore it further), was their fortitude in times of suffering. The Puritans had been so persecuted at nearly every stage of their history that they became a people who not only endured in the face of hardship but accepted and embraced their struggle as an inevitable part of their triumph. Puritan pastor John Gere summed up this sentiment when he declared that "he who suffers conquers." Recognize the embedded assumption of sacrifice and suffering as a good thing? We mentioned it in Chapter 1. Hello, Work Devotion!

The Puritans considered suffering to be a path for redemption from original sin. It's one of the biggest foundations of our "no pain, no gain" philosophies that link hard work with both spiritual and material rewards. No wonder we've grown to take work seriously—it was once considered an act of Godliness, directly linked to one's moral character, and potentially the fate of your immortal soul. When the President of the United States condemns laziness as an immoral act, it becomes clear how deeply these belief systems are baked into our modern-day beliefs and attitudes.

RAGS TO RICHES

The next big evolution of the American Dream would happen in 1776, upon the founding of the United States as a nation, when the Declaration of Independence would ratify the optimism and potential of frontier life with the devoted work ethic of the people who had come to call this wild land home. The idea that a person was entitled to "life, liberty, and the pursuit of happiness" as an inalienable right would reaffirm the philosophy that had defined the New World, formally integrating it into the identity of the United States of America. The notion that a person's ambition can be used to create a better life for themselves became more than a powerful idea—it was written into law.

The concept of the self-made man would also become popularized during this time. One of its greatest archetypes was Benjamin Franklin, the "original self-made man," whose rise from a humble son of a candlemaker to one of the most respected figures in science and politics would cement the mythology of the American Dream. Franklin himself perpetuated it through his own writings, mixing advice with Puritan wisdom to encourage each man to pursue his own dreams.

Other authors picked up the theme. In 1858, Charles C. B. Seymour profiled sixty individuals in his book *Self-Made Men*, including Benjamin Franklin, Immanuel Kant, Andrew Jackson, Alexander Wilson, and more, publicizing the real-world viability of rising above your circumstances.[8]

The California Gold Rush of 1849 added a new dimension to the American Dream—that of overnight success. Historian H.W. Brands wrote about the power of this idea, noting that "The old American Dream...was the dream of Puritans, of Benjamin Franklin's 'Poor Richard'...of men and women content to accumulate their modest fortunes a little at a time, year by year by year. The new dream was the dream of instant wealth, won in a twinkling by audacity and good luck."[9]

One interesting historical note that we found (which might be a bit controversial) links the work ethic and the American Dream to the Civil War. In a 2009 article entitled "Whatever Happened to the Work Ethic," Steven Malanga contrasted the Protestant work ethic of the Northern Colonies to the aristocratic ethos of the southern settlers, who sought only economic opportunity. "Rather than viewing all honest work as honorable, the [southerners] developed what historian C. Vann Woodward calls the 'Southern Ethic' which saw some work as fit for only slaves," he wrote. "In the end, these attitudes proved the South's greatest vulnerability, as the North, shaped by the work ethic, brought to bear its industrial might against the narrow economy of the South, built precariously on tobacco and slave labor and a cavalier rather than Puritan ethic."[10] After the war, the Protestant ethic became something that was universally American.

The Horatio Alger Myth: Hard Work Pays Off

On the cultural front, the rags to riches archetype was further cemented by authors like Horatio Alger Jr., whose young-adult novels offered variations of the same story again and again: a boy born into impoverished circumstances who bettered his lot through hard work and determination. The protagonist of his breakout novel *Ragged Dick* is a homeless fourteen-year-old boy who impresses his bosses with his work ethic and his honesty.[11] When a thief snatches his savings account passbook and threatens the financial security Dick has built through his honest labor, bank officials recognize him from his regular visits to make deposits and the thief is arrested. Dick is rewarded not only for his honesty and hard work but his thriftiness. The theme became so recognizable (Alger would write over 120 books) that it's now known as the "Horatio Alger myth."[12] The spirit of the myth Alger wrote about is alive and well today: every year the Horatio Alger Association recognizes distinguished Americans who "exemplify dedication, purpose, and perseverance in their personal and professional lives."[13]

And who could forget "The Checkered Game of Life," a Milton Bradley board game sold door-to-door in the 1860s, in which players were rewarded for getting an education and starting a family and were punished for gambling or idleness.

This was a turning point for the American Dream, as the pursuit of happiness was firmly linked with the accumulation of material things, an attitude that was only amplified by the economic boom of the Gilded Age and later by the decadent prosperity of the booming 1920s. If hard work was a virtue, prosperity was a right. One of the first presidents to put this belief into practice was Franklin Delano Roosevelt, who through the New Deal and the Economic Bill of Rights advocated for equal opportunity for home ownership, financial security through a well-providing job, universal health care, and access to education, calling these things "a right" and stating that "we have come to a clear realization of the fact...that true individual freedom cannot exist without economic security and independence."

This formalized the promise of a prosperous future for every American and introduced a more collective-oriented understanding of the American Dream. The Social Security Act of 1935, which ensured a "safe old age" for workers via a mandated pension, would be the first piece of legislation that was linked to the promise of the American Dream.

During the Second World War, American participation was seen as a way to extend the American Dream to other nations. FDR would capture this aspiration in his 1941 State of the Union address, in which he laid out the four essential human freedoms: freedom of speech, freedom of religion, freedom from want, and freedom from fear. These would be captured in the now iconic Norman Rockwell paintings. Arguably the most recognized one, Freedom from Want, is often called the "Norman Rockwell Thanksgiving." WWII became an opportunity to demonstrate the moral righteousness of the American Dream, making America a true City on a Hill.

President Truman expanded the American Dream even farther after the war with his GI Bill, which rewarded veterans with a government-paid college degre, and facilitated home ownership through low-interest mortgages. Making education accessible to a whole generation was seen as proof that the American Dream was real. Once a privilege that was only available to the wealthy, higher education was now within reach of the average Joe.

This postwar social contract would, in combination with a booming economy, create an environment where it was indeed possible for the general public to gain some level of prosperity.

The emergence of suburbia introduced a new aspirational lifestyle for the masses. At its core a simple but powerful idea, "making a house a home" became a powerful ideology that embodied living the American Dream and was powered by consumption. Americans had access to an endless stream of new products and services from dishwashers to televisions that were designed to help facilitate this new metric of success.

According to the US Department of Housing and Urban Development, between 1940 and 1960, the percentage of Americans who owned their own homes rose from 43.6 percent to 61.9 percent thanks to accessible financing, the GI Bill of Rights, and a rush to build affordable housing.[14] As a society, we were moving away from Adams's broad vision of a dream in which each and every American could attain the "stature that they are innately capable of," toward one in which a set of specific markers denoted success.

The 1940s and '50s also ushered in some important legislation that created very stable economic conditions and favorable working conditions. In 1948, General Motors and the United Auto Workers Union negotiated the Treaty of Detroit, a labor agreement that guaranteed annual income increases, access to health benefits, and monthly pensions, leading the way for other companies to follow, and ensuring that both labor and management benefitted from the economic growth. This period has been called "The Great Compression," because the income gap between upper and middle classes shrank significantly (it would never be that narrow again). This economic heyday was buoyed by the notion of the "virtuous cycle"—because companies were paying higher wages, workers had a disposable income they could now spend on products and services. This demand would create more jobs in order to fill this increased need, and the cycle would continue.

THE MODERN AMERICAN DREAM:
TELEVISION AND MEDIA

Television created a new set of cultural narratives that reinforced these norms. Just 3 percent of households owned a TV set in 1949. By 1956, 72 percent did.

Interestingly (but perhaps unsurprisingly), some of the most iconic TV shows, including classics like *Father Knows Best* and *Leave it to Beaver*, were created after the production side of the business traded in gray New York for the endless summer of Los Angeles. Television's sun-lit view of the "real American family," with its detached home, car, white picket fence, dog, and 2.5 kids, is still influential today. Television did much to perpetuate gender roles as well, with its hardworking fathers and stay-at-home mothers. June Cleaver vacuuming in pearls provided an indelible image of the "perfect mother and wife," who not only had time to cook and clean but to look great doing it.

One of the most popular shows of that time was *The Adventures of Ozzie and Harriet*, a radio program turned into a television show that aired between 1952 and 1966. It perfectly captured an idealized version of a white, prosperous family, ensconced in a comfortable home that was filled with shiny gadgets.[15] What's interesting is that television historians note that the Nelsons' living standards were relatively modest, at least when compared to ours today.

That modest interpretation of the American Dream would soon get a big upgrade through the introduction of personal financing via credit cards, giving American families the ability to reach, just a little, beyond their means. Joe Nocera, the author of *A Piece of the Action: How the Middle Class Joined the Money Class*, called this a "money revolution," noting that the doubling of consumer credit from $45 billion USD in 1945 to $105 billion USD in 1970 was tantamount to the middle class "betting that tomorrow would be better than today." And indeed, why not? Up to this point the socioeconomic ascension was not only possible but expected and seemingly without limit.

Up until the 1960s, the promise of the American Dream had been reserved for white people. Like his namesake Martin Luther, Dr. Martin Luther King would offer a new vision of the American Dream, one that was inclusive of all races. The notion of work ethic was also questioned during this turbulent decade, as many Americans embraced an ethos of instant gratification and hedonism. The social upheavals of the '60s would be followed by a series of economic shocks in the '70s, including double digit annual rises in inflation that devastated savings and reinforced a culture of free spending.

It seemed that after the protests and the energy crisis, people were ready to live in the moment and not worry too much about the future. This tendency was reflected in shows like *The Brady Bunch*. The Bradys' two cars, big house, annual vacations, and housekeeper stood in stark contrast with the Nelsons' thriftier lifestyle.

With inflation under control and the markets recovering, by the 1980s Americans were embracing materialism with gusto. Thanks to Reagan era deregulation, especially in the financial industry, credit was easier to access than ever before. As the American Dream refocused itself toward the accumulation of wealth, television's families became richer than ever.

This new lifestyle standard was reflected in *The Cosby Show*'s Huxtable family, or, in far grander style, the Carringtons from *Dynasty*, which brought the images and trappings of wealth into the living rooms of millions of Americans each week. Culturally, we saw the emergence of the "yuppie," a college-educated Boomer with a well-paying job and expensive tastes. We had moved into an era where living the American Dream meant having fun, enjoying life's excesses, and trying to make as much money as possible. Norman Rockwell's Freedom from Want had shifted into the Freedom to Want, and we wanted lots of things. The Home Shopping Network (1982) and QVC (1986) made it easier than ever to consume from the comfort of your home.

During this time, movies were still creating narratives about individual accountability and the transformative power of work. *The Karate Kid* and *Rocky* would give us iconic video montages of the need to push ourselves harder in order to triumph. Perhaps reflecting the wild abandon of the '80s, promos for *Scarface* bore the taglines "The World is Yours" and "He Lived the American Dream—With a Vengeance." Tony Montana's ascension to power was not based on his moral standing but on violence. His famous quote "In this country, you gotta make the money first. Then when you get the money, you get the power. Then when you get the power, then you get the women," is an explosion of the mythology of the self-made man but without the moral compass of Horatio Alger's deserving characters. Tony's eventual downfall would become an early warning sign of trouble to come, a reflection of what the future would hold.

CALLING OUT THE JONESES

By the 1990s and early 2000s, the economic data showed that life in America was pretty good. Even adjusted for inflation, households were earning nearly double what they had in the '60s, and nearly three quarters of Americans owned their houses. But something strange was also happening. Though more people than ever before were living the American Dream, there was a growing sense of unease. In March of 1995, *Business Week* published the results of a poll that showed that two out of three respondents believed it was harder to achieve the American Dream than it was ten years ago, and three quarters of respondents believed it would be harder still to achieve the American Dream in the next decade.[16] This sentiment was echoed in surveys taken in the early 2000s. A CNN poll conducted in both 2003 and 2006 found that 54 percent believed the American Dream was no longer attainable.

This confused us. Why were people feeling this way in a time of unprecedented income stability and home ownership? This same question puzzled economist Gregg Easterbrook, author of *The Progress Paradox: How Life Gets Better While People Feel Worse.*

The innate expectation for ever-improving circumstances and opportunities had engendered the dangerous notion that nothing was ever enough, that success was a constant and steady motion upwards, and that to truly achieve the dream, one had to constantly want for more of everything. "For at least a century, Western life has been dominated by a revolution of rising expectations," Easterbrook wrote. "Each generation expected more than its antecedent. Now, most Americans and Europeans already have what they need, in addition to considerable piles of stuff they don't need."[17]

We have become a society defined by our property. We link our worthiness to our bank accounts and then constantly expect both to grow. According to Easterbrook, the rise of our standard of living had been accompanied by a rash of mental health research that showed that more and more Americans were unhappy. Instead of being happy that they owned a house, Americans now dreamed of a bigger house. Of another car. Of a fancier television. The American Dream was inexorably tied to the accumulation of material goods. To live it, we had to keep buying, keep consuming. And if we couldn't afford it? That's what credit cards are for.

REALITY TV: FAME AND SOCIAL MEDIA

Ironically, many of our struggles with these issues would be reflected in television's boom of reality programming. *Survivor* created a literal rags to riches story, in which participants competed with each other to survive on a remote island so they could win a cash prize. Other franchises, such as *X-Factor*, *American Idol*, and *America's Next Top Model* sold the same premise: fame and success can happen to you if you're willing to work for it. Shows like the *Real Housewives of Beverly Hills* and its subsequent spin-offs exposed the hyper competitiveness of people who were desperate to prove to the world that they were "successful." For the MTV generation, shows like *Laguna Beach* and *The Hills* revealed another aspect of the American Dream—the desire for fame. These shows would follow the "real lives" of affluent teenagers in Southern California (there's that mythical gold rush state again!), simply to showcase their wealth, evidenced by flying on private jets to Cabo, driving expensive cars, and living a high-style life. *My Super Sweet 16* documented the often ridiculously excessive celebrations that wealthy teens threw for their sixteenth birthdays.

In 2014, a new show called *The Rich Kids of Beverly Hills* followed teenagers whose parents were very wealthy, including Dorothy Wang, whose family is estimated to be worth billions, as they bought new apartments and spent their parents' money. Wang described herself as "funemployed," and her social media feeds were full of pictures of shopping sprees and luxury vacations aboard yachts. These teens didn't even have to do anything to become famous—they were simply rewarded for having rich parents. In 2005, the *Washington Post* published a survey that showed that two thirds of teens predict they will one day be rich, with 31 percent of teens saying it's highly likely that they will be famous one day to boot.[18] Jake Halpert, author of the book *Fame Junkies,* interviewed a group of girls who said they would rather be in proximity to fame, like a celebrity's assistant, than be the CEO of a company.[19]

Coupled with the rise of social media, the most contemporary version of the American Dream has become so mutated that Adams would have a hard time recognizing it. It was no longer enough to be rich; now we wanted to be famous, too. Andy Warhol said that in the future everyone would be famous for fifteen minutes, and that's never been truer today. Justin Bieber, one of the biggest recording artists of all time, was discovered by his future agent, Scooter Braun, on YouTube after uploading videos of himself busking on street corners. He would go on to win a Grammy and have platinum albums—a digital retelling of a Horatio Alger myth, rags to riches thanks to the web. The Internet is the latest gold rush, complete with a new set of heroes, including comedian Bo Burnham (his comedy videos racked up more than 70 million views and earned him a full-length comedy special on Comedy Central at just eighteen years of age, followed by two successful Netflix specials), model Kate Upton, and musical artists including The Weeknd, Charlie Puth, Ed Sheeran, and Shawn Mendes—all who got their start on social media.

Karen Sternheimer, a sociology professor and the author of *Celebrity Culture and the American Dream: Stardom and Social Mobility*, posits that it's because of the current economic instability that so many young people (who were in their formative years during the 2008 recession we wrote about in the last chapter) are flocking to the web. "In this economic environment, fame might seem a reasonable escape from financial responsibilities. For someone with few other options, a reality show based on being in a relationship with a celebrity or someone who gets drunk and fights at bars could be one of their only likely means of social mobility," she writes. "And while it may seem that this environment of instant celebrity offers many a shot at moving up economically, it has largely served to reinforce an illusion that anyone—no matter where they come from—can still make it big in America. The messages seem to be that if they can do it, so can you."[20] Even as their economic prospects have worsened, the

Internet has created a new platform of opportunity for a generation who sees technology as a pathway to fame, recognition, and
fortune. It's the American Dream 2.0.

BEWARE THE SHADOW DREAM

Our belief that anyone can make it in America if they work hard
enough doesn't represent the full picture. In reality, a dark corollary of the American Dream also exists that is often unsaid and
unexpressed but felt all the same: if you're not successful, then
you must not have been working hard enough. It is the shadow
of the American Dream, and the inescapable consequence of carrying its logic through to its conclusion. After all, if we as individuals believe so strongly in our vaunted status as "self-made"
people, then that would mean that those who don't achieve the
trappings of success bear the responsibility for their failure.

Even though we know this is not the truth, that there are
very real socioeconomic limitations that can severely limit
a person's upward mobility, an irrational part of us looks at
someone's inability to succeed and thinks that it must be their
fault. But perseverance and resilience *are* important factors in
the overcoming of obstacles and the achievement of success, we
can hear you saying. Of course they are, but those are just pieces
of the puzzle and certainly not the biggest or most important.
For the first time in American history, an up-and-coming generation—Millennials, the most educated generation to date—
will be financially worse off than their parents.[21]

Productive Creative Millennials face increasing student
debt, wage stagnation, and a prohibitively expensive real-estate
market. Not to mention the devastating impacts of the 2008
financial crisis that put such a huge dent in our lifetime earning
potential. As the economist Steven Rattner puts it, "Those who

graduate in weaker economic times typically earn less than those who enter the workforce during more robust periods. Starting behind often means never catching up."[22] Many of the challenges Productive Creatives face today simply cannot be solved by working harder. As you saw in the last chapter, we're already working harder than ever before—and it's not working.

Our point here isn't to paint a dark picture but to shine light on a stark reality: that the systems we are working in are at odds with many of the stories our society tells itself about work, success, and effort. We cannot seem to fathom the existence of a challenge that cannot be solved by trying harder because we've been culturally programmed to think that way for a century and more.

We want you to step back, take a look at those forces, and recognize that the burden of your success does not lie solely on your shoulders, despite the cultural myths and values that are trying to convince you otherwise.

In his best-selling book *Outliers*, Malcolm Gladwell documented the two big factors that went into famous people's successes: a dedication to acquire an intense level of mastery (his famous 10,000 hours rule) but also serendipity: favorable economic conditions, lucky opportunities, fortuitous encounters that helped propel them to fame. Consider the story of Bill Gates, who was lucky enough that the proceeds of his school's bake sale were used to purchase a PC and that his high school was next to the University of Washington, which provided both the computational facilities he needed to keep improving his skill set and the opportunity to meet his future business partner Paul Allen. Not to mention the fact that his father, Bill Gates Sr., was the attorney for many of Seattle's top technology start-ups. The addition of a technologically savvy, well-connected father was another bonus that helped serendipity along.

It's funny, but despite Gladwell's insistence that successful people "are invariably the beneficiaries of hidden advantages and extraordinary opportunities and cultural legacies that allow them to learn and work hard and make sense of the world in ways that others can not," the concept that really resonated with most readers of *Outliers* was the 10,000-hour rule. Of course, we would be drawn to a number that quantified the payoff of the work ethic!

We couldn't help but laugh. As we mentioned in the beginning of this chapter, humans are exceptionally skilled at interpreting stories in ways that bolster their existing worldviews. We see what we want to see.

Our social identities are shaped by our jobs (and the political and economic systems they sit within), and in turn, we make choices based on those identities to perpetuate those systems. We are caught in a loop.

Even with a net worth of $1.4 billion USD and a resume that boasts founding the social network Twitter (which employs nearly 4,000 people and serves 368 million active users), and Square (a mobile payment platform which employs over 1,000 people and is valued at $6 billion USD), Jack Dorsey still wants to be Steve Jobs.[23] Even the 1 percent aren't exempt from the cultural magnetism of icons; they are just as susceptible to the narratives of success that the rest of us are constantly bombarded with.

We spend an average of one third of our lives (80,000 hours) at work. The time that we spend in a particular social and psychological environment shapes how we make sense of the world. Rarely do we ask ourselves how we have been shaped at the deepest level by our jobs, but beyond our professional identities, our characters and our worldviews are deeply influenced by our work environments.

In reading all of this historical evidence, we wondered if we hadn't in some ways trained ourselves to be unhappy—that much of the discontent that we feel today stems from our deep-seated belief that suffering is ennobling, that idleness is immoral, and that owning a lot of stuff is a visible sign of grace. We have been programmed to believe that home ownership is a right and that economic mobility is as constant as the law of gravity. No wonder the 2008 recession was so psychologically devastating for us.

Summary of Big Ideas

➡ The American Dream is one of the most fundamental and deeply held beliefs about work that we have today.

➡ The Puritan roots of the dream intertwine suffering and sacrifice as key moral markers of success.

➡ The iterations of the American Dream as portrayed in the media have slowly taken to encompass an increasing level of consumerism.

➡ The Shadow Dream: the unspoken belief that if you are not successful it's because you didn't work hard enough.

5.

THE MYTH OF THE SELF-MADE MAN

You might be wondering why a book that is supposed to be about the future of work, especially the future of Productive Creative work, has been so focused on the past. We didn't intend it to be that way. In fact, we wanted to do the opposite, to dive into the future disruptions and possibilities, but every time we did we'd come up against something that didn't make sense, a behavior, a narrative, a reaction that confused us. And so, we'd tug at that thread, unraveling it bit by bit to see where it came from, and how it was impacting us. In a world where innovation moves lightning fast, it might seem counterintuitive to keep looking backwards, but something wonderful happened: in making sense of our past, in really understanding how and why our ideals and notions about work are the way they are, the future became clearer. It was easier to spot the trends and patterns that have governed our behaviors for generations.

In the last chapter, we spent a lot of time documenting the different iterations of the American Dream and how they shaped the concepts of self-made men, of moral purity through hard work, and of the entitlement of prosperity through work ethic.

In this chapter we'll take a look at how the rise of entrepreneurship and the popularity of purposeful work dogma have combined and spread via the amalgamation of celebrity culture and social media to create a new explosion of symbols and narratives. Because here's the thing: while the American Dream might have evolved, its foundational roots are still strong. For example, a report from the National Association of Realtors showed that most Millennials still dream of home ownership, despite unfavorable economic conditions.[1] So while we've wandered away from the American Dream's original spirit, its echoes still linger, and we are still being influenced by them: a weird alchemy of the Puritan work ethic, materialistic spending, and self-worth linked to work.

When we examine stories in the media today, contemporary symbols emerge that are reinforcing those old narratives in new ways. Let's take a look at a few of them.

1. The Next Big Thing: The Self-Made Man 2.0

The rags to riches story that we've been told since the nineteenth century has become updated with a global perspective. Our definition of riches has expanded to include a new breed of billionaires—the creators of global corporations and brands that have changed the way we live. As we move from the Industrial Revolution to the Information Age and knowledge work (as mentioned in Chapter 1), our new heroes reflect those changes.

Today, technology provides the latest gold rush of opportunity, on both a macro and a micro level. On a macro level, we have stories like Bill Gates's and Steve Jobs's, who founded Microsoft and Apple, multi-billion dollar companies that changed the face of personal computing. From the creation of Windows OS to the launch of the iPhone, these two powerhouses would redefine American success and the cultural appeal of the CEO. For Millennials, it is Jeff Bezos, the founder of Amazon, and Mark

Zuckerberg, who as a university student created Facebook, the most powerful social network in the world, connecting two billion people and changing our relationships permanently. Oprah Winfrey, an African American woman who rose from poverty to become a billionaire media personality and mogul, also embodies the accessibility of the American Dream. J.K. Rowling, the Scottish author of the Harry Potter series, was rumored to have been living in her car before she became successful and is now listed as a billionaire.

Because of their adherence to the rags to riches narrative, and their unwavering work ethic, the stories of these new heroes inspired the world. They hit all the right notes: Work Devotion, sacrifice, struggle, unrelenting focus, and the rewards of unimaginable material wealth. More than that, they whisper to us about our own potential. They reinforce the same themes that have been shaping our work perspectives for centuries.

We took a cursory glance (read: very quick Google search) of some of the media coverage that these celebrated entrepreneurs have received. Here's some snippets:

- A *Vanity Fair* profile of Bill Gates quoted him as saying, "I was quite fanatical about work. I worked weekends, I didn't really believe in vacations," and told how he memorized the license plates of his employees, so he could track when they arrived and left work each day.[2]

- When asked how many hours he works in a day, Zuckerberg said, "If you count the time I'm in the office, it's probably no more than 50-60 hours a week. But if you count all the time I'm focused on our mission, that's basically my whole life."[3] Another article said he routinely works fifteen-hour days.[4]

- Jeff Bezos worked twelve-hour days, seven days a week in the early days of Amazon.

- Current Apple CEO Tim Cook is a "workaholic who begins emailing his underlings at 4:30 a.m. each day. . . The [then COO] prides himself on being the first into the office and the last one out. At IBM he volunteered to work in the factory on Christmas and New Year's day."[5]

- Marissa Mayer, then-CEO of Yahoo, is described by colleagues as someone who will "literally work 24 hours a day, 7 days a week."[6]

- Starbucks CEO Howard Schultz pulls thirteen-hour days at the office and then continues to work when he returns home. An article comments that he "rarely socializes" and works on Sundays.[7]

- Jeffrey Immelt, then-GE CEO, works out every morning at 5:30 a.m. and has been logging one hundred-hour weeks for the past twenty-four years.

- Indra Nooyi, CEO of Pepsi, told employees that her regular day starts at 7:00 a.m. and doesn't end until 8:00 p.m.

Now you might read these and think to yourself, "Well, I don't want to be Bill Gates." And that's a fair point—to be honest, neither do we. But it's not so much about wanting to emulate Bill Gates (though many people do) but about looking at the impact of what happens to our own notions of work, however subtle, when we are continuously being fed the same message about work and self-worth.

Read enough of these articles and over time, you will absorb some of the values; even if they don't have to do with you personally, they will inform your view of the world. These figures are cast as the prominent heroes of our time, as the people we should aspire to emulate. It says a lot about our society that we are idolizing a very specific type of personality, a personality that not coincidentally seems to embody the same notions surrounding the work ethic that we've been drawn to since the Puritans fled Europe in search of wealth and adventure on the American Frontier. Except now, industry has become celebrity—and CEOs have become brands in their own right, promoting their values to a global audience.

Thanks to technology, those figures now include media icons as well as CEOs: supermodels, rappers, singers, and athletes. For the next generation, figures like Kim Kardashian, worth hundreds of millions of dollars because she leveraged a sex tape into a multi-million dollar media empire including apps, a game, and a long-running television reality series, is the latest spin on our cultural obsession with rags to riches. The tech boom has created a new wave of hopeful entrepreneurs who hope to launch their careers using apps and leveraging social media platforms to become "influencers." Going viral has become the latest gold rush in today's attention-obsessed world.

In some ways, the over-availability of content gives the illusion of accessibility. I can ask Bill Gates a question on Quora, and he can answer me, which makes the distance between us seem small. If entrepreneurs are just like us, why can't we all become entrepreneurs?

The rise of influencers or microcelebrities has been an interesting addition to the celebrity/entrepreneur ecosystem because it is a modern-day version of the Steve Jobs garage start-up story, except instead of a garage, it's a person who is streaming video content to YouTube using their webcam. The latest wave of YouTube celebrities includes Yuya, a twenty-five-year-old beauty vlogger from Mexico who records beauty product reviews and tutorials for her 17.8 million subscribers. At what other point in history could a regular twenty-five-year-old have a platform to earn millions of dollars and reach millions of people? Or consider Felix Kjellberg, a twenty-nine-year-old

Swede who goes by the username of PewDiePie. He leads the pack of YouTube content creators with 54.1 million subscribers and annual revenues of $15 million USD.[8] Other Internet celebrities have successfully launched books, products, and businesses, further cementing the idea that the accessibility of the Internet means the only thing separating you from ultimate online fame is how hard you're willing to work.

2. DWYL—Do What You Love

Confucius once said, "Choose a job you love, and you will never have to work a day in your life."[9] Joseph Campbell wrote, "Follow your bliss and the universe will open doors for you where there were only walls." In 2005, Steve Jobs famously told a stadium full of new college graduates that the "only way to do great work is to love what you do," and warned them not to settle for anything less. The Holstee Manifesto, which has been shared 160 million times, starts off by saying, "This is your life.[10] Do what you love and do it often." The American writer Marsha Sinetar captured the essence of this sentiment when she wrote, "Do what you love, and the money will follow."

This is one of the biggest themes in modern-day work culture, and it's intimately linked with the American Dream, leading people to believe that if they do what they love hard enough or for long enough success will be inevitable. As we wrote earlier, it places the burden of success on the individual, and any lack of achievement can therefore be blamed on that person for "not wanting it bad enough" or "not working hard enough."

This is especially true with Millennials and younger people today, who face the paradox of having more career choices available to them but without any of the economic stability enjoyed by previous generations. They can pursue whatever profession they are interested in, but their chances of making a viable living, never mind a fortune, are more limited than their parents'. Even so, they believe that if they're not achieving their goals, the problem is with them, not with the host of shifts that have happened on an international and national level that have made it more difficult than ever for people to achieve their desired level of financial security.

And when work doesn't live up to our expectations, when it doesn't deliver the personal fulfillment we're told it should, that also sends a message that the problem is with us. A 2015 marketing survey reported that 76 percent of Gen Z wanted to "make their hobby their job" and 72 percent wanted to start their own businesses.

The work myth of DWYL is dangerous. Miya Tokumitsu, author of *Do What You Love: And Other Lies about Success and Happiness*, describes DWYL as the "unofficial work mantra of our time."[11] Its individualistic focus makes it easy for us to be so obsessed with our own work fulfillment that we ignore what beliefs like this mean for others. "The problem," she writes, "is that it leads not to salvation, but to the devaluation of actual work, including the very work it pretends to elevate—and more importantly, the dehumanization of the vast majority of laborers." Being able to do something out of love instead of financial necessity is still largely a privilege that's reserved for the elite. But thanks to the DWYL myth, we assume that people who don't love their jobs are lacking in passion and determination. And we turn that same criticism on ourselves.

The most ironic thing of all is that Work Devotion takes on an exploitative edge when it is combined with notions of "doing what you love." This is particularly true of creatives, who work in what many would consider to be "desirable" industries and are expected to not only demonstrate a solid work ethic but to be only too happy to work hard without the right compensation. Working for free, or working for not much money, has become a new norm within a media landscape where everyone is struggling to produce content to sell to consumers.

Because these industries are in demand, there is no shortage of people who are willing to work for free or for very little. The notion has become accepted that a job isn't something you do for wages, it's something you do because of your true sense of love for the work itself. And that notion has created another narrative: that if you pitch in and do more work for the same or less pay, you will be rewarded with job security. After all, if you really love what you do, why wouldn't you want to do it on weeknights and weekends and while on vacation? A labor of love has very different economic implications—and boundaries—than a job. It is important to recognize that while it might seem that the pursuit of this type of fulfilling work is an important part of our personal development, the reality is that those who are truly benefitting are the organizations which are able to cash in on this cheap labor, while convincing us that we are the ones lucky to have the chance to do such "important work."

The absurdity of our preoccupation with Do What You Love becomes a little more visible when extended to other industries, where traditionally "loving the job" has not been an express requirement and/or the jobs themselves are merely a means to pay for rent—not a path to self-enlightenment or pseudospiritual purpose. During our research, we came across a fascinating 2013 essay in the London Review of Books by Paul Myerscough that documented the organizational culture that has grown around being passionate and happy at work at Pret a Manger. One of their recruiting guidelines includes a list of seventeen undesirable behaviors for working a minimum wage job, including being "just here for the money."

Take a moment and think about that. To work at a minimum wage job at a fast food restaurant you must demonstrate that you are not, in fact, there to earn a paycheck so you can live your life but to find some sort of inherent joy and passion in the work that you do. And the organization demands that this happiness be authentic. "It isn't clear which is the more demanding," writes Myerscough. "Authenticity or performance, being it or faking it, but in either case it's difficult to believe that there isn't something demoralizing, for Pret workers perhaps more than most on the high street, not only in having their energies siphoned off by customers, but also in having to sustain the tension between performance of relentless enthusiasm at work and the experience of straightened material circumstances outside it."[12] It gets more depressing: employees are routinely evaluated on their "happiness" at work through the use of Mystery Shoppers, whose ratings determine whether or not the team gets an additional bonus at the end of the week. It should be noted that the article mentions that the average wage of a Pret employee is 6.25 GBP, which is lower than the recommended living wage, defined as 8.55 GBP by the Greater London Authority. Yes, nothing makes people happier than working at a job that doesn't actually pay them enough to live in the city they are working in. We'll deep dive into the implications of happiness as a metric in Chapter 9.

3. Special Snowflake Syndrome: Finding Your Calling

An interesting byproduct of the intermixing of Do What You Love, Self-Made Man propaganda, and the rise of social media, is a culture where we have become intensely focused on the personal fulfillment of work and what it means to our own sense of self. Essentially, Millennials and Gen Z were raised in a world where they were told repeatedly that they were capable of becoming anything they wanted, with the idea that each person is special and unique and, more importantly, deserving of success. We were also raised within a cultural narrative that assumed unlimited growth and consumption, that everyone could have access to the upward socioeconomic mobility we've previously described.

The Special Snowflake Syndrome is a term used to describe an unfounded sense that an individual is more special and unique than others and is therefore entitled to a different (often priv-ileged) treatment. Often applied to Generation Y (Millennials), it comes from the notion that each snowflake has a unique con-struct. Amusingly, a recent use of the term was in an article about the Brexit vote (the referendum that decided whether the United Kingdom should remain in the European Union). Its headline read, "Want the UK to Leave Europe? You're Suffering from British Special Snowflake Syndrome." Apparently, it can be applied to nations as well as individuals.[13]

While the causes of Snowflake Syndrome are nuanced, much of it comes from Boomer parents, whose formative years coin-cided with a time of unprecedented economic prosperity but whose own children face a very different reality. Still, the notion of being unique is one that is constantly marketed to people, especially within the context of work. It's an additional layer of pressure that one must contend with to not only achieve a certain level of financial success but to achieve said success through the use of a very special talent and highly individual-ized talent.

The mythology of the calling has become a staple of con-temporary work myths and is spread by such influential figures as Oprah Winfrey (who herself, as previously mentioned, em-bodies the archetype of the self-made woman entrepreneur). In her book, *What I Know For Sure*, Winfrey writes that she's come to believe that "each of us has a personal calling that's as unique as a fingerprint—and that the best way to succeed is to discover what you love and then find a way to offer it to others in the form of service, working hard, and also allowing the energy of the universe to lead you."

There is so much to unpack in that short quote, which so accurately combines everything we've written about so far. The notion of being special, of having a unique calling, of doing work that we love, and of developing a work ethic, and all of it straight from the mouth of the heroine of one of the most legendary rags to riches stories of contemporary culture. It's powerful stuff, and it resonates with a lot of people. The elevated importance of a purpose is also reflective of an individual-centric view of the world where everyone is striving for an ambiguous pinnacle of achievement that doesn't reflect the reality of most people's working lives.

Historically, work has been considered either a job, a career, or a vocation. What Winfrey is talking about, and what the entire Special Snowflake/Find-our-calling movement is built upon is the notion that everyone's work should be a vocation.

Being lovers of etymology, we were intrigued (and then depressed) to learn that the origins of the words career and vocation convey very different messages. The word career is derived from both the Latin word for cart and the Middle French word for racetrack—it refers to moving in a circle and never getting anywhere. Before the rat race and the hamster wheel of the corporate grind, there was that pesky cart! In contrast, the word vocation is much more poetic—it comes from the Latin word *vocare* or "to call." It's used to describe a voice that summons a person to a unique purpose.[14]

In modern terminology, an extension of finding one's vocation is the romantic career advice of "following your dreams," a phrase that originated in the '90s and became a popular refrain in the 2000s. Millennials' formative years were flooded with notions of uniqueness and the possibility of unlimited potential. Cal Newport, the author of *Deep Work*, argues that verbs like "follow" imply that "you start by identifying a passion and then match this preexisting calling to a job. Because the passion precedes the job, it stands to reason you should love your work from the very first day."[15] Newport rightfully points out that even Steve Jobs, who encourages us to "do what we love," followed a long and nonlinear path to his own dream gig. That part of the story is often glossed over in favor of the image of the entrepreneur who is driven by a singular vision of what he wants to achieve, a myth that occludes the reality of chance and circumstances that allowed Jobs to stumble upon what later would become Apple.

The notion of "the calling," then, becomes attached to the more modern interpretation of the American Dream—specifically, getting rich quick—and the result is a slew of expectations that have collectively disappointed a generation used to being praised just for being themselves. Not only do we expect success as a given but we expect it instantly, simply for being special.

In 2010, a story in the *New York Post* called Millennials "The Worst Generation," quoting research from the University of New Hampshire that showed that Gen Y respondents exhibited 25 percent more psychological entitlement and narcissism than those aged 40-60.[16] The article concludes that "Gen Y-ers are characterized by a 'very inflated sense of self' that leads to 'unrealistic expectations,' and ultimately 'chronic disappointment.'" We should point out, as Millennials ourselves, that the label of the "me me me generation" dates back to the '70s, before any of us were born. (*New York Magazine* had a cover story in 1976 that called the '70s the "ME" decade—so there!)

A *Psychology Today* article published in 2015 entitled "Declining Student Resilience: A Serious Problem for Colleges" identified the increase of anxiety and depression among college students as a nationwide problem in the United States. The article described how students display alarming levels of emotional fragility, particularly when it comes to receiving critical feedback, such as grades. Some educators reported having "grown afraid to give low grades for poor performance because of the subsequent emotional crises they would have to deal with." Interestingly, it was the response to poor grades that underscored the entitlement issue: many students reacted by blaming the institution for having unclear guidelines, or had their parents complain, instead of seeing the feedback as an opportunity to strengthen certain skill sets.[17]

It's sad—our whole generation was led to believe a worldview which turned out not to be true, and now we feel like we've been tricked. This isn't a world where "everyone wins," and that is fueling some of our discontent and some of our lingering unrealistic hopes around what we want work to be and who we want to be while working. Chasing the ideal of some grand divine plan is a recipe for disappointment—it puts a lot of pressure on ourselves for no reason.

To be clear, this doesn't mean that we shouldn't find meaning and purpose in what we do. As you'll see in Chapter 9, contributing to work you see as meaningful is a surefire way to be happier at work. But finding a purpose doesn't have to involve universal divine intervention. Working for a company that has a product you believe in, building strong relationships at work, or even being able to provide for your family are all valid purposes on their own. We don't need divine intervention telling us that the path to fulfillment is in discovering the mysterious and singular reason we were put on this earth. (Which, if you'll remember from Chapter 4, also comes with the unspoken rule that if you haven't found your purpose, then you're simply not looking hard enough.)

One of our favorite philosophers, Ralph Waldo Emerson put it best when he said, "My life is not an apology but a life. It is for itself and not for a spectacle. I much prefer that it should be of a lower strain, so it be genuine and equal, than that it should be glittering and unsteady."

We couldn't have said it better ourselves. You don't need to have a capital P—Purpose. We need to break free of this seductive narrative and enjoy life for what it is: a random, thrilling, often inexplicable ride.

4. Pseudo-Spirituality Self-Help

Did you know that figuring out your best career is a spiritual endeavor? Neither did we, but *Forbes* seems to believe that this is the case, having recently launched a series entitled *Spirituality and Success*.[18] In one article, a reformed corporate professional turned career success coach and leadership developer interviews Lodro Rinzler, author of *The Buddha Walks into the Office*, for tips on how to let spirituality lead the way to the right career. The most notable takeaway is that "No matter what work you are engaged in you have the ability to approach your 9-5 as a spiritual path."

This premise is threaded through Rinzler's work. He promises that "you'll discover practical ways to bring mindfulness into administrative support, cabinet-making, financial management, nursing, truck-driving, or latté-brewing. You'll also learn leadership skills that apply compassion to management in a way that increases happiness along with efficiency."[19] Rinzler's premise also characterizes a new, ever-popular breed of self-help that first emerged in the mid-'90s.

Self-help gurus have been around for a long time. In 1936, Dale Carnegie outlined a road to success through self-confidence in *How to Win Friends and Influence People,* which sold 15 million copies and still sits on Amazon's list of best sellers. Napoleon Hill's *Think and Grow Rich* (1937) touted positive thinking as a key to attracting wealth and happiness. Norman Vincent Peale's *The Power of Positive Thinking* (1952) argues that better thoughts make better salesmanship. These titles were joined by countless others, and by the late twentieth century the booming industry of self-help publishing was estimated at $11 billion (USD).

A pseudospiritual subgenre within the self-help category seems to contradict the work-hard message of the last several hundred years. Though these books might be tempting to dismiss, they (and the people behind them) actually give us an intimate and telling snapshot of the contemporary American character. Whether rigorous in their research or not, they are hitting on a cultural current and providing something that people are hungry for.

Take, for example, the New-Age and self-help author Marianne Williamson, who has sold millions of copies of books aimed at reconnecting people to their spirituality. Six of her eleven published books have been *New York Times* best sellers, four of which reached #1 status. In her 1993 audiobook *On Money*, she says, "Money is energy, and energy is infinite in the universe," as well as, "Seek ye first the kingdom of Heaven, & the Maserati will get here when it's supposed to." The connection between the mystical (in this case, the infinite energy of the universe) and the material (thy Maserati) is one that seems to contradict the rhetoric of hard work we've been researching. Believing trumps working.

Similarly, Rhonda Byrne's *The Secret* (2006), which sold 19 million copies worldwide and was translated into forty-six languages, lays out how the Laws of Attraction can be used to "obtain anything you desire." (If you haven't read the book, a perusal of its Twitter account will give you a quick overview. @thesecret recently tweeted, "The magical power of gratitude turns your life into gold! #gratitude.") *The Secret* is known mostly for its emphasis on visualization and the power of the mind to make us magnets for anything we might want in life. When it comes to weight loss, for example, Byrne writes, "Food cannot cause you to put on weight, unless you *think* it can."[20]

Spiritual powerhouse Deepak Chopra wrote a pocket-sized self-help guide in 1994 entitled *The Seven Spiritual Laws of Success: A Practical Guide to the Fulfillment of Your Dreams*. Chopra introduces the concept of his book by challenging our deeply ingrained belief that achieving success requires relentless hard work. Instead, he explains that "the universe operates through dynamic exchange...giving and receiving are different aspects of the flow of energy in the universe. And in our willingness to give that which we seek, we keep the abundance of the universe circulating in our lives."[21] He offers seven principles, ranging from the Law of Pure Potentiality (taking the time to meditate) and the Law of Karma (understanding that every action has a consequence).

It may seem like we're being facetious with the quotes we're choosing to pull, but we're really trying to emphasize the interesting diversion from "hard work as a virtue" to "just believe." The overwhelming popularity of these titles truly gives us pause.

The pseudospiritual world of self-help believes in the power of commitment, positivity, and manifestation to help you achieve anything, just as the Protestants believed in the virtue of hard work as the path to success. In this case, however, if you don't succeed, perhaps you haven't believed hard enough.

DARE TO DREAM?

While this chapter has explored some complicated factors that play a role in our understanding of the cultural influences that have shaped (and continue to shape) our notions of work, it can all be summed up with this: The American Dream is crumbling in the face of a very real socioeconomic context that is making it impossible for many Americans to attain something that was once considered an "unalienable right." Things like Doing What You Love have become more of a sign of socioeconomic privilege than an uplifting motto to embrace your creative pursuits.

In 2012, the PEW Charitable Trusts, which tracks economic mobility across generations, showed a mixed outlook. Erin Currier, the program's director, described these metrics as absolute mobility and relative mobility.[22] Absolute mobility compares the level of income or wealth between generations; it looks at how your earnings compared to those of your parents when they were the same age. Relative mobility looks at how much your income brackets changed compared to your parents.

In her report, "Pursuing the American Dream," Currier reported that while the majority of Americans had higher incomes than their parents, those who were born into lower socioeconomic brackets were more likely to remain there. Nearly half of those who start out in a lower bracket remain there even after a generation has passed. When looking at those who had successfully moved from the lowest 20 percent to the upper 20 percent within a generation, the number was very small: just 4 percent were able make the rags to riches transition that so many dream of.

"Recent polling shows that Americans feel increasingly financially insecure, perhaps in part because of this lack of mobility out of the bottom rung of the economic ladder," Currier said. It turns out that despite making more than their parents, for the most part Americans have been unable to translate their earnings into more wealth. This is an important point because the two factors are interrelated—more wealth means the ability to invest in things like education, which has a correlation with higher income.

Despite this grim reality, nearly 64 percent of Americans reported that they still believe in the American Dream, down from 72 percent in 2009 but still counting for nearly two thirds of Americans.[23] The belief that each generation will do better than the one that came before persists. Economist Paul Taylor, author of *The Next America: Boomers, Millennials, and the Looming Generational Showdown*, says that Millennials will be the first generation to do worse economically than their parents.[24]

If you're wondering how this can be when corporations are reporting record profits, the answer lies in an often neglected measure: wage stagnation. In 2014, Goldman Sachs's chief economist Jan Hatzius reported that the lack of wage increases meant that organizations were able to pocket more of the profits, leading to what he describes as a "remarkably strong performance."[25] So while household incomes for many people declined after the 2008 crisis, a select few experienced the opposite effect: some of the wealthiest Americans enjoyed skyrocketing increases in wealth.

Fivethirtyeight.com's Ben Casselman documented the stagnation of the American Middle Class over the past fifteen years. He also says the dream is fading. "In early adulthood, these Americans out-earned their parents, those born in 1950," he wrote. "But their gains stalled in the 2000s, when they were in their 30s. Now in their 40s, their earnings have fallen behind those of their parents at the same stage in their lives."[26] Even though worker productivity increased nearly 40 percent since 1995, median wages lagged behind with a mere 9.6 percent increase, meaning that we were producing more output but getting paid less. Between 1950 and 2000, the American economy saw a steady rise in household income, but the following decade would see the beginning of a decline that coincided with Millennials entering the workforce.

Try looking for some of these themes in the world around you. We bet you'll find them all over the place. From your Facebook feed to the covers of the magazines you peruse at the airport, the messages are all there: work harder, find your calling, dare to take a risk, anything is possible, find your dream job, uncover your purpose, etc.

We think the new focus on spirituality and finding that all-powerful purpose is a coping mechanism to make the current economic realities palatable. After all, it's much easier to convince ourselves that we're searching for our purpose than to admit that for most people today, lower-paying jobs and wage stagnation are the norm.

That's not to say that any of these beliefs are inherently bad but understanding and seeing their influence can help us identify the ideas about work that we actually want to pursue, instead of the ones that we've unknowingly subscribed to as a part of a larger cultural message. And that really is the point of this book: to give us the awareness to be able to decide for ourselves.

It's not just limited to work. What we're really talking about is our identity, our sense of self. And as you'll see in the next chapter, it's not at all easy to separate the two, no matter how self-aware you think you are.

Summary of Big Ideas

➡ The myth of self-made men is pervasive today, especially in entrepreneurial culture, which uses technology as a means to achieve the "rags to riches" narrative that has been at the heart of the American Dream.

➡ The idea of a "professional destiny" infuses current narratives about work with the idea that every person has ONE thing that that they are meant to do in order to achieve happiness and fulfillment (and that they should absolutely LOVE doing it).

➡ The Special Snowflake syndrome is characterized by an individual feeling that they are special or more unique than their peers and therefore are deserving of opportunities, success, and recognition.

6.

I WORK, THEREFORE I AM

"You are not your job. You're not how much money you have in the bank. You're not the car you drive. You're not the contents of your wallet. You're not your fucking khakis." —Tyler Durden, *Fight Club*

During our research for *Hustle & Float,* we came across an interesting quote, attributed to Abraham Lincoln, that said: "Great things come to those who wait, but only the things left by those who hustle." We were immediately skeptical, since the Internet does have a spotty record for accurately citing who said what. Interestingly, as we traced the quote back to its source, we found that it had shifted over time, from simply saying "things may come" to "good things may come" and finally, the latest iteration, "great things come." Good things are no longer enough. We now demand great things, but we understand that we deserve them only if we hustle. There's a lot of symbolism here: a respected historical figure, a man of unimpeachable character, plus the notion of working harder than those around us, woven together via pixels and bytes to push a very specific narrative about self-worth and value. As you might have guessed, Lincoln did not say those motivating words. According to a 2003 newsletter from the Abraham Lincoln Association, in Lincoln's time the word "hustle" would have been understood to mean "to get up" or to "obtain," as in "hustle me up a few chips to start this fire."[1] The word hustle as used in this quote refers to an energetic effort. Yet this usage did not appear until very late in the nineteenth century, well after Lincoln died.

The article helpfully concludes that "Lincoln may have been ambitious, but he did not hustle."

Much like Lincoln's non-quote, the meaning of the word hustle has also changed. The dictionary defines the verb form as "to push roughly or jostle," as well as, "to obtain illicitly or by forceful action." As a noun, it's used to describe a "state of great activity," or a "fraud or swindle." It almost always connotes a heightened energy and usually an element of dishonesty, of taking advantage of a system through underhanded means.[2] Historically, it often referred to activities like rigged gambling games, prostitution, and drug dealing. Hustle became embedded in popular culture with the disco song, "The Hustle," by Van McCoy and the Soul City Symphony, which sold eight million copies in 1975. It also began to be used in the context of professional sports.

Today, it has entered the vernacular of a new generation of entrepreneurs and creatives, who use it to describe the high level of hard work necessary to achieve success. It has been injected with a dose of morality, ambition, and, in recent iterations, is the ultimate expression of "doing what you love." We stumbled across a blog post describing hustle as "one of the greatest traits anyone can possess" and "doing the extra work, and caring enough to do the right things in the right manner."[3] An article in *Forbes* declared that "both a verb and a noun, 'hustle' implies that you're constantly moving, or pushing towards a goal, be it money, a job or a personal target."[4]

Author Tom Morkes devotes a page on his website to hustle, writing, "Hustle means doing the hard creative work even when you're mentally and emotionally exhausted. Hustle means putting in the long hours others aren't willing to put in." He posits that hustle is what differentiates professionals from hobbyists and points to the example of a person who manages to work on their novel for forty hours each week, even while working a 60+ hour job.[5] The themes are clear and easily spotted: the trendiest new buzzword of our day captures the latest iteration of the American Dream.

This may seem ironic, considering that the original meaning was all about taking shortcuts and acting in a dishonest way. But for contemporary work culture, hustle has become synonymous with work ethic, and in our hashtag happy world of social media, a digital version of Work Devotion that is cool and hip.

We used it in our title because it has become a rallying cry, a symbol for success, particularly for a generation of workers that are grappling with challenges and are responding with new ways of working. They are embracing new technologies and pursuing entrepreneurial opportunities. But they are also grappling with unrealistic expectations and the shame that comes from not living up to impossible standards.

Gary Vaynerchuk grew his family wine business from $3M to $60M in five years and then went on to co-found the digital media agency Vaynermedia and to write multiple best-selling books. A dominating presence in social media with over one million Twitter followers, Vaynerchuk has become our leading apostle of hustle. In 2014, he released a five-minute film on YouTube in which he called hustle "the most important word ever." In the video, he rails about the need for a work ethic, telling his viewers that if they aren't seeing the types of results that they want in their lives, then they aren't hustling.

"I think that people claim that they work hard and smart, but they aren't putting in the work, and they work 9–6—and it's just not enough," he says, looking into the camera, his words punctuated by a hip-hop beat and black and white images of a busy city. "There is no reason to do shit you hate," he is seen telling an audience a little later on. "Promise me you won't. Look yourself in the mirror and ask yourself what do I want to do every day for the rest of my life? Then do that. Then hustle your face off 15 hours a day and get people to care." It all culminates in Vaynerchuk being filmed in front of a Christmas-tree-lined street telling his viewers that while everyone is going to their holiday parties, he has three meetings coming up and is planning to spend his evening reviewing his email. "So, while everyone is drinking eggnog," he says, "I continue the hustle."

To be clear, this is nothing personal against Vaynerchuk! We admire his talent and his dedication to creating great content for his network. We just believe his brash honesty perfectly captures so many of the work myths that plague our culture: that success is proportionally linked to an individual's hard work; the imperative to do what you love; and finally, the excessive Work Devotion, demonstrated through working on holidays.[6] He has embraced this modern-day definition of hustle and has incorporated it into his own brand and work philosophy—to work harder than ever.

SACRIFICE, SUCCESS, AND "HAVING IT ALL"

As a cultural discourse, films reflect enduring themes about life. There is, for example, the theme of "love conquering all"—despite class, distance, politics, or otherwise—as depicted in some of the most popular movies of all time, such as *Titanic, Pretty Woman, Dirty Dancing, Breakfast at Tiffany's,* and *The Princess Bride*—just to name a few! Despite its prominence, the theme has been analyzed (and often criticized) for its impacts on the expectations that people have about love and their relationships. Unrealistic ideal or inspiration?

In the same vein, ideas around work ethic and the American Dream take shape on screens in stories about industrious heroes who overcome any and all obstacles on their journeys to success. Baked into this narrative is "one of the primary myths of the American Dream—that virtue and hard work are central to an individual's success and that neither unemployment, structural poverty, hiring discrimination nor a recession can get in the way of this extraordinary individual."[7] Think of cult classics like *Rocky* (a struggling boxer stops at nothing to go from nobody to somebody), *The Pursuit of Happyness* (a single father struggles to make a life with his son), or *Whiplash* (an emerging jazz drummer overcomes emotional abuse and isolation to meet his potential) and you will recognize the formulaic pattern of ruthless work ethic surmounting the epic challenges at hand.

The American Dream supposes a nation with unparalleled opportunity and personal liberty. But as it is depicted in films, its corollary is that failure to achieve success is due to a lack of hard work or virtue. If you really want success, the myth tells us, you must be prepared for sacrifice.

It's hard to overstate the power the American Dream has on shaping our understanding of work. At the time of this writing, there are 67,000,000 results for a Google search on success and sacrifice, many of them charting the keys to success with titles like "8 Things Successful People Sacrifice for their Success," or "Why Success is about Sacrifice, Not About Finding Happiness."[8] It's evident that making the dream a reality requires work ethic and sacrifice—the fundamental units in the equation for success—but how does this intersect with the heavily contested but ever-present notion of "having it all?"

HAVING IT ALL = CONSUMING IT ALL

Author and fellow at the Institute for the Study of Social Change, Ruth Rosen has written extensively on the history of the women's movement and the origins of having it all. Rosen argues that the original women's movement was a demand for economic and social revolution that would create the conditions for real equality at home and in the workplace. "American social movements tend to move from a collectivistic vision to one that emphasizes the success of the individual," writes Rosen. "The fact is, activists in the women's movement knew women could never have it all, unless they were able to change the society in which they lived."[9]

Rosen argues that original activists in the women's movement knew that "having it all" was impossible unless society changed. The movement was always anchored in the interests of all women, not individuals—and this was echoed in the demands of the Women's Strike for Equality march in 1970, where the preconditions for women's liberation had to include child care, legal abortion, and equal pay.

As the movement grew in the 1970s and 1980s, the media sought to make feminism palatable to the American public by addressing the individual instead of women as a group.[10] The focus shifted away from "sisterhood" and moved toward the "superwoman." This archetype—built on the idea that women could have families, careers, sparkling homes, and vibrant sex lives—collided with the rise of consumer culture. Everything was possible with the right outlook and the right products. As Rosen explains, "Self-help books and magazines ignored the economic and social conditions women faced and instead emphasized the way in which each individual woman, if only she thought positively about herself, could achieve self-realization and emancipation."

Today, other prominent public figures are weighing in and adding to the media momentum. Anne-Marie Slaughter, a high-profile international lawyer, political scientist, foreign policy analyst, and public commentator, exploded the debate in 2012 when she wrote a controversial article for the *Atlantic*

entitled "Why Women Still Can't Have it All" about her decision to resign from her demanding job at the State Department
in order to spend more time with her teenage sons.[11] Slaughter
describes feeling lucky to have worked for an understanding
office such as Hillary Clinton's—which nonetheless required
eleven-hour work days and permitted one day off a month—instead of the other more demanding offices of her peers. While
Slaughter responded candidly to the pressures that modern
women face while trying to negotiate work and life, the issue
itself is too multifaceted to be simply a gender issue. Firstly, the
fight against long working hours has been one that men have
historically battled since the Industrial Revolution (as we covered in Chapter 1). Secondly, the speed-up of jobs (especially at
the top) is very much a symptom of an economic issue at large
and a big part of what we discussed in Chapter 3.

Slaughter's piece acknowledges the fiction in the notion of
having it all for women (and men), particularly for her demo-
graphic, which she describes as "highly educated, well-off women
who are privileged enough to have choices in the first place." The
general response to the article was that equality isn't about the
ability to do everything but about making choices that promote
physical, emotional, and spiritual well-being. As Millennial
coach Christine Hassler puts it, "An empowered woman is not
burnt out, stressed out, and freaking out over accomplishing a
million things on her to-do list. An empowered woman knows
how to conserve her power by not chasing after external validation or obligations."[12] Shouldn't this go for everyone?

So, if "having it all" was never intended to be a goal of the
women's movement, and if the structural constraints of
"achieving it all" go beyond gender, why do we continue to try
so desperately to unlock the flawed ideal of the perfect work/
life? This pursuit is conceivably the very source of our dissatis-
faction and unhappiness, and yet we are inundated with adap-
tations of this same theme.

In her book *Thrive: The Third Metric to Redefining Success and Creating a Life of Well-Being, Wisdom, and Wonder*, Arianna Huffington, the mogul behind the *Huffington Post*, argues that in order to be fulfilled we need to look beyond money and power as a metric of success. Huffington makes a case for an equal weighting of personal growth and well-being when it comes to the demands of work. In practice, this translates to leaving work on time each day, avoiding work and emails outside of business hours, daily meditation, banning technology from the bedroom, and going to bed by ten every night. Ranked by *Forbes* as one of the world's most powerful women and the best-selling author of twelve books, Huffington is no stranger to burnout. In 2007—two years after she launched the *Huffington Post* and four years before she sold it to AOL for $315 million—the concept for *Thrive* hit her when she broke her cheekbone on her desk after fainting from exhaustion.

And yet, according to Huffington, we can, in fact, have power, money, and well-being. In an interview with *Entrepreneur* magazine, she said, "There's absolutely no trade-off. That's a collective delusion, that in order to climb the ladder we have to sacrifice. Not at all."

Huffington presents an accurate portrait of work culture today but has a platform to do so *because* of her many sleepless nights. As she evangelizes for her Third Network movement, which includes a conference and ample speaking engagements, it's hard to imagine that any of that has changed. Her former personal assistant has said, "She's insane! She works all the time. Literally all the time!"[13] While she may have identified ways to treat the symptoms, the solution—which at the offices of the *Huffington Post* is nap pods and yoga classes—only addresses them at a surface level.

It seems that "having it all" and the American Dream fit hand-in-hand—we believe that a virtuous work ethic can attain an almost ridiculous standard of personal and professional success. This goes not just for women (who certainly bear the brunt of the pressure) but for men, who are also increasingly measured against a widening scope of success. Put quite simply, we're constantly told that in order to have it all, we must do it all ourselves. Books like *The Outsourced Self: Intimate Life in Market Times* show the measures we must take to manage that pressure. It offers countless approaches to "having it all" but almost never asks why we want it all to begin with.

Both Rosen and Slaughter argue for institutional changes to eliminate gender biases, including government investments in education, universal childcare, support for caregivers, and the building of infrastructures of care within the workplace. Most telling, Slaughter argues that we won't see real change until we get serious about addressing and changing the culture (in this case, resocializing men).

The tensions between our deeply rooted desire to self-actualize and the systemic challenges we come against in trying to do so are obvious. We believe that wherever there is tension and conflict, there is a misalignment of expectations. What's interesting in this case is that some of the strongest and most pervasive social drivers that are encouraging us to strive grew out of efforts to change the system and make it fairer—to, in short, eliminate the need for so much hustle and sacrifice. They were never meant to be a manifesto for individual success.

MY JOB, MY WORTH

The ideas about work we've covered in prior chapters have trickled into our deepest beliefs. Our occupation and the work we do make up a fundamental part of our identity. From childhood, we are asked what we want to be when we grow up. Despite the statistics that document low engagement and fulfillment levels at work in America, working remains such a cultural bedrock that "unemployed adults and those not working as much as they would like are twice as likely to be depressed as Americans employed full time."[14] Being out of a job is more troubling to our sense of self than being in a troubling job.

As the author and critic Joanne Ciulla puts it, "We have gone beyond the work ethic, which endowed work with moral value, and now dangerously depend on our jobs to be the primary source of our identity, the mainspring of individual self-esteem and happiness."[15]

It certainly wasn't always this way. In their book *Time Without Work*, Walli Leff and Marilyn Haft explain that it was "family, descent, such as religion and place of origin" that governed identity in the traditional societies from which American immigrants came.

This complicates our relationship with work. Work is considered to be a means to an end—success, fame, or maybe simply retirement. Though we may envy those who don't work, they are simultaneously derogated. Leff and Haft explain, "If poor, they are regarded with contempt for not wanting to work. If rich, they are tolerated, but not respected." Despite the rhetoric around working to live and freedom from labor, those who do not work are viewed as idle and/or frivolous. In the libertarian working culture of today, it seems like people can't just take time off; they take "health sabbaticals" or "research secondments" instead.

As an organizing principle in our lives, work can be incredibly useful. It not only provides us with social markers, structure, discipline, influence, and agency, it tells us what to do every day.[16] It's hard for many people to imagine how they would find fulfillment and satisfaction without working.

Psychotherapist Charles Allen attributes the alignment between self-worth and working to the way that jobs continuously provide us with the sense that we are contributing members of society.[17] More than this feedback, we also look to work as a place for feelings of belonging and a sense of purpose, much as the farmer takes pride in his land and animals.

But what happens to work-based self-esteem within systems of work where the worker neither owns nor controls their workplace? What happens within the accelerated pace of work today? From *Psychology Today* to the *Harvard Business Review*, a steady stream of articles about the need to regain or protect our sense of self-esteem and self-worth in today's work culture signals a serious problem. Technology makes it difficult to disconnect, and with the growing demands on productivity, accomplishments are weighed against unfinished business, leaving many feeling inadequate.[18] A recent study confirmed that the most significant spikes in stress-inducing cortisol levels happens when there is a threat "to one's social self, or threat to one's social acceptance, esteem, and status."[19] As desperate as we are to find ourselves in the midst of our work, it's no wonder that we're burning out. The phrase "it's not personal, it's business," seems to have been turned on its head: it *is* personal, and it *is* business. This makes the stakes so much higher.

The expectations we set on ourselves are not only products of the system, they are cultural. In her book, *Overwhelmed*, Brigid Schulte used the expression "busier than thou" to describe the attitude and belief that being busy is the ultimate status symbol for middle-class professionals. We've all been a part of conversations in which friends or colleagues boast about their busyness, which they wear like a badge glittering with the sweat of the hustle. Busyness is a social currency, inside and outside the office. While some people are dying of white-collar overwork, others embrace unrelenting busyness as a way to survive workplace politics and culture. *New York Times* contributor and author Tim Kreider has described busyness "as a kind of existential reassurance, a hedge against emptiness."

In a 2015 global study of over 10,000 adults, Havas Worldwide concluded that "pretending to be busy has become a vital workplace survival skill, thanks to our modern society's tacit celebration of being overloaded."[20] Its research showed that 42 percent of respondents often overstate their obligations at work while 60 percent believe that that their peers are pretending to be busier than they are. This isn't an issue of morality or deceptiveness; this is a response to the flawed way workers are able to prove their value.

Though the busy-trap is often self-imposed and driven by ambition (work, social, family, or personal obligations that aren't "essential"), the more interesting insight is how anxious and guilty most people feel when they *aren't* busy. "Free time is now seen as an admission that you're non-essential," says Tim Maleeny, chief strategy officer for Havas Worldwide.[21] Once upon a time, your wealth and affluence was measured by how much free time you had. Those days are long past.

According to the Havas study, the predominating attitudes toward the productivity paradox vary across three general groups. Workers in countries like Brazil, China, Japan, and India are stuck between the desire for both success and leisure and are "most likely to pretend to be busier than they actually are, even though they wish they could relax more." Conversely, in countries like Canada, France, the United Kingdom, and the United States, "the new pace of life isn't viewed as a threat to be dealt with so much as a new reality to work around as one sees fit." Finally, in Australia, Belgium, and Italy, workers are skeptical of the value of busyness and are more likely to question whether or not it is worthwhile.

The trend toward freelance work (the rise of the "free agent nation," in Daniel Pink's coinage) only exacerbates this. According to the Bureau of Labor Statistics, 16.7 million people were self-employed in the United States as of spring 2017, a number that is expected to quadruple by 2020.[22] More and more, the expectations and pressures for accomplishment fall squarely and solely on the shoulders of individuals.

Here we uncover a great irony: the work environments that define us (and push us to push ourselves) are in fact alienating us and draining our energy and doing so at the expense of the engagement, productivity, and performance that we covet.

NICE TO MEET YOU, WHAT DO YOU DO?

Picture meeting someone for the first time at a cocktail party. Right after you learn their name, what's one of the first questions you ask? If you're like most people, it will be a variation of "So, what do you do?"

Let's think about this for a minute because there's a lot of meaning embedded in those four little words. By now, we should be able to spot some of the productivity legacy that still lingers in our language, as the emphasis is on doing, or in other words, producing. Even in social situations, we use a person's output, their professional contribution, as an initial frame of reference. We take a complex, layered individual and reduce their worth to their job title.

At first glance, this might not seem like such a big problem. After all, many Productive Creatives are successful and very proud of what they do, in which case answering the question becomes a pleasant opportunity for them to validate themselves. But the person who has succeeded in doing a job they love is no better or worse than the person who shows up to work to collect a paycheck, or the person who is currently unemployed, or the person who had to take on two or more jobs simply to survive. But think about the status we accord to each of them. As the authors of the capitalism chapter (aptly entitled "You Are Not What You Earn"[23]) in the School of Life's online *The Book of Life* puts it, "Our income is the source of information, crucial, decisive information, about our character, our intelligence, our moral fiber: in short, money is the key indicator of our worth in human and just financial terms. The more money we make the more we deserve to exist. By extension, it feels impossible to imagine ourselves as good, decent—and still poor."

We hope this last sentence made you sit up and cry out, "That is a legacy of Puritan beliefs that saw material wealth as a divine symbol of moral superiority—it is embedded in the American Dream!" (If so, please email us and let us know, so we can give you a digital high five.)

We find ourselves asking the "What do you do?" question, too. Part social convention, part habit, but also, we are embarrassed to admit, part laziness. After all, jobs are easy labels that we can use to slot each other into convenient and easy-to-understand categories. In its most innocent version, the question is an easy way to break the ice, to find some common ground and hopefully find other, more interesting topics of conversation. But the danger in asking this question is the unspoken implication that who we are is determined by what we do. So, this question also carries with it connotations about success, money, and status (a subject we will be diving into extensively in Chapter 10). It's not the question itself that is so problematic but linking someone's work to their identity, which, within our current culture of overwork, is only natural. After all, with work consuming more and more of our personal time, is it any wonder that we have developed these deep and binding ties?

In 2013, Elle Huerta, founder of the app Mend, published a post on *Medium* outlining the reasons she chose to leave a well-paying, highly prestigious job at Google. Despite feeling unhappy and anxious, Huerta felt a strong resistance every time she contemplated quitting. "When I sat down and really thought about why I was resisting, I realized something about myself that I didn't like, something that I'm ashamed to even admit now," she wrote. "The main reason I was resisting was because I would be giving up the safety and prestige associated with life as a Googler.

When I reflected more, I realized that external recognition had unfortunately become a primary motivator for me."[24]

She's definitely not alone. We believe most Productive Creatives have at one point or another in their careers come up against the same feeling. When we link who we are with what we do, we are hanging our self-esteem and self-worth on a precarious ledge. When you're doing well professionally, your identity is rock solid, but what happens when something goes wrong? This also links up with the notion of the Shadow American Dream that we wrote about in Chapters 4 and 5.

What if you suffer a health issue that forces you to take extended time off? What if there's another recession and jobs get cut across the board? What if a big disruption in the market (hint, hint, automation and new technologies, which we will talk about in Chapter 14) suddenly makes your position redundant? Do these things make your worth any less? The answer is no. And yet so many people inexorably link their jobs and, by extension, their output to the core of their identities and then become lost, depressed, or anxious when that source of self-validation (security, safety, happiness) is threatened. If we believe that we are our jobs and that it is completely within our power to succeed, then what does it say about us when we fail?

I AM THEREFORE I AM

After recognizing the danger in falling back on work-related questions, we decided to try a different approach. At cocktail parties and networking events, we started asking people to tell us something about themselves that had nothing to do with their jobs. Hobbies ranging from rock climbing to breeding crickets emerged. Other skill sets like building furniture, restoring old cars, and playing musical instruments were discovered. It seemed we needed to be reminded that what a person does for a living is often the least interesting thing about them. This was a particularly helpful lesson for us, especially as Productive Creatives, whose jobs often seem misleadingly glamorous to outsiders. Whether it's tech companies like Google, prestigious law firms, well-known international organizations, or just work in one of the creative industries, at the end of the day, it's just a job. And a job is not the sum of our identities.

We must focus on finding and cultivating other aspects of ourselves that are not related to our work. As you'll see in later chapters, the technology landscape is changing so drastically that the very nature of work is morphing into something we might not be able to recognize. If we don't ready ourselves for this transition, if we don't begin the slow and steady work of separating our self-worth and identity from our job titles, then we will be wholly unprepared for the massive wave of change that is coming.

Pay attention to how you introduce yourself to people. What words do you use? How do you describe your work? Are there other things you can say that would express a different part of yourself?

This was a particularly hard chapter for us to write because as Productive Creatives so much of what we do is linked to our sense of self. At our core we are creators, we bring things to life through the force of our ideas—and there's a heady power in that. As writers, nothing compares to the thrill of seeing a book evolve from an idea, to a belabored draft, and finally, to something physical that you can hold in your hand. It's the same way for Productive Creatives who are building businesses, and in service industries where we tackle challenges through our intellect and creativity—what could be more personal than that?

But still, we must remember that while our job is a part of us, it is not the only part. In our success and performance-driven culture, where ambition and consumption reign supreme, it can be very counterintuitive to stop, to stand against the constant pressure of momentum, to be more and do more, and say, I am enough.

At the end of the day, that's what it's all about: to feel valued and seen. For too long, we have used our careers as a crutch, as a way to prevent people from seeing who we truly are. Only if we're successful and have lofty job titles, we think, will we be recognized as worthy of belonging.

The irony lies in the fact that we have imposed these limits on ourselves. In truth, we've always been worthy.

Summary of Big Ideas

➡ Our culture of overwork has elevated working into an important and deeply personal part of our identities. Who we are is often irrevocably intertwined with what we do.

➡ In tying our sense of self-worth to our jobs, we are now grappling with maintaining a strong sense of self in the face of challenging economic conditions and the disruption of industries across markets.

OUR IDENTITY AND BIOLOGY [SELF]

7.

THE PRODUCTIVE BRAIN

Thanks to advancements in fields like molecular biology and computational neuroscience, scientists have a much deeper understanding of how our nervous system works, revealing a fascinating connection between the electric signals firing in our neurons and our emotional states and behaviors. New fields specializing in these intersections are being developed, including neuroeconomics, social neuroscience, and decision theory. Our scientific understanding of the brain has expanded, and the intermingling of insights from behavioral economists, psychologists, neuroscientists, and cognitive therapists (amongst many others) have shown us the power that our mind has over how we work.

We looked at some of the latest scientific thinking to gain a better understanding of how our brains react to contemporary work culture. In this chapter, we share some of the most important ideas that are reframing how we Productive Creatives view our relationship with work.

1. IN DEFENSE OF DOWNTIME

While we continue to adapt to new types of work, our brains are having some trouble keeping up. Much of knowledge work requires long periods of extended focus, and the brain just isn't wired that way. Not only we do we get fatigued, we get bored, which lowers our ability to efficiently complete our tasks.

Now, we're not arguing for a lack of deep focus. On the contrary, periods of heightened concentration, most commonly described as "flow," demonstrate the power of the brain to problem-solve and tackle creative challenges, but they occur within a limited time frame. Our periods of flow can't last forever, and yet our ballooning to-do lists and ever-expanding job descriptions ensure that we are all under pressure to keep that rigid focus in order to properly do our jobs.

One of the biggest scientific breakthroughs in the understanding of our productive brains was the discovery of the Default Mode Network (DMN). The DMN is the complex system of neurons and circuits that are activated when we daydream. The DMN is one of many networks (the latest research pins the number at a minimum of five) that are activated during slower periods of brain activity. These systems are called resting-state networks.

According to a team of researchers from the University of Southern California, those episodes when our minds wander are essential mental states that help us develop our identity, process social interactions, and even influence our internal moral compass. When we daydream, our brains shift their focus from the outside world to a rich inner landscape where we can explore our desires, dreams, and hopes while working out our tensions and conflicts.[1] We need the time to reflect and think and to try to make sense of the world and our place in it.

Research confirms that introspection is the foundational tool for building a sense of self-identity.

DMN episodes or downtime also provide the brain with opportunities to focus on some pretty important responsibilities: consolidating newly learned information and transferring important skills from short-term to long-term memory. We now know that sleep is critical to memory and learning processes.[2] According to another study by Tamami Nakano of Osaka University, the brain has the ability to switch to a DMN state faster than you can imagine: every time you blink, that tiny nanosecond is enough for the DMN to power up for a tiny but measurable burst.

In her book *A Mind for Numbers: How to Excel at Math and Science (Even If You Flunked Algebra)*, engineering professor Barbara Oakley describes the brain's two modes of operation. In the "focused mode," we use our prefrontal cortex for tasks that require a good amount of cognitive energy and concentration, like learning, reading, or solving math problems. In the "diffuse mode," we might be daydreaming or taking a walk or doing something that doesn't require that same amount of mental effort. This model is very similar to what Daniel Kahneman labelled as System 1 (diffuse mode) and System 2 (focused mode) in his book *Thinking, Fast and Slow*.

Historically, the diffuse mode has had a bad reputation. Did you know that it was once believed that when you daydreamed your mind went dormant? Activities like "spacing out" were considered to be signs of laziness. Many scientists thought it was the most unproductive state your brain could be in, the equivalent of being "offline." Turns out, they were completely wrong.

According to a 2009 study from the University of British Columbia, some of the parts of the brain that we use for complex problem-solving become highly stimulated when our minds wander. Professor Kalina Christoff, who led the UBC study, explained that "our brains are very active when we daydream—much more active than we focus on routine tasks." This is useful knowledge to have, considering that we spend nearly one third of our lives daydreaming!

We now know that this "diffuse state" isn't just important but essential for our ability to solve problems, come up with ideas, and spark new creative outputs. Professor Christoff advises those who are struggling to solve complex problems to switch to a simpler task, like taking a walk and letting their minds wander.[3] Even though it might seem like you're not doing anything "productive," your brain is still humming away in the background, making new connections and processing what you've learned that day. You're far more likely to come up with that great idea, or that solution for your client project, when you're relaxed than when you're stressing out at your desk.

The harder we push ourselves to increase our productivity at work in the form of more solutions, more ideas, and more creativity, the more likely they are to elude us. The busier we are, the less creative we become, which by extension translates into less productivity. "When you're focusing, you're actually blocking your access to the diffuse mode," Oakley explained. "And the diffuse mode, it turns out, is what you often need to be able to solve a very difficult, new problem."

The key is to strike a balance between the two states, the "hustle" and the "float," one could presume to say. And yet, if you've learned anything from the past few chapters, you can guess at how easily a person will surrender their devotion to incessant busyness. Centuries of brainwashing are hard to undo; most people rebel against the idea of taking a break, since they believe it amounts to a display of weakness, an admission that one is not worthy of their job. We're not only prisoners of a historical narrative that predisposes us to a Puritanical focus on continuous output—we're forcing ourselves to operate in a way that runs counter to the optimal functioning of our brains. Cool.

The need for a break flies in the face of so many of our cultural signals of ability and competence. The notion of Work Devotion that we mentioned in Chapter 1 is defined by demonstrable acts of struggle and sacrifice—a contemporary display of masculinity and strength, eliteness, and moral character. Work is sometimes treated like an extreme sport in which powering through is the only way to win.

But as we learn more about the intricacies of our brain, two things are becoming very obvious: first, that when we are daydreaming or relaxing, our brain is still working and in fact is conducting many essential mental processes that we need to stay happy and healthy. Secondly, that those periods of rest are an absolutely nonnegotiable element of work performance—and that they in fact increase our creativity.

2. SOCIAL DYNAMICS AND NEUROLEADERSHIP: A MATTER OF SURVIVAL

Henry Ford once famously complained, "Why is it that when I need a pair of hands I have to get the whole man?" (Don't worry Henry, we'll talk about how AI, robots, and drones might make that sentiment a reality in our near future in a later chapter.) This brings us to one of the biggest developments in neuroscience, one that should have been blindingly obvious but wasn't. And that is the discovery that we humans are not, in fact, machines but social animals, susceptible to a myriad of psychological, physiological, and neurological factors that can dramatically influence our performance at work.

While many managers, both blue-collar and white-collar, have long recognized the importance of a worker's emotional landscape, researchers like Daniel Pink and Dan Ariely are now giving us real insights into why we behave the way that we do, and in particular, why intrinsic motivation is such a powerful driver of productivity. Short version: we are complex creatures that are far more irrational in our responses than we think we are. It turns out that human beings need not just rest but things like purpose, security, and meaning in our lives in order to perform well.

Two consistent themes emerged when we looked at the state of the art in social and integrative neuroscience and psychosocial sociology.

1. The bulk of the motivation that governs our behaviors can be reduced to the desire to **maximize rewards and minimize threats.** At our core, we are hardwired to increase pleasure and avoid pain, and those survival instincts are still active today, even though they might be triggered by stimuli that would have befuddled (or probably terrified) our ancestors. Facebook can't overwrite our instincts, but it can activate them.

2. To our brains, our **social needs are as essential for our survival—and as threatening to it—as any other basic need.** From a neuron perspective, our interactions with others are not secondary systems of behavior that are imposed upon us after our basic needs have been met but are basic and can trigger the same flight or fight responses that we have when facing predators.

David Rock, author of *Your Brain at Work,* has created a model that captures how these two tendencies interact and impact behavior in a modern workplace environment. His SCARF model proposes that there are five domains that cover the human social experience: Status, Certainty, Autonomy, Relatedness, and Fairness.

"Status is about relative importance to others. Certainty concerns being able to predict the future. Autonomy provides a sense of control over events. Relatedness is a sense of safety with others, of friend rather than foe. And fairness is a perception of fair exchanges between people," he explains.[4] "These five domains activate either the 'primary reward' or 'primary threat' circuitry (and associated networks) of the brain."

He goes on to describe how someone who feels their social status is being threatened (either at work or in personal relationships) will experience the activation of the same networks in their brain as someone whose life is being threatened. Someone who perceives that they are receiving fair treatment will experience the activation of the same reward centers in their brain as when they receive a monetary reward. The point here is to underscore that these situations trigger genuine threat or pleasure responses that are deeply felt, even if the circumstances seem superficial. (Who cares if Susan bad mouthed you at the meeting?)

Do you remember getting into an argument with your friends when you were a teenager and feeling like your life was over? Interpersonal conflicts like those can very well trigger elemental survival instincts that are no different in kind from the ones that kick in when you must outrun a bear or a tiger! So, you can call you mother and tell her that you weren't, in fact, being overly dramatic.

The SCARF model is based on the principle of the Approach and Avoid response, which is a survival instinct that helps us stay alive by being able to very quickly categorize anything we encounter as "good" or "bad." If we determine it's good, we can approach and engage with it; if it's bad, we'll avoid it.

It gets interesting because this categorization is made by the amygdala, an almond shaped cluster of nuclei located in the brain's temporal lobe, which is part of the limbic system that operates in the background, without your conscious awareness of it. The amygdala is like the brain's alarm system—it controls responses linked to fear, arousal, and heightened emotional states. It tells you if you should fight or flee.

Once a new external element has been tagged by your brain as one to either approach or avoid, your body will respond in kind, without your conscious control. People who suffer from anxiety disorders or phobias are examples of what happens when this categorization ability malfunctions. This is why exposure therapy, where a person is slowly exposed to the thing they fear in a safe and controlled environment, works as well as it does. Essentially, the purpose is to retrain the amygdala so that it changes the label of something it had categorized as "bad" to "good."

This is important because the amygdala's responses are driven by our own categorizations. If you perceive something as being a threat, your brain will react to it as such and flood your system with the chemicals you need (like adrenaline) to survive. How does this translate back to our working environment?

Well, it turns out that these responses can have a very dramatic influence on our abilities to perceive, make decisions, manage our stress, stay motivated, collaborate, and much more.[5] A person's ability to be creative and productive can be severely derailed if their threat responses become activated due to a dispute with colleagues, a perceived act of unfairness by management, or a lack of job security.

Furthermore, if one of these interactions is labeled as "bad" by the amygdala, then even when the immediate crisis has passed, that lingering unease will remain, as a person's response system remains activated even if they aren't fully cognizant of it. If your brain is sending threat signals, then it will divert resources like oxygen and glucose from your prefrontal cortex (the area responsible for logic and problem-solving) and divert them elsewhere in preparation for your having to react or escape quickly.

If you've ever been put on the spot unexpectedly in a meeting or presentation and found yourself unable to answer questions that you definitely knew the answer to, that's because your brain rerouted resources away from your "thinking" brain and into your "feeling" brain, that primitive part of ourselves that has kept us alive and safe for hundreds of thousands of years.

Threat responses will not only inhibit your ability to complete a task (and raise your odds of making mistakes) but can also inhibit your ability to spot solutions, while making you more risk-averse and thus less likely to innovate or try something new. Scientists have noted that our brain is also more partial to negative information because that information was historically more likely to have kept us safe (e.g., the knowledge that a tiger is hiding behind a tree is much more useful than the knowledge that the fruit on that tree is ripe and delicious). So we're not just susceptible to these unseen neurological and psychological forces—we're actually more sensitive to avoid/threat than reward stimuli.

On the flip side, fostering a reward mentality creates the opposite working conditions. The brain that perceives its working environment as "safe" is more likely to be creative, come up with solutions faster, and be more collaborative with colleagues. The important thing here is to recognize that we have to pay attention to our own categorizations lest we unintentionally sabotage our creative and productive potentials.

Rock points to common organizational patterns that can limit productivity, such as performance reviews that are intimidating and unpleasant. If a performance review calls up threat responses, employees won't accept even constructive criticism and will fail to make needed changes.

3. ALL THE FEELS: THE EMOTIONAL BIAS AND DECISION-MAKING

From a neuroscience perspective, work cultures have traditionally encouraged and favored the rational brain, represented by the prefrontal cortex. Think about the modern standards of professionalism: cool, rational, logical, methodical—the opposite of our messy emotional selves. It was easier to maintain this persona during the age of the Ideal Worker, when you had a spouse at home to shoulder most of the household and child-rearing responsibilities, worked regularly from 9 to 5, and, thanks to the fact that digital media hadn't been invented yet, were able to leave work behind at the end of the day. You could turn off the "personal you" when you came to the office and turn it back on when you left.

But as we've seen, economic instability, the changing demographics of working families, the increase of work responsibilities, and the rise of a constantly connected culture has made it far more difficult to maintain strict borders between our professional and private selves. And while our personal selves have suffered, as we answer email during the evenings and on weekends, we are still expected to maintain our stoic facade at work. So much of the discussion about productivity is sterile, focusing on metrics, outputs, and systems. We think it's important to acknowledge the ways that our emotions can frustrate our goal of achieving a "machine-like" output.

Emotions Are Contagious

As social creatures, we've developed the ability to read body language and other nonverbal cues to determine how the people around us are feeling. This allows us to synchronize our feelings and moods with the people around us, a necessary aspect of living in cohesive and harmonious social groups. Research has shown that we can not only read these signals, we can "catch" them. This phenomenon is called Emotional Contagion.[6]

In a workplace setting, this means that the moods and emotional states of our colleagues, and especially our bosses, can have a measurable and lasting influence on us. As we mentioned earlier, the amygdala is always scanning for potential danger and is more likely to raise the alarm in response to a negative emotion, kicking our threat responses into gear and making it harder for us to concentrate. These responses often happen automatically, compromising our performance without our even being aware of it.

Rahaf once worked with a colleague who was always caught up in some personal or professional drama. Despite the fact that she got along well with him and had no problems with him directly, she started to notice that after they worked on projects together, she was more irritable and had a harder time concentrating. Once he was transferred to another department, she found her productivity nearly doubled.

It's important to mention that a threat response can be subtle—it doesn't always have to be a heart-pounding, adrenaline-rushing burst of feelings. The unconscious response you have to that one negative colleague who is always undermining your effort can have an impact on your creativity, but it's so slight that you might not even be aware of it. The negativity of a toxic team can spread and infect a whole organization.

Normally, we focus exclusively on our own performance and abilities. These new insights mean that we have to be concerned about the behavior and moods of those around us, as well. This is important because we tend to be punitive toward ourselves and oblivious to the external factors that might have contributed to our less-than-stellar output. We need to remember that our personal relationships can also have a tangible impact on our performance.

It's not just emotions that are getting shared but habits, behaviors, and even medical conditions. One study that analyzed the correlations between weight and social relationships among 12,000 people over the span of sixty-five years discovered a shocking link. "When a friend became obese, a person's own future risk of becoming obese increased by 171 percent," the study reported. "A woman whose sister became obese has a 67 percent increased risk, and a man whose brother became obese had a 45 percent risk." As crazy as it sounds, obesity is something that can be "caught" from your social network, along with sleep deprivation, drug use, and even depression.[7]

In 2014, Facebook released the results of a controversial study that revealed that they had been deliberately manipulating the News Feeds, and hence the emotions, of 689,003 users. The study reported that "emotions expressed by others on Facebook influence our own emotions, constituting experimental evidence for massive-scale contagion via social networks."[8] The study was a breakthrough because it had previously been presumed that emotional contagions could only be transmitted through in-person interactions and nonverbal cues. It turns out we are just as emotionally vulnerable to social media as real-life meetings. This becomes even more troubling when we think about how technology has made it impossible to disconnect. We are being influenced by our bosses and colleagues even when we aren't in the office and, if we are on social media, by people we don't even work with.

The Cost of Suppressing Emotions

One of the norms of modern business cultures is the idea that emotions have no place at work. Even though science tells us a different story—that our emotions are just as essential to our ability to function as our rational processes—most of us frown on colleagues who wear their emotions on their sleeves, and we are just as hard on ourselves.

Frederick Taylor and his cohorts wanted people to be as efficient and reliable as the machines they were operating, but that's an unrealistic expectation. It's not as easy as we think to leave our emotional states at the door when we clock into work. It turns out that you can't separate your personal and professional self, at least not without paying a price.

Suppressing emotions requires resources, and the brain will get them by diverting energy from the prefrontal cortex (the part responsible for analytical thinking and problem-solving). Our prefrontal cortex has a limited amount of energy, so using it to suppress your emotions means there is less left over for you to actually do your job. Additionally, research shows that denying your emotions can make them stronger and that there is a link between poor memory and emotion suppression.[9]

We are not suggesting that we need to enable an emotional free-for-all within workplaces; rather, we need to find different and better ways of managing our emotions. Our emotions are an essential part of an integrated system, and there is a way to maintain a balance between being a corporate robot and the office hulk.

This technique is called "labelling." It's bizarrely simple, but it can work wonders. According to a series of experiments by UCLA researcher Matthew Lieberman, simply acknowledging a feeling and associating a word (or a label) with it has a measurable impact on the brain, calming down the amygdala and increasing prefrontal cortex activity. "In the same way you hit the brake when you're driving when you see a yellow light," explains Lieberman, "when you put your feelings into words, you seem to be hitting the brakes on your emotional responses."[10] If you're feeling uneasy before a meeting with your boss, you can just say to yourself: I feel anxious about this meeting. The old adage of naming your fears so they lose power holds a neurological truth to it.

Just the act of labelling forces your brain to stop and think, giving it enough time to calm down and assess the situation, working through the emotion rather than wasting valuable resources trying to suppress it. Interestingly, the technique is only effective if you use one or two words for your labels. If you discuss the emotions at length, you end up amplifying their effects.[11]

When we consider how our emotions at work are natural and normal expressions of ourselves, we can better understand the deep appeal of the "Do What You Love" mantra. It feels liberating to be able to attach an emotional component to the work that we do, to bring passion and liveliness into our often sterile work environments. Sadly, our cultural conditioning militates against our experiencing this satisfaction—though we gravitate toward emotionally fulfilling experiences, we are biased by the modern signals of material worth to behave in ways that make such experiences elusive and that, at the same time, detract from our ability to produce anything of real value.

Perception & Decision-Making

Finally, there is a strong emotional component that comes into play, even when we make seemingly rational decisions. How we perceive new information, the ways that it is colored by our experiences, beliefs, routines, social standing, and relationships, plays an essential part in how we react to it. Often times, this emotional assessment occurs in the back of our minds, and we're not aware of how it's impacting our ability to choose the best course of action. And here's where it gets interesting: we can't process new information logically until we've assessed it emotionally. Or, to put it another way, the prefrontal cortex (our higher functioning, problem-solving brain) will only evaluate the information it's presented with after this emotional read has taken place. If the information is perceived as emotionally good, then we're much more likely to evaluate it objectively. If it's not, then we're more likely to dismiss it without a thorough analysis.

Unlike the amygdala threat response we wrote about earlier, where threat responses actually reduce cognitive functions, cognitive function in this instance isn't reduced—it's simply funneled through a perspective that aligns with our individual worldview. You experience this phenomenon whenever you have a knee-jerk, gut level reaction to a new idea or a proposed policy change. Social aspects come into play, as the source of the news makes a difference—that is, whether or not it is coming from someone you trust.

Ultimately, the right brain/left brain dichotomy is not reflective of the deeply interconnected neural systems that use both emotions and logic to govern our interactions with the world. We need to acknowledge these unseen emotional forces and understand their influence on our behavior, so we can make better-informed decisions. The brain is a social organ. If we are truly committed to creating humane work environments for ourselves, that's something that we need to accept.

THE MULTITASKING LIE

Finally, we want to address one of the most steadfast myths of modern work culture, the notion that multitasking is not only possible but an essential skill for surviving in today's hectic work environments.

As we chronicled in Chapter 3, the 2008 recession created an unfortunate opportunity for corporations to demand more work from employees without paying them for it. Since most people will put up with too much work rather than risk the possibility of not having any work at all, we were forced to figure out how to get more done in a day than what is possible. Multitasking— the ability to do more than one thing at once—seemed to provide the answer. The ability to multitask effectively is a delusion that helps us support our belief that we are equipped with the skill set necessary to handle this new level of work-and-life pressure. We can definitely chat with a friend while writing that report or check our email while out for drinks—it's killing two birds with one stone, right? Well actually, no. Multitasking is something that we like to think we're good at but, in reality, we're very bad at it.

Science tells a quite conclusive story: we cannot multitask. We won't go into the enormous body of work that has been done on multitasking (check the endnotes and online resources for a comprehensive list of reading materials, should you be interested in deep-diving into some of the materials we found), but at a high level, we know a few things about how our brains work:

We switch between tasks. Our brains utilize five main mental processes that help us when working, problem-solving, or completing a task: understanding, decision-making, recalling, memorizing, and inhibiting. These systems activate in a linear fashion, meaning that one operation has to be completed before the next one can begin. You can't skip steps here; you have to follow that process step by step.

When you try to do two tasks that require a high level of cognitive focus at the same time, you're not multitasking. Instead we are very quickly switching our attention back and forth from one task to the other. Even if we're switching at incredibly high speeds, the switch is still there.[12] So, contrary to what you might think, we're not actually doing two things at the same time. Have you ever lowered the volume of your car's radio when you're searching for an unfamiliar address? That's because your brain can't focus on listening to the lyrics and attempting to navigate at the same time. You see, the part of our brain that switches and processes the necessary information that makes it possible to get through the day is called the Executive System, and while it can switch between a few things quickly, eventually, it can get overwhelmed.

David Rock calls this phenomenon "dual-task interference." As he puts it, you're simply draining your brain's energy. Rock describes experiments where people who were asked to multitask showed a decline in their cognitive abilities comparable to going from the level of a Harvard MBA to that of an eight-year-old child. And this isn't just a Boomer thing or a Gen X thing. Despite an emerging narrative that younger generations have brains better suited to "multitasking," the truth is that they have become more adapted to rapid switching but can still suffer from the same drawbacks as the rest of us.

It all depends on focus. If one of the tasks is significantly lower in difficulty than the other, it will be possible to do both activities at the same time because the easy task (say washing the dishes) will be relegated to the routine section of the brain, running in the background, while your focus is on the more difficult task, like talking to your mom on the phone or listening to a podcast. If both processes are equally difficult, the cognitive ability to complete your tasks will be compromised.[13] Additionally, if you're switching between two (or more) high-focus tasks, it could take you some time to get back into the groove once your attention is diverted elsewhere. This is what Mihaly Csikszentmihalyi, the author of *Flow*, has proven. The way to get a difficult task done is long periods of uninterrupted work and singular focus. That means every time you're interrupted during a period of flow, say by a notification on your phone or an email, it could take you up to an hour to get back to that place of peak concentration.

We underestimate the costs and over-estimate the benefits of multitasking. It turns out that when we try to multitask, not only do we waste more time (the aforementioned time lost in needing to refocus) but we end up doing both tasks less well.

A BEAUTIFUL MIND

We'd wager that despite reading the paragraphs above, you'll still find yourself multitasking, even though rationally you know you shouldn't, simply because you believe you can. That is the beauty and the burden of our complicated brains.

We know now that our brain is wired for taking breaks. Our performance and achievements are not accomplished despite our breaks but because of them. Without taking the necessary time to rest and recharge, our productivity suffers disastrous consequences, along with our ability to remember, to learn, and to evolve. In a world where information is a constant stream of interruptions, the person who rests and recharges will triumph over those who think the path to success can be attained through sheer force of will.

However advanced our gadgets, however sophisticated our jobs, however cool our projects, we are still being governed by social evolutionary forces that impact the way we relate to each other at work. Whether you're dreaming up a new ad campaign, drafting a press release, solving a programming problem, or managing a team, there are real chemical reactions that trigger deeply emotional responses that have to do with our perceptions of status and safety. It's funny to think that the same instincts that helped our ancestors grow socially cohesive groups are still in evidence at the weekly manager's meeting.

Finally, our emotions at work can be powerful allies, and suppressing them in support of outdated work archetypes isn't doing anyone any favors. This isn't to say we advocate for over-the-top emotional responses, but we do need to stop villainizing emotional reactions at work as a sign of weakness.

Our brains have helped us survive for tens of thousands of years, and now, we've inadvertently created a system that works against our brain's natural processes. The push for continuous output, and the transition of work into a type of psychological and physical endurance sport, goes against everything we now know that the brain needs to thrive.

In the tension between productivity and creativity, our brain is firmly caught in the middle, trying desperately to keep up with our constant demands while we ignore the very protocols that are required to keep it running at its best.

The fight for the future of Productive Creative work doesn't just turn on social or cultural issues but on biological ones as well. And as we'll see in the next chapter, scientists and researchers have also expanded our understanding of our brain's impact on our creativity.

Summary of Big Ideas

➡ Downtime is an essential necessity in order for the brain to recover and operate.
➡ Humans cannot multitask effectively. Don't believe the lies.
➡ Perceived status (linked to our jobs and work) trigger the same fight or flight reactions as if we were facing a physical threat.
➡ Suppressing your emotions will negatively impact your ability to make good decisions.

8.

THE CREATIVE BRAIN

In the last chapter, we addressed some of the important findings that have helped scientists reframe our brain's relationship with productivity. In a nutshell, we learned that a work model that is based on continuous output is misaligned with our natural neural processes and in fact can interfere with our ability to produce.

In Chapter 2, we saw that creativity was mostly ignored by the sciences until the 1950s. In an industrially focused economy, creativity was not a needed skill. Deviating from set standards, in fact, was mostly frowned upon. In today's knowledge economy, in contrast, original ideas are the most valuable currency, and creativity is a necessary attribute for professionals across disciplines. But despite the avidity of contemporary scientists to understand creativity, the trait is much harder to quantify than productivity—which is a measurement of output in and of itself.

Creativity posed other challenges, too. For starters, it took scientists a long time to reach a consensus on the concrete phenotype (the complex mix of genetic and environmental influences, nature and nurture) that underlies its development. Researchers labored for decades to define all the characteristics of creative individuals, painstakingly laying the groundwork for the investigation of creativity on a neurological or molecular level.[1]

To highlight how nuanced these efforts must be, consider the many attributes that schizophrenia and creativity share in common: "delusional thinking (divergent, loose associations), jumping from idea to idea (flexibility), and over-inclusive thinking patterns (attention to irrelevant stimuli and detail, or lack of latent inhibition)."[2] By studying the different brain activities in people who are both creative and schizophrenic, researchers have been able to explore the deep link between creativity and our genetics (which we will get into later in this chapter).

The study of creativity is especially challenging for neuroscientists because creativity tends to be elusive. Creative thoughts appear when we least expect them, and they are difficult to force on the spot. That makes it difficult, if not impossible, to capture a moment of pure creativity in a laboratory setting. This is part of the reason that ideation is often used as a proxy for creativity in scientific studies. It is common to employ exercises that measure how many ideas, combinations, or associations one can produce in a given time in order to map creativity and the brain.

THE RESEARCH DILEMMA: LITTLE C OR BIG C?

One of the biggest challenges scientists researching creativity faced was the lack of consensus on what creativity actually is, or more specifically, how we define and measure it. In reviewing much of the literature, two clear approaches emerge. One strategy treats creativity as a process; the other looks at its products.

"Little c": The Process

Those who see creativity as a process try to break it down into a series of tasks that can be measured, tracked, and analyzed. Experiments often task subjects with identifying all the uses they can find for a commonplace item, such as a paperclip, in order to measure their "divergent thinking." You can try this yourself: set your phone timer for one minute, and challenge yourself to come up with as many possible uses for a paperclip as possible. Common answers include things like removing the SIM card from an iPhone, piercing your ears, or making a necklace. When we've done this with our MBA students, they've come up with some pretty unique answers. One guy suggested bug jousting (we have no idea what that is, but he got points for extra-divergent thinking). The results are then evaluated based on their originality, complexity, and function.

What makes these tests useful is the ease with which they can be administered across large groups of people, allowing researchers to assess a person's relative level of creativity (based on the assumption that having some degree of creativity is a universal human trait). The results generally fall into a bell curve, with those at the extreme edges representing the highest and lowest levels of creativity, and the bulk of the population falling somewhere in between.

Several models of the creative process have been proposed over the last ninety years. One of the earliest is Graham Wallas's four-phase process (preparation, incubation, illumination, and verification), which was developed in 1926.[3] Wallas's model was one of the first to connect the notion of incubation (setting aside an idea for a time) to illumination (the "aha" moment, when inspiration strikes). Wallas's successors would tweak or modify his model, but its basic suppositions hardly changed. In 1931, Joseph Rossman would attempt to demystify the incubation and illumination stages of the process by adding three

additional steps.[4] His phases were: observation of a need or difficulty, analysis of the need, a survey of all available information, a formulation of all objective solutions, a critical analysis
of all available solutions, the birth of the new idea, and finally,
the experimentation to test out the the best solution and implement it. Rossman's work, in turn, laid the groundwork for Alex
Osborn's, the inventor of "brainstorming." Osborn's seven-step
model included: orientation, preparation, analysis, ideation, incubation, synthesis, and evaluation. Osborn placed special emphasis on ideation, which continues to influence many of the
"little c" process-based approaches to creativity and divergent
thinking today.[5] Consider, for example, the four-step model
that Frank Barron introduced in 1988 (conception, gestation,
parturition, and "bringing up baby"—the actual and very much
unexpected name of the last step).

The main drawback of the little c approach is this: in order
for us to take its measure of divergent thinking as an accurate
representation of creativity, we have to believe that divergent
thinking is indeed a legitimate proxy for creative ability and
that a high score does in fact correlate with a higher creative
process. But while divergent thinking is an incredibly useful
skill, it clearly does not capture the whole gamut of creativity,
some of which turns on the opposite skill—the ability to home
in on the one correct solution to a problem.

"Big C": The Product

Other scientists have sought to measure and understand creativity in reference to its products, rather than the processes
that created them. Their research is usually focused on a specific sample of the population, such as authors, artists, musicians, innovators, and people who have been recognized for their
unique contributions to their fields (Nobel Prize winners, for
example, or recipients of MacArthur "genius" grants). Instead

of assuming that creativity is evenly distributed throughout the population (albeit in greater and lesser quantities), Big C research focuses on outliers—the Steve Jobses, Albert Einsteins, and Duke Ellingtons of the world—whose talents are in a completely different realm from those of us mere mortals.

The trouble here is in establishing a definition of creativity that encompasses such a diverse set of products. That is, can you compare a great literary novel to the invention of the iPhone or a scientific breakthrough? Do these types of output share any commonalities, or are we trying to compare apples and oranges?

Creativity has become an overused catchall; can just one concept, no matter how broadly defined, really capture the intangible magic that happens when a spark of inspiration hits? While the debate continues to rage, some interesting developments have emerged. Back in the age of the Muses, we would light incense and chant to entice the goddesses of creativity to bless us with some inspiration. Today we have the benefit of a significant body of scientific research that is shedding light on how we problem-solve and come up with new ideas.

But despite their different approaches, big and little c theories run up against the same complex, messy questions: how many of these skills are inherited versus learned? How much influence does nature have vs. nurture? While we already know that the nature vs. nurture debate is moot—the answer almost certainly involves an alchemy of the two—we were curious to see what else science has discovered about the ways that creativity actually works. Since the field is full of questions, we clustered our research around the three biggest questions we had.

1. Is there such a thing as a creative personality?
As we mentioned in Chapter 2, our concept of creativity evolved over time from something you have into something you are, and, finally, into something you do. But since our work culture

intertwines what we do with who we are, and at the same time puts such a high premium on creativity, our identity as creatives is an important part of how we define ourselves.

Many lay people think that creativity is a feature of one's personality, that you are either born with it or not. Between the 1950s and 1970s, much of the literature surrounding the nature of creativity was based upon the assumption that it was an innate trait that was amplified in geniuses and lacking in others—that if you weren't born with it, you were basically out of luck. Most of the research conducted during those years compared high performance creatives with their less prolific peers and concluded that the first group had distinct differences in their abilities, backgrounds, and personalities. In 1966, psychologist E. Paul Torrance, known as "the father of creativity," introduced the Torrance Tests of Creative Thinking (TTCT), a series of tests that focus on four scales: fluency (the number of relevant ideas generated), flexibility (the number of different categories), originality (the rarity of the response), and elaboration (the level of detail in the responses).[6] Now one of the most widely used tests in the world, the TTCT is available in over thirty-five languages and is highly regarded in both the educational and corporate worlds.

Personality research turns out to be just as complicated as creativity research, meaning that there are a great number of theories and models that attempt to account for the traits that define us. In order to understand the value of creativity within an identity setting, it's important to have a general understanding of personality theory.

The most widely agreed upon definition of personality is a "pattern of characteristic thoughts, feelings, and behaviors that distinguishes one person from another and persists over time and situations."[7] There are many different ways to study and measure personality, and we could probably devote an entire book to the pros and cons of each of them. We thought it would be useful to begin with a general overview of the main ones before returning to the issue of creativity. If you're already familiar with some of these approaches, feel free to skip ahead and meet us on page 180.

■ **Type Theorists** classify people into mutually exclusive categories, classifications that are binary and either/or. While trait theorists argue that such attributes as introversion and extroversion exist along a continuum, with people having more and less of each, type theorists believe that you either have them or you don't. As you can imagine, the debate in type theory is about how many classifications there should be and what those classifications actually are. One model you might have heard of is the Type A vs. Type B personality theory proposed by Meyer Friedman in the 1950s.

The most famous test from this school of thought is the Myers-Briggs Type Indicator,[8] which recognizes sixteen distinct personalities based on four binary categories:

1. Extraversion vs. Introversion
2. Sensing vs. Intuition
3. Thinking vs. Feeling
4. Judging vs. Perceiving

■ **Psychoanalytic Theorists** or Freudians believe that our behavior is determined by the interplay between the three different parts of our personality. The *id* is motivated by immediate gratification, and as such is our inner child. The *superego* is our higher self; it acts as a moral compass and is essentially our conscience. The *ego*, or our conscious, everyday self, is influenced by both to greater and lesser degrees and spends much of its energy negotiating its boundaries with them.

- **Behavioral Theorists** believe that our personalities are the products of our environmental conditioning. B.F. Skinner was the best-known and most influential member of this school.[9] As he saw it, a child throws a temper tantrum because they have learned that it is an effective way to get what they want.[10] Ivan Pavlov, who famously trained dogs to salivate at the ringing of a bell by pairing the sound of the bell to the delivery of food, is another famous behaviorist.

- **Social Cognitive Theorists** believe that behavior and personality stem from a person's cognitions (expectations or beliefs) about the world. They build on behavioral theory by factoring in things like memory and emotions. This field was founded by Albert Bandura, who was known for his famous "Bobo doll experiment," in which a group of young children kicked and abused a doll, imitating the behavior they had seen in a video shown to them just before.[11] This field is all about narratives, especially the stories we tell ourselves to explain the world around us. Interestingly, one discovery that you might find familiar was made by educators in the 1970s, who saw a high correlation between the belief that hard work results in the attainment of your goals and improved performance.[12]

- **Humanistic Theorists** focus on the notion of free will and an individual's active and conscious engagement with the world around them. Personality and behavior, in this view, are products of a person's subjective experiences. The giants of this field include Abraham Maslow (of Maslow's Hierarchy of Needs fame) and Carl Rogers, who argued that personality was complex and holistic and influenced by a host of factors. At their core, humanistic theories are optimistic in that they presume that individuals can take charge of their lives and make positive changes in them.

■ **Trait Theorists** use various models that measure character-istics along a continuum. Trait theory models assume that traits remain stable over time, that they differ from individual to individual, and that they play an important role in behavior. Critics of Trait Theorists argue that the traits are superficial as described and that there is a paucity of concrete evidence that proves that they shape personalities.

The best-known model within this field is Lewis Gold-berg's "Big Five,"[13] which is also known as the OCEAN model. Its five traits are:

1. Openness to Experience: Imaginative, independent, and interested vs. practical and interested in routines.
2. Conscientiousness: Organization and discipline vs. carelessness and impulsiveness.
3. Extraversion: Sociable and outgoing vs. retiring or reserved.
4. Agreeableness: Soft-hearted and trusting vs. suspicious and uncooperative.
5. Neuroticism: Anxious and insecure vs. secure and self-satisfied.

So how does this relate to creativity? Openness to Experience is the strongest predictor of creative ability,[14] which makes sense, considering that new experiences can fuel idea generation. But other personality aspects also play a part.

After conducting an extensive review of past research on personality and creativity, psychologists Guillaume Furst, Paolo Ghisletta, and Todd Lubart presented an overarching integrative model that explained personality's influence on creative ability through three super-factors: plasticity, divergence, and convergence.[15] Each super-factor was linked to the Big Five. Plasticity, for example, defined as a "tendency to explore and engage flexibly with novelty in both behavior and cognition," is found in individuals who have high levels of both Openness to Experience and Extraversion.[16] Divergence, on the other hand, or nonconformity thinking, is found in those who rank low on both Agreeableness and Conscientiousness.[17] People who rank highly on Convergence tend to have a high level of Conscientiousness, coupled with strong precision, persistence, and critical sense. As you can see, the features of creativity aren't clear-cut; many characteristics must overlap to produce the most favorable conditions for it.

And so, at long last, we arrive at the answer to our question. Simply put, in terms of personality traits—that is, those stable tendencies that are core to our identities—there is no one "creative type." According to David A. Owens, author of *Creative People Must be Stopped: 6 Ways We Kill Innovation (Without Even Trying)*, creativity is something that we individuals do have some control over.[18] "Research suggests that our habits of perception and thinking drive creativity more than some mysterious genetic trait," he writes. "And habits are things we can do something about." Owens believes that individuals who are creative possess excellent skills of perception (observation), intellection (thinking and making connections between ideas), and expression (communicating their findings).

These findings are echoed by Professor Oyvind L. Martinsen at the BI Norwegian Business School, who conducted a study to determine the characteristics of a "creative" personality."[19] His findings showed that "creative personalities" were motivated, flexible, and ambitious. Even respondents who didn't display traditional characteristics of creatives could improve their creativity through behavioral changes. "You can change the way you behave in relation to the world around you," he said in a Fast Company interview.

Of course, certain personality types are more likely to develop the habits that can lead to increased creativity, such as an extrovert's curiosity, or an open-to-experience person's appetite for new ideas.[20] But these attributes aren't set in stone. On the contrary, creativity is a skill, a habit, that can be cultivated and strengthened. While some people might have more of an aptitude for it than others, that doesn't mean that if you're born lacking some of the skills that go with it that it's game over for you.

2. Is there a link between creativity and genetics?

As one of the most prolific writers of all time, Stephen King is in the top echelons of Productive Creatives.[21] Over the course of his career, King has published fifty-four novels, almost two hundred short stories, and has sold over 350 million copies of his books, which include *The Shawshank Redemption*, *The Green Mile*, *Carrie*, and *It* (responsible for our lasting, very real fear of clowns—thanks Mr. King!).[22] This is impressive enough, until you consider the artistic output of his family: his wife Tabitha is a poet, the author of eight novels, and several short story collections.[23] His son Joe (pseudonym: Joe Hill) has written three best-selling novels, several short stories and comics, and has received numerous awards, including the 2006 William L. Crawford Award for Best New Fantasy Writer and Bram Stoker Awards for both Best New Horror Short Story and Best First Novel.[24] Not to be outdone, his other son, Owen, released his debut novel in 2013 and has published short stories, comics, and a screenplay. He's also the recipient of the John Gardner Award.[25] That's a lot of creative talent in one family.

Obviously, one could argue that environment, not to mention the financial privilege that allowed them to pursue creative endeavors, also played a role in the King children's success, but artistic talent often shows up in family clusters. Consider, for example, the renowned British writer Kingsley Amis, who has produced twenty novels, numerous short stories, scripts for both television and radio, and six volumes of poetry. Amis was ranked nine on the list of 50 Greatest British Writers Since 1945 by the *Times* in 2008. That list also included Amis's son Martin, who carried on the family's literary tradition by publishing fourteen novels (and counting), seven works of nonfiction, several collections of short stories, and one screenplay. The father-son duo count five Man Booker Prize shortlists between them.[26]

And then there are historic powerhouses, like the Brontë sisters (their father Patrick Brontë was himself a writer, poet, and polemicist, and their less famous brother Branwell was a painter and a writer as well).[27] Interestingly, it was the Brontë children's aunt, Elizabeth Branwell, who was responsible for raising them and taught them how to read and write—another point for the nurture aspect of this equation.[28] Whether it's the Dumases (father and son, both named Alexander) or the Jameses (Henry and William), the concentration of creativity found in specific family clusters has been a long-standing source of fascination and curiosity for scientists, cementing the notion that creativity is an inherited gift, something you either have or don't have.

One of the earliest thinkers to tackle this question was Francis Galton, the father of the discredited field of eugenics, who published *Hereditary Genius* in 1869. Galton researched the historical backgrounds of about four hundred talented people, grouping them by category (writer, statesman, etc.) and then searching their family trees for any relatives who were also successful in their field. There were indeed strong connections: 50 percent of authors and painters, 40 percent of poets, and 20 percent of musicians had relatives who were also successful in the same artistic pursuit, leading Galton to write, "I conclude that each generation has enormous power over the natural gifts of those that follow, and maintain that it is a duty we owe to humanity to investigate the range of that power, and to exercise it in a way that without being unwise towards ourselves, shall be most advantageous to the future inhabitants of the earth."[29]

Funny fact: Galton was himself cousin to Charles Darwin. While his theories are considered an oversimplification of the creative process today, he was accurate in his assertion that creativity involved some heritability (though not in his assertion that genetics was the be-all and end-all of creative ability).

Some emerging science makes a better case for a genetic link. After examining 300,000 individuals suffering from mental illnesses, as well as those individuals' siblings, over the past forty years, scientists from the Karolinska Institute in Stockholm made an interesting discovery:[30] individuals who had been diagnosed with neuropsychiatric conditions such as bipolar disorder or schizophrenia demonstrated increased creative skills compared to mentally healthy individuals. Not only did a large portion of respondents indicate that they worked in creative and artistic fields but first-degree relatives who didn't have any mental illnesses had a higher likelihood to also be engaged in creative pursuits. In a follow-up study of more than one million people, the authors further studied the link between pathology and creativity and the results were a mixed bag. The good news: individuals in creative professions are not more likely to suffer from mental disorders than controls, with one exception: authors. Sigh.

In fact, authors were twice as likely to suffer from schizophrenia and bipolar disorder than control subjects and, if that wasn't bad enough, were more likely to suffer from unipolar depression, anxiety, and substance abuse. Even those authors who didn't suffer from any of the disorders the researchers were screening for were at a higher risk to commit suicide. Yeesh. (Hilariously, the study goes on to reassure us that those in accounting or auditing professions could rest easy, as there was no association between psychopathology and those particular professions.)

Another study examined the link between genetics and musical aptitude and discovered a direct correlation between individuals who display musical talent and the presence of a group of genes associated with the brain's ability to form and break new connections between its cells, also known as neuro-plasticity.[31] Many musical individuals also had a genetic quirk known as Copy Number Variations (CNVs), meaning they were either missing certain genes or had duplicate copies.

There is an especially strong link between CNVs and com-posing and singing and having perfect pitch.[32] In this case, participants had duplicate copies of DNA strands that aid in serotonin processing (we'll have more to say about serotonin in just a moment).[33] Some research suggests that these same genomic variants can indicate an increased risk of developing certain neuropsychiatric conditions.

Seneca the Younger was hardly exaggerating when he said that "there was never a great genius without a touch of mad-ness." History has no shortage of notable figures who strug-gled with demons (though we can only speculate as to their actual diagnoses), such as Tolstoy, Beethoven, Poe, Hemingway, and even Isaac Newton, the father of calculus and the laws of motion, who is believed to have suffered from autism and bi-polar disorder. Virginia Woolf battled ongoing bouts of depres-sion and bipolar disorder and Polish scientist Marie Curie was thought to have Asperger's.

But for all the anecdotal evidence, the verdict is still mixed. While new papers and research findings improve our under-standing of the connections between our creative abilities and our genes nearly every day, the field is still in its infancy.

There is enough evidence to suggest that some elements of creative talent are indeed inherited. Yes, some people—like Steve Jobs and Stephen King—are born with what seems to be an unfair amount of raw talent. But we use the word "raw" deliberately because the advantages that their genes give them are unrefined. Without the benefit of an environment that in-stills discipline, hard work, practice, and instruction, even their immense natural talents may remain untapped. Genetics play a role in creativity but not the only role.

That's the flip side of this coin: that a person's conscious and strategic efforts can also influence their creative abilities and output. We are all born with a certain level of innate skills that we can augment to some degree with practice and study, but we have an upper limit as well. After all, we could wake up every day and practice shooting hoops for one hundred years and while we would dramatically improve our current nonexistent skills, we would never be as good as Lebron James on his worst day.

3. How do our brains facilitate our creative abilities?

We've covered personality and genetics, but we can't leave out the last piece in our investigation of the sources of creativity: biology. How do the workings of our brains help or hinder our creative processes? There have been some interesting recent discoveries about the links between creativity and brain structure.

Much of the research we found was in its early stages, highlighting how much we still need to learn. This is something we find both liberating and frustrating. Liberating because it seems like there is a whole frontier of discoveries that are yet to be made, and frustrating because it often feels as though we are living inside a machine that didn't come with an owner's manual.

For example, take the posterior cingulate cortex (PCC), a structure in the cerebral cortex. Scientists know that this part of the brain plays an important role in supporting processes responsible for memories and emotions.[34] They also know that the PCC acts as a central node in the Default Mode Network. If that last name sounds familiar, it's because we mentioned it in the last chapter—it's the internal network that is activated when we are doing things like daydreaming, planning, or remembering events.

Researchers at Duke University discovered that the PCC plays an important part in helping us maintain motivation, by monitoring our performance and redirecting our attention as needed.[35] Essentially, it is a control gate between our internal and external attention spans—as a part of the DMN, it activates when we let our mind wander and deactivates when we need to focus on external stimuli.

During meditation, for example, the PCC dials down, giving us the ability to focus our cognitive attention on being present and on our breathing.[36] It is therefore hypothesized that the PCC region plays an important part in divergent thinking,[37] one of the chief attributes of creativity.

How is this important to our search for understanding creativity and our brains? Well, it turns out that creative individuals have bigger PCCs. Those Duke researchers also noted that they have higher levels of serotonin, a neurotransmitter responsible for connectivity between brain cells and mood stability. Because it enhances connectivity, high serotonin levels are associated with increases in abilities like pattern detection, symbol comprehension, and the ability to come up with unique and new solutions to problems.[38] At the same time, abnormalities in serotonin production can lead to problems. Low levels of serotonin are associated with depression, anxiety, and suicidal behavior (in extreme cases).[39] Similarly, PCC abnormalities have also been linked to a variety of diseases and disorders, including schizophrenia, autism, depression, ADD, and Alzheimer's.[40]

And that's only the PCC—there's still the rest of the brain to examine! When scientists at Cornell University examined the brains of writers, musicians, and other creatives, they discovered that on average they had a smaller corpus callosum, the mass of nerve fibers linking the left and right hemispheres of the brain together. Decreasing the connection between the two hemispheres results in what scientists call "an incubation of ideas," basically giving each side of the brain the opportunity to fully explore and develop ideas.[41] This also can lead to an increase in divergent thinking.

In 2015, a study published by Stanford University implicated the cerebellum, the part of the brain responsible for movement and coordination, in the creative process, a new development in the field. Its authors speculated that the cerebellum does more than simply coordinate our movements. It also activates when we are learning a new behavior and models it, allowing other parts of the brain to focus on new challenges.[42]

Left Brain/Right Brain

One of the most enduring models for understanding creativity has been the dichotomy between the left and right hemispheres of the brain. The left hemisphere has been described as the rational part of ourselves, the no-nonsense, practical part that helps us navigate the endless logistics that a self-sufficient adult in the modern world must master. In contrast, the right brain is seen as your flaky aunt—the one that lets you paint on the walls and have chocolate cake for breakfast. This is the fun side of your brain, often called the creative side, whose skills are intuition and imagination. These two parts, as we have just seen, are connected by the corpus callosum, which enables the brain to work as a cohesive unit. But according to a recent paper from the University of New Mexico's neurosurgery department, this view is an oversimplification.[43] While certain types of mental tasks do cluster in their respective hemispheres, creativity depends on the interplay of regions all over the brain and is more akin to a network. In fact, as we have seen, there are a number of such neural networks that we depend on. Since we're not cognitive neuroscientists, we found the following analogies helpful in organizing our thinking around those various networks and their uses.

The Sprinter—Officially called the Executive Attention Network, the Sprinter is called upon when you need to completely focus on your goal, usually to complete some challenging, highly cognitive task. As you move with single purpose toward your goal, much like a runner racing toward the finish line, your lateral prefrontal cortex region and posterior parietal lobe are called into action. When you're concentrating in a meeting, learning something new, or actively thinking about something, that's when the Sprinter jumps into focus.

The Flaneur—Flaneur is a French word that describes someone who is wandering in a leisurely way. This is the Default Network (also called the Imagination Network) we mentioned in the last chapter. It's what kicks into gear when your mind wanders in a daydream or when you're imagining a future scenario. It's internally focused, much as if you are taking a stroll through your own mind. The Default Network involves the prefrontal cortex, the medial regions of the temporal lobe, and the parietal cortex.

The Conductor—Imagine an orchestra full of musicians. The Conductor carefully monitors everything that is going on—in this case, both the inner thoughts and any external stimuli—and then it chooses the network that is best suited to address the matter at hand. Need to focus? The Conductor activates the Sprinter. Bored on a long commute? The Flaneur gets called up. This is also called the Attentional Flexibility Network, and it uses the dorsal anterior cingulate cortices and the anterior insular.

Within the framework of cognitive creativity, we tend to switch back and forth between the Flaneur and the Sprinter. This notion is supported by the findings of Arne Dietrich, professor of psychology at the American University of Beirut. Dietrich, who authored *How Creativity Happens in The Brain,* considers the prefrontal cortex the anchor of creativity, positing that, depending on the task at hand, certain brain regions will either slow down or ramp up. In other words, when we're trying to come up with new possibilities, we should let the Flaneur lead the way. When we need to critically assess our new ideas to see if they are actually useful or not, it's time to call on the Sprinter.

But you can't force the process. Research shows that trying to make yourself creative might actually backfire. If you force your Executive Control (the Sprinter) to look for needed solutions, you might find yourself frustrated and blocked. Instead, you might have to undertake another activity to help your inner Flaneur take a look. As we mentioned earlier, despite our work culture, which encourages us to "push through," the most productive thing you can do might be to take a break, step away, and let your mind wander.[44]

As with all things, Dietrich reminds us that much of this research is still in its infancy; a certain degree of skepticism is appropriate. "Even for the wilderness of human thinking, creative ideas seem to be deliberately designed to defy empirical enquiry," he said in an interview with the *Atlantic*.[45]

A GIFT AND A JOB

The French novelist, playwright, journalist, and political activist Émile Zola summed up our conclusions best when he said, "The artist is nothing without the gift, but the gift is nothing without the work." At its core, creativity is a dizzying mix of genes and environment, inherited traits and finely honed skills. What we do know is this: creativity has been at the heart of human evolution since our ancestors first climbed down from trees. We are all creative, to lesser or greater degrees, subject to the exigencies of our genes, our upbringing, and our educations.

The definition of creativity itself has contracted and expanded over time. Once reserved for artists, it is now wide enough to include the millions of people working in knowledge economies who are creating their own forms of art, be it through language, numbers, visuals, problem-solving, or any number of other highly-cognitive activities. However, there still exists a hierarchy of creative jobs that have a higher level of perceived legitimacy. We reject that; we firmly believe that Productive Creatives can be found across all organizations, whether they work in finance or HR, marketing, communications, strategy, or in leadership positions.

As Productive Creatives ourselves, we believe that it's critical that we recognize our own innate potential while making every effort to develop, hone, and improve our skills. For most people, this involves a commitment to regular and challenging practice.

When was the last time you dedicated time (other than reading this book right now) to honing your creative skills? Or did you just assume that your ability to problem-solve or come up with creative ideas was simply a part of your nature?

Summary of Big Ideas

➡ "Little c" approach to studying creativity focuses on the process you use to create.
➡ "Big C" approach to studying creativity focuses on the end product.
➡ There is no such thing as a "Creative Personality." Some people have a higher aptitude for the characteristics that facilitate creativity (openness, flexibility etc.), but everyone can improve their creative abilities to a point—though some people are obviously more gifted than others.

➡ There are genetic links in creative traits running in family groups, but the other factors (privilege, access to mentoring, financial support) also play a part when successful offspring follow the creative footsteps of their parents.

➡ The left brain/right brain dichotomy is an outdated model for understanding creativity. The creative process uses processes and functions on both sides of the brain.

9.

DON'T WORRY, BE HAPPY

When we first started this quest to understand our relationship to work, we didn't realize what a mammoth topic it was, spanning cultural, social, biological, and historical elements, or how challenging it would be to wrap our heads around it. Work has become an elite status symbol and a coveted social signal as we more and more define our identities and values through our job titles.

We've developed a long list of expectations of what work means and what it's supposed to give us. In addition to financial security, we expect our jobs to deliver meaning and purpose. As we dug deeper, we spotted a new addition to our list of expectations: happiness.

Employers have recognized this too, and as they confront the challenges of talent attraction, management, and retention, they have made efforts to keep their workforces more engaged by ensuring their happiness. Yes, following in the footsteps of creativity, another abstract metric is gaining importance within organizations. As you'll see in this chapter, happiness is being co-opted, quantified, and industrialized as a way to maximize productivity and efficiency. In the wake of all those "Most

Creative Places to Work" lists, we are now seeing "Happiest Places to Work" lists, an interesting distinction and one that has a lot of ramifications.

As the most popular phrase in the Declaration of Independence, the "pursuit of happiness" is a core piece of the American identity.[1] Yet happiness is an abstract concept that is hard to define precisely. Yes, we all want to be "happy," but what we mean by that can vary wildly from person to person. The one thing we *do* share is the compulsion to chase this societal ideal, which is now being absorbed into our work lives as well.

Specifically, the introduction of happiness as a metric is relevant because it contradicts so many of the other feelings we associate with both productivity and creativity. On the productivity front, Work Devotion and the fetishization of suffering has long been embedded in our psyches. Creativity is complicated, too. The familiar archetype of the "tortured" artist is very much at odds with the happiness that companies are now trying to instill.

In this chapter, we'll take a look at what the commercialization of happiness means for the way we work, as well as its specific impacts on our productivity and creativity.

THE COMMERCIALIZATION OF HAPPINESS

The idea that happiness leads to higher productivity wasn't always so widely accepted. Over the past several decades, the connection between happiness and productivity was debated. As early as 1989, there were researchers who hypothesized that happiness could result in **demotivation** at work, since the happier workers were, the more likely they were to be complacent and disengaged.[2] Others theorized that hard work doesn't make us happier, but that happiness motivates us to work harder.

By now there is a large body of research that shows that companies with happy employees enjoy stronger financial performance and higher customer satisfaction.[3] After years of resisting employee demands for better working conditions, it seems that organizations are finally waking up to the tangible economic benefits that come with positive work environments.[4] Happiness is good for business.

The integration of "happiness" into the corporate world has been fascinating to watch. The last time we checked (mid-2018), there were over 1,654 job postings for "Chief Happiness Officer," a role popularized by Chade-Meng Tan, a software engineer who became his company's official "Jolly Good Fellow." Tan, who was the 108th employee hired at Google, was inspired by the Buddhist monk Matthieu Ricard, an advocate for the transformative power of mindful meditation focused on compassion. In the estimation of a group of scientists who studied him, he may be "the happiest man in the world."

Let's unpack this a little, starting with Matthieu Ricard, a molecular geneticist who became a Tibetan monk and a prolific writer on, among other things, happiness. (His book, *Happiness: A Guide to Developing Life's Most Important Skill*, came out in 2006.) In 2008, he participated in a study conducted by the Laboratory for Affective Neuroscience at the University of Wisconsin that used MRI scans to measure the levels of positive emotions in people. Ricard scored off the charts, with -0.45, where others barely approached -0.3.[5] This not only means that Ricard is as happy as he claims to be—it also means that cognitive scientists have figured out a way to quantify happiness, much like their creativity-focused counterparts that we mentioned in the last chapter. Though we should also mention that this was just *one* experiment that generated a number, and who's to say that an MRI scan can measure something as subjective and intangible as happiness, anyway? But that's neither here nor there.

Ricard's story caught Tan's attention, who wanted to apply some of Ricard's meditation practices within an organizational setting. In a 2010 TED Talk, Tan spoke about seeing the benefits of inner peace and compassion and translating them into an organization's value. "Matthieu's brain scan shows that compassion is not a chore. Compassion is something that creates happiness. Compassion is fun," he said. "And that mind flowing insight changes the entire game. Because if compassion was a chore, nobody's going to do it, except maybe the Dalai Lama or something. But if compassion was fun, everybody's going to do it. Therefore, to create the conditions for global compassion, all we have to do is reframe compassion as something that is fun."

He saw this as a unique business opportunity. "Fun is not enough," Tan continued. "What if compassion is also profitable? What if compassion is also good for business? Then, every boss, every manager in the world, will want to have compassion." In order to institutionalize happiness, Tan created a program called "Searching Inside Yourself," which teaches Google employees techniques to calm their minds, be more aware of their thoughts, and create more positive mental habits.[6]

We don't deny that valuing compassion only within the context of profitability rubs us the wrong way, but we were willing to give Tan the benefit of the doubt. If mindful compassion can make you a better and happier person, improve the world, and also deliver some business benefits, then isn't it worth a try?

Zappos CEO Tony Hsieh followed suit with the publication of his 2010 *New York Times* bestseller *Delivering Happiness,* which outlined the strategies he implemented to create a happy work environment at his online shoe store. Whether it was because his people were happy or not, Amazon was certainly impressed with his business results—they bought the company for $1.9 billion in 2009. Hsieh has also launched a global consulting firm that has spread his happiness gospel to 160 companies, including Hilton, General Mills, Audi, and Lowe's.

So far, so good, right? We would wholeheartedly agree that helping people become happier at work and increasing the levels of compassion in the world would be a good thing. Working in a company where a positive work environment is a priority is, at first glance, a big benefit to employees everywhere.

But things start to get murky when we attach these concepts to financial performance, when it becomes someone's responsibility to transform an emotion into a corporate resource. Happiness becomes yet another sacrifice at the altar of productivity. A metric used to attain a singular purpose: to push employees to produce more.

Let's stop and think about what it means that "happiness" has been added to the mix of business health metrics. William Davies, author of *The Happiness Industry: How The Government and Big Business Sold Us Well-Being*, is concerned about the co-optation of happiness by organizations. "Happiness, in its various guises, is no longer some pleasant add-on to the more important business of making money, or some New Age concern for those with enough time to sit around baking their own bread," he writes. "It has penetrated the citadel of global economic management."[7]

Companies have become hyper-invested in tracking, measuring, and analyzing happiness as a way to control their product output, or, to put it another way, to get Productive Creatives to grind out more work. Productivity as a practice is centered around the idea of having control of the process to determine the output, only this time we're not calibrating machines but people. While happiness is good for business, you certainly can't force it on your employees, though it hasn't stopped a few companies from trying.

In 2016, the US National Labor Board Review heard a case that involved the American telecom giant T-Mobile's employee handbook, which stated that all workers were required to communicate "in a manner that is conducive to effective working relationships with internal and external customers, clients, coworkers, and management," in order to maintain a "positive work environment."

There were also other work regulations that prohibited workers from arguing or making detrimental comments about the company. Taken together, it was reasonable to assume that a worker wouldn't risk losing their job by violating these policies and would therefore self-censor, depriving themselves of their legal protected right to communicate their grievances at work,[8] which is an essential part of raising awareness of issues and organizing around unfair work conditions.

The National Labor Board Review sided with the employees, likening the demand of constant positivity as an infringement on free-speech rules, and declared that employers can't police their employees' on-the-job happiness. Legally speaking, you don't have to be happy at work.

This is not a book about happiness, and we are not happiness experts (though we would humbly take an accreditation on our knowledge of our Lady Queen Bey). We don't want to dive into the mechanics of what exactly makes us happy and how to cultivate it. There are far more qualified people who have written about this whose work we recommend on our website.

We simply want to point out that happiness has migrated from something that philosophers once mused about to a bottom-line business metric. Everyone has happiness on their minds. In 2011, the United Nations launched their first edition of the World Happiness Report, which was quickly followed by the OECD's Better Life Index. Consider the fact that Matthieu Ricard, our Buddhist friend, has been attending the annual meetings of the World Economic Forum at Davos to share his insights on mindfulness with government leaders and CEOs. "Ten years ago, doing morning meditation sessions at Davos would have been unthinkable," Ricard said in an interview with the AFP. "Now it has become fashionable."

Formed in 2017, the newly launched Global Happiness Council brings a diverse group of academic specialists and key practitioners together to identify the "best practices at the national and local levels to encourage advancement of the causes of happiness and well-being." We were encouraged to read that the 2018 Global Happiness Policy Report moves away from using GDP per capita as a measure of human progress. Council members, including the famed economist Jeffrey D. Sachs, Martine Durand, the chief statistician at the OECD, and the father of positive psychology Martin Seligman, focus on six areas instead (education, workplace, personal happiness, public health, city design, and management) and produce a report containing policy recommendations on how to promote happiness and well-being. "Skeptics of the happiness movement believe that power, not happiness, is the (inevitable) business of government," writes Sachs in the introduction to the nearly three hundred-page report. "Yet pursuing happiness is not only idealistic; it is the world's best and perhaps only hope to avoid global catastrophe."[9]

But, in making happiness such a central tenet of our companies and governments, are we also transforming it into a burden? If you recall from Chapter 2, the concept of productivity morphed over time to become an important personal responsibility. Now we are responsible for our happiness as well. In his book, *Perpetual Euphoria: On the Duty to Be Happy,* Pascal Bruckner argues that our right to pursue happiness has become an obsession that is making us more unhappy. "Gripped by the twin illusions that we are responsible for being happy or unhappy and that happiness can be produced by effort, many of us are now martyring ourselves—sacrificing our time, fortunes, health, and peace of mind—in the hope of entering an earthly paradise," he writes. "Much better to accept that happiness is an unbidden and fragile gift that arrives only by grace and luck."[10]

According to June Gruber, an associate professor of psychology and neuroscience at Yale University, setting happiness as a goal could make you feel worse in the long run, especially if the intent is to solely increase happiness. "When you're doing it with the motivation or expectation that these things ought to make you happy, that can lead to disappointment and decreased happiness," she says.[11]

HAPPY COWS MAKE HAPPY MILK?

A recent study led by Andrew Oswald, professor of economics at Warwick University, explored the connections between happiness and productivity. Researchers asked participants to add single digit numbers together for ten minutes and paid them for their performance as well as their participation.[12] Once their task was completed, one group was shown a short video of a well-known British comedian and the other a "placebo" video of colored sticks. (Side note, we love imagining the thinking process that goes into structuring these experiments. A video of colored sticks?) Feeling happier, the comedic group did 12 percent better on their second round of arithmetic while the placebo group did 10 percent worse. When researchers questioned the participants about their personal lives, it emerged that those who'd experienced illness or a recent death of a loved one also performed on average 10 percent worse than the rest of the group. Human emotion, they concluded, is an important consideration and driver in the equation for optimal productivity. As Oswald put it, "companies like Google have invested more in employee support, and employee satisfaction has risen as a result. For Google, it rose by 37 percent under scientifically controlled conditions, proving that making workers happier really pays off."[13]

Outside of the economics laboratory, there is plenty of other data that confirms this notion. Shawn Achor's *The Happiness Advantage* describes multiple experiments across neuroscience and management studies that prove happiness drives a higher level of productivity among workers. This is demonstrated through better sales performance, stronger leadership, and, consequently, better performance ratings and pay, as well as more job security. The brains of happy workers are 31 percent more productive. Happier workers are also less likely to take leave, sick days, or quit. An intensive and thorough review of happiness-related studies by the *Harvard Business Review* also found that happiness had a strong impact on work performance.[14] To quantify the realities of an *unhappy* workforce, research firm Gallup estimates that America's "disengagement crisis" results in $300 billion in lost productivity each year (once again, we point out that the metric that is really being measured is productivity).[15]

Just like we've done with creativity, we are forcing our happiness to conform to productivity standards. According to Emma Seppala, science director at Stanford University's Center for Compassion and Altruism Research and Education, and the author of *The Happiness Track: How to Apply the Science of Happiness to Accelerate Your Success*, happiness, much like creativity, requires space and not simply an exertion of effort. "People generally have the misconception that, in order to be successful, they have to postpone their happiness. Ironically, what research is showing is that happiness is the fast track to success," she said. "If, instead of overworking and burning out, you take time to relax, to cultivate calmness, to stay present, and to be more compassionate to yourself and others, you will be more productive, resilient to stress, charismatic and influential, and more creative and innovative."

Our long hours and other displays of Work Devotion can actually harm us and work against our creative best interests. "People think that success requires extreme sacrifices in the present—foregoing personal happiness, enduring negative feelings and tremendous stress—because the eventual payoff is worth it," Seppala continues. "They get addicted to productivity; they are driven by perfectionism. The result is workaholism. What they don't realize are the costs of workaholism: damaged physical and psychological health, decreased productivity and performance, decreased attention span, sleep problems and even family problems."[16] We cover the other economic costs of burnout in Chapter 12.

To sum up, being happy has a positive impact on your productivity, but chasing happiness for its own sake can make us very unhappy.

WHISTLE WHILE YOU WORK:
THE HEDONIC TREADMILL

While happier people are indeed more productive, does productivity make us happier? It may give us a fleeting sense of satisfaction, but it's not enough.

In his book *Stumbling on Happiness,* Harvard psychology professor Dan Gilbert notes that humans tend to overestimate how happy or sad certain events or outcomes will make them.[17] You've certainly heard the cautionary tales about lottery winners who don't report being happier than anyone else. This theory applies to losing weight, winning an election, getting a promotion, and yes—even reaching Inbox Zero. These conditions don't have the lasting impact on our happiness that we think they will. Gilbert uses the image of a "hedonic treadmill" to explain why this is. We are adaptive creatures, and our desires and expectations adjust to the changes around us. When we make our happiness conditional, we forget that our adaptive nature significantly minimizes the lasting effects of even our most desired outcomes. We are effectively running in place. What we want, and what we believe will make us happy, is what we *don't* have.

Part of this can be attributed to what psychologist and researcher Richard Eckersley calls "cultural fraud"—the compounding impact of images we're constantly exposed to that define the "good life" but have more do with economics than psychological well-being.[18] For a long time, we didn't have a common, critical lens to help us understand that we might be encouraged to chase after the wrong things (fame, fortune, etc.), but that's changed. Today, you probably don't need the findings of a research study to tell you that materialism doesn't breed happiness and can actually create depression and anxiety (though there are plenty of them out there, if you do).

The over-ripe rhetoric around productivity, and the promise of the happiness we can achieve through it, has simply replaced an older, outdated status marker: wealth. A focus on productivity for its own sake is like a focus on accumulating wealth— sad people are still sad, even when they become rich.

We know that happier people are more productive, but science does *not* show us that **productivity is the trigger for happiness**. What the data *does* strongly suggest is that while work provides us with a mechanism to define and express meaning and purpose in our lives, it's the pursuit of that self-identified purpose that really makes us happy.

It's important to note that having purposes like resume-building, earning money, and gaining professional status are very different than the divine professional destiny we wrote about in Chapter 5. Feeling like you are contributing toward something that is bigger than you and that deeply matters is a more powerful motivator than a raise, a promotion, or even more vacation time.

Does happiness make us productive? The science says yes— happy people are more productive. But it's possible that our actual pursuit of happiness is making it harder for us to find. Perhaps it's time to start focusing on another marker instead.

HAPPILY CREATIVE?

As you well know by now, creativity is a complex and ambiguous process that requires the cooperation of several different neurological, biological, and social mechanisms. Does creativity make us happier? Does being happy make us more creative? And what about all of those tortured artist tropes that convince us that we must suffer for our art?

Researchers in a collaborative experiment between Kent and Sussex Universities did a thorough review of ninety studies conducted over the past sixty years that explored creative processes across diverse fields of expertise. They were able to identify fourteen distinct components:

1. Active involvement and persistence
2. Dealing with uncertainty
3. Domain competence
4. General intellect
5. Generating results
6. Independence and freedom
7. Innovation and emotional involvement
8. Originality
9. Progression and development
10. Social interaction and communication
11. Spontaneity and subconscious process
12. Thinking and evaluation
13. Value
14. Variety, divergence, and experimentation

Each of these interacts in varying degrees at different points in a person's creative process. Bill Keller, a linguist at Sussex University and one of the authors of the study, made sure to specify that these fourteen components represent elements of the creative process and not a definition. As you'll recall from Chapter 8, the items on this list span both the little c (the process) and Big C (the output) as well as a mix of other skills and competences. You might have been surprised to see that happiness didn't make the list.

That's because in some cases, especially when focusing on problem-solving or completing challenging and difficult tasks, creative work can make you feel angry and frustrated. As we're sure we can all attest, some part of the creative process involves banging our heads against a wall as we try to figure out how to move our projects forward. This can be stressful and infuriating and, sometimes, depressing, but these emotional states are unavoidable when producing creative work.[19] The other benefit of emotions that fall on the more unpleasant side of the spectrum is that feeling unhappy about something not only signals that there is a problem needing to be solved but can often motivate us to figure out how to fix it. This line of thinking was also reflected in the T-Mobile labor ruling we mentioned earlier in the chapter: that preventing workers from expressing "negative views" at work could deprive them of the opportunity to raise these issues in an effort to fix them and potentially improve work conditions. So, in some cases, negative emotions that get a bad rap in the race to infuse organizations with happiness do come in handy and serve an important purpose.

Echoing these findings, psychology professors at Rice University studied the correlation between mood and creativity in 160 employees.[20] The experiment required workers to keep a journal documenting their moods, while their bosses measured their creative performance. It turns out the ideal creative state is one where a person can swing between positive and negative mood states. This was great news for us, who alternated between exhilaration and doubt that we could ever do justice to such a complicated topic during the writing of this book.

Those of us who manage people or who work with teams should also take note: the respondents who reported both good and bad moods combined with a supportive work environment significantly outperformed their counterparts. Having an understanding supervisor created the type of environment where these moods could be focused on making real tangible progress.

To work with or manage creatives can be challenging, especially within a work culture that expects a neutral type of professionalism that meets the Ideal Worker gold standard. Now, we're not saying that we should make it ok for people to scream or express their frustration in inappropriate ways, but we should recognize that these mood states are part of the needed ecosystem for optimized creativity. And with all this new emphasis on happiness in the workplace, we're concerned that organizations are creating conditions that will stifle this essential part of the creative process.

We chose to highlight the above two studies because the bulk of the other research we came across focused on the influence of only one emotional state on creativity, which resulted in contradictory results. There are papers that showed that happiness increased creativity in terms of idea generation and out-of-the-box thinking, while others stated that negative mood states motivate people to address a particular pain point (recall from Chapter 7 that our brains are wired to seek pleasure and avoid pain). Happiness in certain contexts can make us more creative, but it can also make us complacent and less willing to try new things.[21] Before we can find balance, we must acknowledge this variability.

EMBRACING SOCIAL NORMS

The growing interest in happiness coincides with some of the most turbulent economic conditions we've seen in centuries.

As the definition of work moves away from the stable employment enjoyed by previous generations into something a little more volatile and unpredictable, we must also contend with the technological revolution looming on the horizon that threatens to dramatically disrupt every aspect of our lives.

In the midst of all of this uncomfortable change and uncertainty, companies are clinging to happiness as a means to boost their brands. After all, being voted as the happiest place to work sure looks good on paper, doesn't it?

We've turned happiness into a metric, a goal worth pursuing, and a personal responsibility. Anyone who doesn't toe the company line is a troublemaker, or worse, someone who isn't working hard enough to achieve the desired state of happiness. Pressing employees to be happy also allows companies to sidestep real work issues and conflicts.

The corporate happiness esthetic embodies fun and a level of care that is attractive to current and potential talent. But while happiness makes you more productive, creativity requires a fuller, more balanced spectrum of emotions, which can often run against the grain of well-meaning happiness policies and end up hurting more than helping.

In 2016, I visited Dan Ariely, professor of psychology and behavior economics at his research center at Duke University where we chatted at length about this subject. I was especially interested in understanding why human beings act irrationally.

In his book *Predictably Irrational,* Ariely reveals the two mutually exclusive worlds we negotiate when we try to make sense of a situation or make decisions. The first world is that of "social norms," where values like reciprocity, vulnerability, and generosity tend to govern. The second is that of "market norms," the transactional, "you get what you pay for" evaluations of options and actions. When it comes to the workplace, he pointed out that social norms are more effective (and cost efficient) for motivating people than money.

He writes, "If companies want to benefit from the advantages of social norms, they need to do a better job of cultivating those norms. It's remarkable how much work companies (particularly start-ups) can get out of people when social norms (such as the excitement of building something together) are stronger than market norms (such as salaries stepping up with each promotion). If corporations started thinking in terms of social norms, they would realize that these norms build loyalty and—more important—make people want to extend themselves to the degree that corporations need today: to be flexible, concerned, and willing to pitch in."

When it comes to motivation at work, the growing narrative of meaning, pride, and collaboration is moving "work" from the world of market norms to social norms. Taking pride in what we do and experiencing the value of "building something together" and of developing a worthy professional identity are changing the contexts in which we make decisions. Work incentives that reach into the world of social norms, like medical benefits and live/work environments, do this as well. But this isn't happening in anywhere near as many workplaces as it could and should. Even in those places where we pay lip service to the rhetoric around "work-life" balance, our job insecurity, pay incentives, and our drive for recognition and acknowledgment all contribute to the warped relationship we have with our work.

The result is that we overwork in a competitive rush to be the exceptions to the rule (fueled by the notion that our own abilities are all we need to power through any adversity). Understanding this helps us begin to unpack why the relatively simple idea behind productivity, dividing output by input, has spiraled into working smarter, harder, longer, and better than your peers.

Introducing the concept of happiness to a culture that loves to hustle has made it a very tempting lure. We're chasing it with the same fervor and intensity that we've chased productivity and creativity and in doing so have completely missed the point. Happiness seems to be the end goal that we're all striving toward, but does that goal even make sense? Ralph Waldo Emerson said, "The purpose of life is not to be happy. It's to be useful, to be honorable, to be compassionate, to have it make some difference that you have lived and lived well."

Taking this into consideration might help us understand why we are so willing to give ever more to our jobs. This is something we've experienced first hand: there have been periods in our lives that were defined by our commitment to our jobs. Our motivations were a familiar mix of intellectual stimulation, the need to achieve, the desire for a sense of accomplishment, identification with our work, as well as the money and status that we earned.

In retrospect, we were perhaps sightly misguided in our motivations, but we'll admit there is something alluring about being recognized and rewarded for what (or rather how much) we could produce. After all we live in a culture where the workhorse often gets to be the show pony.

Summary of Big Ideas

➡ Happiness is being co-opted by governments and organizations that are trying to quantify this abstract notion through various metrics.
➡ The creative process requires both positive and negative emotions.
➡ Happiness becomes a responsibility where, once again, if you're not happy, then the fault is yours for not "loving your job enough" or "working hard enough."
➡ Research shows that being overly focused on attaining happiness can actually make you sad.[22]

10.

RISE OF THE WORK WARRIOR

BEHOLD THE CORPORATE ATHLETE

In 1999, Jack Groppel, a sports medicine expert, published *The Corporate Athlete: How to Achieve Maximal Performance in Business and Life,* a book that explored what office workers could learn from professional athletes. In 2003 came Jim Loehr and Tony Schwartz's runaway hit, *The Power of Full Engagement: Managing Energy, Not Time, Is the Key to High Performance and Personal Renewal.* And in 2008 came Loehr's solo follow-up, *The Corporate Athlete Advantage: The Science of Deepening Engagement.* All of these books share the same purpose: to elevate business into a spectator sport, with all the hard work, dedication, physical prowess, and status that doing so entails.

While these books did not create the concept of the corporate athlete, which has been around for years, they gave it new prominence, so much so that it's become an archetype: The Work Warrior. It's a natural progression: Athleticism plays into the Do What You Love element of work culture that we discussed earlier, since sports are a form of play and professional athletes enjoy the added bonus of being spectacularly paid for playing. "When you do something you love, you don't consider many things sacrifices that other people would. However, to be the best, you must be willing to go beyond what your competition is willing to sacrifice." The quote comes from a UFC Middleweight Champion, but it could have easily been tweeted by any contemporary entrepreneur.

The Work Warrior is the next iteration of the Corporate Athlete because identity and purpose play such a central role in their personal narratives. Work Warriors may covet fortune, but they seek to achieve it by having a positive impact on the world. They do what they love, and in the process, endure their sacrifices with pride. When you have a sense of duty, they say, "it doesn't feel like work..."

It all goes back to the Puritans and their belief in the dignity and virtue of work. A copy editor is not just a copy editor but an athlete with the honorable task of achieving peak performance. The training that is required to reach peak performance adds a layer of self-importance that companies like EXOS, which use state-of-the-art diagnostic tools to improve the performance of firefighters, military personnel, and police officers, have been quick to commercialize, as they have begun to offer their services to corporate athletes as well. "We deliver a competitive advantage by optimizing the performance of employees through our prescriptive and proven approach," their website states. "We apply the finest performance systems to empower people to upgrade their lives."[1]

We would be remiss to downplay the role of ego in this equation. With their incredible physical abilities, lucrative contracts, endorsement deals, and adoring fans, it's fair to say that professional athletes are the gold standard in our culture for having "made it." Professional athletes are a natural elite that anyone would want to be associated with—even through the way they characterize their work.

Going back to the Work Devotion we discussed in the first chapter of this book, the evolution of the salaryman into the corporate athlete is consistent with the desire to turn work into a display of strength and virility, a modern show of masculine power, which is increasingly reflected in the vernacular of management. Tony Schwartz describes the Ideal Performance State for Executives as the capacity to develop endurance, strength, flexibility, self-control, and focus.[2] Other buzz-phrases include energy management, sustained performance under pressure, "deep inner strength," and "testing your limits."

While there are, in fact, some similarities between the careers of athletes and the careers of corporates, there are some significant structural differences, too. For one, the average career of a professional athlete is about seven years, while corporate professionals work anywhere between 40-50 years.[3] Athletes have an off season that often spans several months, while the average executive takes one 2-4 week vacation per year (if that — as we have seen, vacations are on the decline). While athletes of course train almost full-time, they only actively compete for the length of a game or race. Executives are expected to perform upwards of ten hours per day and to make themselves available at night and on weekends. While athletes spend the majority of their time preparing for a short burst of performance, their corporate counterparts are expected to be training for improvement and delivering peak performances at the same time day after day.

But there's an irony here that few have recognized. If we want to perform like a professional athlete, then we need to train like a professional athlete—and the pros take breaks in order to give their bodies and minds a chance to recuperate. Tony Schwartz has stated that the biggest barrier to high performance is the lack of regular rest. "Chronic stress without recovery depletes energy reserves, leads to burnout and breakdown and ultimately undermines performance," he writes. Executives need to cultivate a balance between expending energy and renewing energy, a process he terms "oscillation." The trick is not to try and eliminate stress but to ensure that periods of stress are managed with systemic rituals that allow for recovery.[4] Schwartz promotes a holistic approach to working, including devoting time to physical fitness, sleep, and emotional and spiritual well-being, which, needless to say, runs counter to modern work culture.

Most would-be Work Warriors fall into exactly the trap that Schwartz warns against. Hard work breeds success, and success breeds more hard work. The *Harvard Business Review* explored the toll of "Extreme Jobs" in their December 2006 issue. According to a study carried out by The Center for Work-Life Policy, Extreme Jobs are held by a category of high-earners (the top 6 percent in the United States) that work more than sixty hours a week and include such characteristics as unpredictability, fast pace with tight deadlines, frequent travel, work-related events outside business hours, and 24/7 client demands.[5]

Extreme Jobs are on the rise, the study found, resulting in intense work pressure for high-earning professionals across the board—regardless of gender, sector, or location. What struck us, however, was that the people who hold Extreme Jobs weren't feeling victimized. As the article poignantly explains, "by and large, extreme professionals don't feel exploited; they feel exalted."[6] Extreme Workers get an incredible amount of self-esteem from carrying distinguished jobs and are willing to endure the characteristics of Extreme Jobs in return for recognition, intellectual stimulation, intelligent colleagues, and large compensation. Many admit that they actively pursue such work because of their Type A personalities.

People who thrive in Extreme Jobs, like people who rise to the top in Extreme Sports, inspire a certain awe—in others and in themselves. Voluntarily challenging yourself to the very limits of your mental and physical capacity, whether by running an ultra-marathon in the Nevada desert or pulling off a caffeine-fueled all-nighter to deliver that pitch in time, creates an adrenalin high that is literally addictive.

There is a certain pathology in some of these behaviors that can be concerning, and many psychologists have begun to categorize overwork as an addiction in the same vein as a dependency on alcohol or drugs. Unlike substance addiction, however, there is no stigma attached to workaholism; in fact, we live in a society that celebrates extreme Work Devotion, and so people who exhibit these types of behaviors are praised and idealized. Their dysfunctional behaviors are rewarded instead of treated.

There are some safe havens for those of us who find ourselves compelled to work, however. Workaholics Anonymous has been providing support to workaholics and their friends and families for the past two decades.[7] Its literature sounds a sobering theme: workaholism can cause its victims to lose the very things they are working so hard to secure: their relationships with spouses, children, lovers, and friends. Psychologist Dr. Cecilie Schou Andreassen from the University of Bergen in Norway developed a framework to identify the syndrome. The Bergen Work Addiction Scale is a series of seven criteria:

1. You think of how you can free up more time to work.
2. You spend much more time working than initially intended.
3. You work in order to reduce feelings of guilt, anxiety, helplessness, and/or depression.
4. You have been told by others to cut down on work without listening to them.
5. You become stressed if you are prohibited from working.
6. You deprioritize hobbies, leisure activities, and/or exercise because of your work.

7. You work so much that it has negatively influenced your health.

If you answer Often or Always to four or more, then you may be suffering from workaholism. If, like us, you looked at those questions and thought to yourself, *who hasn't done these things?*, then congratulations, you have helped us prove a conclusion that all of our research has been leading us to: that we are becoming a country of workaholics.[8]

Dr. Bryan Robinson, psychotherapist and author of *Chained to the Desk: A Guidebook for Workaholics, their Partners and Children, and the Clinicians who Treat Them*, draws a sharp distinction between workaholism and hard work. "The Puritan work ethic is not a bad thing," he says. "It's a good thing, but anything carried too far is a bad thing. That's what addiction is, it's a personality thing." This brings us back to what we covered in Chapter 5. Extreme Jobs happen at the intersection of culture (the rise of Special Snowflake plus Do What You Love) and macrolevel structure (increased competition, rise of knowledge work, constant connectivity).[9] The two are mutually reinforcing.

It's important to recognize that the stresses that go with workaholism are as damaging to employers as they are to employees. Employees who are focused on improving their health not only perform better but lower their company's health care costs. One corporate wellness program called (wouldn't you believe it) Corporate Athlete has been implemented by companies like Procter & Gamble. 8,500 people have gone through the program at P&G since 2003, and 61 percent of them reported that they were better able to focus at work, 59 percent said they were more engaged at home, and 51 percent said their physical health had improved overall.[10]

Not surprisingly, workers are more willing to embrace the concept of ritualized rest when it is tied to a promise of improved productivity. In general, people seem more willing to make changes when those changes are tied to an improved picture of themselves—be it warrior or athlete—than they are simply because doing so would be good for their health. That was one of our most important takeaways from this research— that it is far more effective to change work behaviors when you work within embedded belief systems rather than against them.

And, as we will see, it is impossible to overstate the role of ego.

THE CREATIVE EGO

"At the age of six I wanted to be a cook," Salvador Dalí is quoted as saying. "At seven I wanted to be Napoleon. And my ambition has been growing ever since."

If there's one thing we've learned so far on this journey, it's that creativity is a messy process, a wild mix of biological, genetic, social, cultural, and environmental factors that all interact together to help us find inspiration and to come up with ideas. The process is complicated because human beings are complicated. Mihaly Csikszentmihalyi, widely regarded as *the* expert on understanding flow, put it best when he named complexity as the one unifying trait that often separates those who are highly creative from those who are not.[11] "I have devoted 30 years of research to how creative people live and work, to make more understandable the mysterious process by which they come up with new ideas and new things. Creative individuals are remarkable for their ability to adapt to almost any situation and to make do with whatever is at hand to reach their goals," he wrote. "They show tendencies of thought and action that in most people are segregated. They contain contradictory extremes; instead of being an 'individual,' each of them is a 'multitude.'"[12]

Creating something, whether it's a book, a new branding campaign, or a new system, requires a leap of faith, a belief in your ability to create something of value. There is, however subtle, an arrogance in thinking that we can write a story or build a product that has never been tried before. Simply put, a certain level of insolence is required to fuel progress and invention.

The self-absorbed actor, the insufferable writer, the tyrannical CEO who always knows best—we recognize these cultural tropes because there is some level of truth to them. Often times, immense creative talent brings with it an equally out-sized sense of entitlement and arrogance. From Steve Jobs and Kanye West (who, interestingly, described himself as the "Steve Jobs of music"), to Donald Trump and Mariah Carey, there are countless examples of successful people who are infatuated with their own genius. "I hope that posterity will judge me kindly," Descartes wrote in a moment of grandiose self-reflection, "not only as to the things which I have explained, but also to those which I have intentionally omitted so as to leave to others the pleasure of discovery."

We should note here that it's not just traditional creatives (writers, artists, painters, etc.) who are susceptible to this kind of egotism but workers in any field where a high concentration of talent is required for success, like law, medicine, and professional sports. We would actually argue that doctors, lawyers, and even professional athletes are, in fact, creatives.

Do inflated egos help or hinder creativity? Interestingly, it depends what kind of egotism is at play. Though they all stem from the same source, egotism can manifest itself in varying ways.

WHERE EGO HELPS

We know from the previous chapter that when looking at the big five personality traits (Openness to Experience, Conscientiousness, Extraversion, Agreeableness, and Neuroticism, or OCEAN) only Openness to Experiences has a large influence on a person's creativity. In 2011, researchers conducted yet another study looking for links between personality and creativity, but this time, they added another factor into the mix: honesty-humility.

After administering a range of personality and creativity tests to more than 1,300 students, researchers discovered that honesty-humility had a negative influence on creativity. The study's lead author, Paul Silvia, an associate professor of psychology at the University of North Carolina, was quick to reassure us that this doesn't mean that all creatives are as conceited as Kanye West or Salvador Dalí.[13] "Our research didn't find a huge effect, and we certainly aren't claiming that all creative people are insufferably arrogant, but on average, people with a lot of creative accomplishments were less humble and modest," he said.[14] In fact, Silvia argues that in many cases, a certain lack of humility can be a useful asset for people who are pursuing creative endeavors, especially when it comes to the ability to take criticism or discouragement in stride (have you read the comments on a YouTube video lately?).

Success inevitably attracts detractors, so having a thick skin is essential. It's only natural that the advantages of being more curious and open minded would come with some potential drawbacks—for example, being a bit of an ass.

Things get especially tricky when creative success is accompanied by power, as within an organization. According to research conducted at the Kellogg School of Management, the possession of power actually diminishes a person's ability to consider the thoughts, feelings, and perspectives of others, fostering a greater reliance on their own viewpoints and belief systems.[15] This helps explain the many horror stories about leaders like Steve Jobs, who publicly humiliate their subordinates.

Those of us who manage other creatives must remain cognizant of the influence that the behavior of someone in a position of power can have on the people working around or for them. In one study, researchers observed that when an individual witnessed an act of rudeness by an authority figure, their own performance on both routine and creative tasks subsequently suffered.[16]

WHERE EGO HURTS

On the flip side, ego can be a powerful block to pursuing creativity as well. Too much ego can lead to inflexibility, an unreceptiveness to new ideas and opportunities. It can also lead to an inflated sense of our own value, which can create all sorts of distracting interpersonal issues, especially if you work with a team or collaborate with others.

Earlier we noted that our brains consider our status to be as important as our survival. If someone links their creative talent and success too tightly to their personal power, then they might consider any questioning of their ideas to be an encroachment on their perceived territory. This can result in an aggressive response, including anger, bullying, belittlement, or a tendency to take credit for other people's ideas. In the long run, suggestions for necessary changes and improvements won't be made, with predictably bad results.

From an emotional perspective, ego can result in fear being the primary motivator in decision-making, meaning that we will fall back on more risk-averse behaviors in order to "stay safe" instead of seizing opportunities to create something new or innovative.

A problematic ego can manifest as an inability to take any action for fear of judgment or failure. Think of all the books that aren't written and businesses that are never launched because their would-be creators hide their lights under proverbial bushels. As Brené Brown notes in her work, to create requires a vulnerability that means exposing our less than perfect sides to a world that seems to favor over-curated, produced moments to authenticity. That can be very unsettling to someone who is just starting out.

These types of behavior often surface in the workplace when there is disagreement over the direction of a creative idea or project that requires collaboration. Playing the victim when our ideas aren't chosen, blaming other people when our ideas don't work, hoarding good ideas, and refusing to contribute are all manifestations of uncontrolled ego.

It's understandable that this would be the case. So much of our work culture is crafted around the notion that our identities and our jobs are inexorably linked together, that in fact, they could be considered one and the same. As we discussed in Chapter 6, this is one of the biggest challenges that professional creatives face today. We cannot produce creative output without making ourselves vulnerable to criticism, even when it is necessary for the overall health of the project. This doesn't mean that we should listen to every critical thing that is said about us or take every rejection or setback as an indication of our lack of ability, but it does mean that we must separate ourselves from our creative output. We are not our brand campaigns, our products, our novels, our books.

We need to screen out the mixed messages that the media sends us, too. While paying lip service to the humility and goodness and character that has been mixed into our work culture from its beginnings (see Chapters 1-4), contemporary media is also quick to lionize the unseemly displays of machismo and power that too often occur in c-suites (see: Mark Zuckerberg reportedly putting "I'm CEO, Bitch." on his business cards). It is stories like these that have allowed the lore of the ball-busting hardass who is willing to do whatever it takes to succeed to become such a destructive archetype.

We wrote this book as a response to several questions we had about our own behaviors and more broadly to examine the unseen forces that were influencing our attitudes and beliefs about work. In writing this chapter, we recognized ourselves in many of the examples of bad behavior.

As embarrassing as it is to admit, we both have been guilty of protecting our turf, of playing the victim, or of overly criticizing a colleague's idea because we were afraid that it might take away from our own perceived performance. As with genius and madness, in the end, there is a fine line between confidence and arrogance. As Todd Henry, author of *The Accidental Creative*, explains, "Confidence is saying 'I'm valuable,' arrogance is saying 'I'm invaluable.'"

THE DECLINE OF LEISURE

We do more than inflate our egos when we view our struggles as the heroic deeds of Work Warriors; we also take a justifiable pride in our ability to push ourselves to our limits. The value that society places on our hard work is reflected by its new status norms, especially in the perceived value of leisure time.

For a large part of human history, leisure was considered to be the ultimate status symbol, a luxury afforded only by the wealthy. But today, economists have noted a startling trend: the rich are logging in more time at work than the poor. For the first time, it seems that leisure has become a marker of poverty instead of affluence.

In a paper entitled "Measuring Trends in Leisure: The Allocation of Time over Five Decades," Professors Mark Aguiar and Erik Hurst looked at time-use surveys and research studies from the past fifty years to track how our concept of leisure time has evolved.[17] Between 1965 and 2003, the average number of leisure hours increased in most households. In the 1960s, a college-educated male reported having just slightly more leisure time than his high-school educated counterpart. By 2005, it was the high-school graduate who was reporting more leisure time than the college grad—nearly eight hours more of it per week. Based on the 2013 results of the American Time Use Survey, those with an undergraduate degree or above clocked in an average of two hours more per day than people who never finished high school.[18] In a 2006 research study, Daniel Kahneman et al. showed that American households earning less than $20,000 annually spent up to 40 percent more time on passive leisure (like watching TV) than households earning $100,000.[19]

There are a few theories as to why this is taking place. One is called the "substitution effect," which posits that since wages are higher now, the opportunity cost in taking time off has also increased: in other words, the less you work, the more money you lose. Since top-earner salaries have continued to rise while working class wages have stagnated, economists argue that financial gains are a powerful incentive to motivate those who are making more money to keep doing so.

Another theory points to the hyper competitive nature of the new "winner-takes-all" global economy, in which spotting new market opportunities can mean an enormous financial gain. The fast-paced nature of innovation has created a constant pressure for organizations and their workers to stay ahead, and that translates into not taking time off for fear of missing out on the next big thing.[20]

None of those explanations are totally satisfying. You'd think that at some point you'd earn so much money that the costs of taking time off would become negligible. After all, if you're already making enough to be able to afford the things you want, then why choose to work more?

This is where our pesky egos rear their heads. Simply put, there's more status in being a Work Warrior than a member of the leisure class these days.

It should be noted that this is a complex and convoluted issue. As we've seen from the devastating impact of the 2008 financial crisis, some of the increase in leisure time among the less educated might be involuntary—unemployment, the rise of part-time work and contingent labor, and the decline of manufacturing industries have all contributed to it. To say that it's simply a question of status would be a drastic over-simplification and one we would never make. We just wanted to make the point that on a whole, the notions of leisure and work have become more intertwined than previously thought, and that sometimes those who have the opportunity to work pleasurable jobs continue to do so beyond their financial needs simply because of the status and enjoyment it confers. The lack of "leisure" time is now seen as an important marker of success, especially within the mythology surrounding entrepreneurship, hustling, and the pursuit of the American Dream. It has become a reflection of the noble pursuit of work.

For a warrior, there is no greater reward.

Summary of Big Ideas

➡ Work is being marketed as an extreme endurance sport where overwork behaviors are celebrated as a sign of prowess and achievement.
➡ The idea of leisure has transformed from being a marker of the wealthy to a marker of lower-income classes.

➡ Ego can be a blessing or a curse depending on how it's applied. In the best-case scenario, it creates motivation and a
resilience in the face of setback. In the worst case, it hinders
a person's ability to receive feedback or be attuned to the
needs of others.

SCENARIOS

11.

BURNOUT

AN ARMY OF INVISIBLE BOSSES

For years, we've been using our cellphones as alarm clocks. As our sleepy eyes sharpen into focus, we compulsively check the activity that has piled up throughout the night. Scanning, browsing, and clicking, we complete a morning triage of all the emails we can safely delete before our feet have even touched the ground.

The implication for work, of course, is that as long as we're reachable, we can be working—and since the smartphone tipping point of 2007, we're always reachable and never quite unplugged. However, burnout caused by connective technology isn't just related to work. When you're done checking your work and personal email (increasingly one and the same), you'll probably dive into the social graph, the content feed, or perhaps a game.

In an article he wrote for the *Atlantic*, game developer and philosopher Ian Bogost reframed many of our social media activities as a new type of hyper-employment. He writes about the feeling of overwhelm many of us experience in the face of never-ending notifications, emails, DMs, statuses, and updates. "Often, we cast these new obligations either as compulsions (the addictive, possibly dangerous draw of online life) or as necessities (the importance of digital contact and an online brand in the information economy)," he writes. "But what if we're mistaken and both tendencies are really just symptoms of hyper-employment?"

Our activities on these platforms—managing the flood of information, contributing value as users, creating new content—are all small bits of work we do for companies like Google, Instagram, Facebook, and Twitter. "Today, everyone's a hustler," Bogost continues. "But now we're not just hustling for ourselves or our bosses, but for so many other unseen bosses." The burden of supporting, reacting, creating, has become in itself a new type of labor in the digital age. Even leisure activities have started to resemble work. This is uncompensated work that goes well beyond simply being the "eyeballs" of traditional media, and we do it for "fun."

Despite what we read about leisure and status in the last chapter, many of us intuitively agree with Aristotle, who said that "We work to have leisure, on which happiness depends," but how does that manifest in reality? For the hyper-employed, productivity may have created the space for more leisure, but we've simply filled it with more work, paid and unpaid alike.

The blurring lines between work and play and the relentless demand of attention and action shape our impulses. Digital burnout has a role to play in feeling overworked, even when we're not "working." The goal, of course, isn't to abandon email and delete Facebook but rather to acknowledge how our expectations of ourselves and others are changing. Perhaps, more importantly, it is to take the momentum of history for what it is: inconsequential. Just because things have been a certain way, that doesn't mean that is how they have to be.

The impacts of a never-ending stream of information are far-reaching and have as many social implications as professional.

Is it any surprise that overwork has become so normalized? Contemporary work culture was built on the notion of constant productivity, which has been reinforced through societal values around the link between work and morality, as well as the idealized archetypes that are widely circulated throughout the media.

However, it is the injection of creativity as an essential business skill and valuable economic unit that has made our current position so untenable. It turns out that to do the work we need to do to succeed, we need to work less, not more. And so today's Productive Creatives (anyone who deals with unstandardized, non-repetitive tasks) find themselves in a paradoxical situation where behaviors that have been touted as symbols of success and achievement are the very things that might be preventing us from reaching our goals.

Here's one undisputed fact: if we don't change our behaviors we will have to deal with more than simply a diminished capacity to produce work. We are putting our health, our relationships, and our whole economy at risk.

THIS IS YOUR BRAIN ON STRESS

The word burnout was originally used as a metaphor for extinguishing a flame—what happens when our own sparks of vitality and creativity are snuffed out. In the early twentieth century, "to burn oneself out" was English slang meaning to work so hard that you die early. It turns out that it isn't just our Japanese friends who have a word to describe death by overwork!

The term "burnout" was popularized in a medical context by Herbert Freudenberger, a German-American psychiatrist, in 1974. While working at an alternative health clinic in New York, Freudenberger witnessed a repeating pattern of exhaustion and fatigue among the idealistic young volunteers who faced a sustained emotional drain from working with drug addicts. He noted that exhaustion and deep fatigue were most often reported by the staffers who were the most committed to the clinic's cause, usually after they had worked at the clinic for one year.

The term was originally used in relation to the symptoms of stress that were experienced by workers at aid organizations, women's shelters, inner-city schools, hospitals, and in the criminal justice system.[1] Today, the term has expanded across professions, industries, and nations to reflect a state of psychological distress that is impacting economies around the world. (One of the more interesting reports we stumbled upon described the "alarming rate of burnout" in pastors and preachers within the Baptist church.)[2]

Despite the many documented side effects of burnout, the underlying mechanisms are still generally unknown, but research is emerging that is proving that burnout—both psychological and physiological—is not only real but a dangerous threat that is heavily impacting the way we work. Symptoms include exhaustion, a reduced commitment toward work in the face of increased demands, an increased risk of depression, the use of aggression as a coping mechanism, impaired cognitive performance, motivation, creativity, and judgment, an erosion in the quality of one's emotional and social life, and finally, despair. One of the most succinct and powerful definitions of burnout that we came across was in "The Burnout Companion to Study and Practice: A Critical Analysis," which described the phenomenon as "the long-term result of an imbalance between investments and outcomes."[3]

While the term itself might be relatively new, the phenomenon it describes is not. In his book *Burnout: History of a Phenomenon*, Flavio Muheim counts early historical examples going all the way back to the prophet Elijah from the Old Testament, who "was famous for his success in accomplishing various miracles and victories in the name of the Lord. However, confronted with persistent obstacles and having suffered a major defeat, even he was suddenly plunged into deep despair, longing for death, and wishing to fall into a deep sleep."[4]

In a 2011 academic paper, Dr. Wolfgang P. Kaschka explains that burnout is often derived from a complex mix of internal and external factors. Personality traits such as a strong need for recognition, a tendency to use work as a substitute for social life, and having an idealistic sense of self can clash with high demands at work, time pressure, and overwhelming responsibilities. While the triggers can differ from person to person, feelings of disengagement, unhappiness, and exhaustion seem to be common outcomes.

So what exactly is happening to the brain and body when someone experiences burnout? Armita Golkar and peers at the Karolinska Institute in Sweden designed a study that suggests burnout affects the parts of the brain that are the most responsible for emotional responses and executive function—namely the limbic structures, the amygdala, and the mesial prefrontal cortex.[5] In short, they found reason to believe that burnout can reduce a person's neurological resilience, compounding stress into a downward spiral.

The study looked at forty participants with formally diagnosed symptoms of burnout—people who had worked 60-70 hour workweeks consistently over several years—as well as a socioeconomically matched control group of seventy healthy, unstressed participants. In the first of two sessions, all the participants were asked to focus on an image. While they focused, a loud, startling noise would sound in the background. An electrode taped to the participants' cheeks recorded their reflex reactions to this stressful stimulus. While both groups were equally startled, the real difference emerged when they were asked to down-regulate their negative response. The burnout group had a much harder time doing so.

In the second session, an MRI was used to scan participants while they sat quietly. The amygdala (the brain king of emotional reactions like fear and aggression) was enlarged in the burnout group, and researchers also noted more connections between the amygdala and other areas of the brain that are linked to emotional distress. Interestingly, the burnout group also showed weaker connections between the amygdala and the mesial prefrontal cortex (a critical actor for Executive Function). The study makes a case for more research but proposes some important hypotheses on the impact of stress on our experience of negative emotions, as well as our ability to regulate them. The results aren't shocking, but with relatively few studies on the neurological impact of burnout, they move the conversation to one that is evidence-based instead of strictly anecdotal.

Dr. Esther Sternberg, director of the Molecular, Cellular and Behavioral Interactic Neuroscience Program at the US National Institute of Mental Health, explores the prolonged experience of stress on the body in her book *The Balance Within: The Science Connecting Health and Emotions*. The research she shares draws powerful connections between memory, emotion, and stress and their role in causing or exacerbating disease.

"As soon as the stressful event occurs," she explains, "it triggers the release of the cascade of hypothalamic, pituitary, and adrenal hormones—the brain's stress response. It also triggers the adrenal glands to release epinephrine, or adrenaline, and the sympathetic nerves to squirt out the adrenaline-like chemical norepinephrine all over the body: nerves that wire the heart, and gut, and skin. So, the heart is driven to beat faster, the fine hairs of your skin stand up, you sweat, you may feel nausea or the urge to defecate. But your attention is focused, your vision becomes crystal clear, a surge of power helps you run—these same chemicals released from nerves make blood flow to your muscles, preparing you to sprint."

"All this occurs quickly," she continues. "If you were to measure the stress hormones in your blood or saliva, they would already be increased within three minutes of the event. In experimental psychology tests, playing a fast-paced video game will make salivary cortisol increase and norepinephrine spillover into venous blood almost as soon as the virtual battle begins. But if you prolong the stress, by being unable to control it or by making it too potent or long-lived, and these hormones and chemicals still continue to pump out from nerves and glands, then the same molecules that mobilized you for the short haul now debilitate you."

When stress becomes chronic, your immune system is impaired and is less able to defend your body. If you're exposed to any kind of illness while you're chronically stressed, your body is far more vulnerable. But tiredness and stress are only skimming the list of symptoms, which also include exhaustion, disinterest, boredom, heightened irritability, feeling unappreciated, loss of concentration, and feelings of detachment. If burnout lingers, it can also lead to depression, substance abuse, and a worsening of overall health.

The motivations around "hustling" aren't completely misguided. Our bodies are wired in a way that pairs stress and efficiency—as the former rises so does the latter. Unfortunately, there is a catch; our efficiency only increases up to a certain point. After that, stress causes our performance to decline dramatically.

Researchers including the American Sleep Disorders Association and Center for Sleep and Circadian Neurobiology have been exploring this topic. Most of the numerous studies on the connection between lack of sleep and performance, creativity, fluent, flexible, or original thought, memory, decision-making, and visuomotor performance don't yield surprising results: the less you sleep, the worse you perform. Make it chronic, and you can cause permanent damage to the neurons that regulate your alertness.

THE COSTS OF A GLOBAL EPIDEMIC

A recent UCL study that surveyed over 10,000 civil servants in London revealed that people who work three or more hours longer than a normal seven-hour day have a 60 percent higher risk of heart-related problems, such as fatal and nonfatal heart attacks and angina.[6] In the United States, Gallup estimates that overworking costs American companies between $450 and $550 billion annually in lost productivity.[7] A report issued by the World Health Organization back in 2000 stated that, "In most countries there is no specific legislation addressing the impact of job stress. Most countries have at least minimum standards for safety and health features of the workplace. These standards tend to focus on the physical aspects of the workplace and do not explicitly include the psychological and/or mental health aspects of working conditions."[8]

Despite the lessons that our industrial-era predecessors learned at such cost, we have chosen to ignore the perils of overwork, as we embrace a culture where work continues to creep into the hours previously reserved for leisure, or, worse yet, sleep. Whether you're a freelance journalist or employed by a tech giant, burning the midnight oil at work has become a touted and/or dreaded reality for many people, and governments are finally starting to address this problem.

- Concerned about the burden on the Canadian health care system, a 2017 survey by the Canadian Medical Association reported that 54 percent of their 80,000 members have symptoms of burnout. That means if you go to the doctor in Canada, you have a 1 in 2 chance that the person in charge of your medical care is experiencing symptoms that could result in compromised cognitive functions.

- A study by the London School of Economics and King's College London estimated that the annual cost of burnout to European businesses was £77 billion.[9]

- In 2012, the French government indicted France Telecom's former CEO, Didier Lombard, and six other executives in response to allegations that the executive had created a toxic organizational culture that promoted overwork, resulting in the suicides of thirty employees between 2008 and 2010.[10] Those who took their own lives had left notes blaming punishing working conditions as the reason for their actions. The case is set to be heard by the courts in 2019. The charge, "moral harassment," can be punishable by up to two years in prison and 30,000 euros in fines.

- Former German labor minister Ursula von der Leyen estimated that overworked employees who fall ill or retire early cost the German economy between 8 and 10 billion euros each year.[11] Ironically (and predictably, as we have seen in earlier chapters), von der Leyen said it wasn't companies' policies that were the issue but the difficulty they had in actually enforcing them.

- In the United States, businesses are losing $300 billion a year due to worker stress and burnout.[12]

The list goes on, but one thing is clear: this is an issue of global proportions.[13] The increase of burnout is accompanied by a host of other ailments that are impacting our ability to work and live well. A 2015 report that looked at the usage of Employee Assistance Programs of 100,000 employees globally found a significant increase in employee stress (up 28 percent), anxiety (up a whopping 74 percent), and depression (up 58 percent) compared to levels measured in 2012. Combined, these issues accounted for nearly 83 percent of emotional health cases, up from 55.2 percent in 2012.[14] Interestingly, Asian respondents had the highest rates of depression, Central and South America led the way for the highest levels of stress, and the Middle East and North America reported high rates of anxiety. The World Health Organization reported that between 1993 and 2012, the number of people suffering from depression and anxiety increased to 615 million from 416 million, a 50 percent uptick. A 2009 research paper entitled "High Anxieties: the Social Construction of Anxiety Disorders," stated that at the beginning of the twenty-first century, anxiety disorders counted as the most prevalent mental health problem around the globe. The World Health Organization predicts that by 2020, depression will be the *second leading cause of disease* and will move into first place by 2030.[15]

The good news is that treatments can and do make a difference. "We know that treatment of depression and anxiety makes good sense for health and well-being; this new study confirms that it makes sound economic sense too," explained Dr. Margaret Chan, the former director general of the World Health Organization. "We must now find ways to make sure that access to mental health services becomes a reality for all men, women and children, wherever they live." The WHO estimates that every US dollar invested in treatment returns $4, as measured by better health and an increased ability to work. To put it in large scale terms, if countries invested the estimated $174 billion that is needed to scale up the availability of their mental health programs, the resulting 5 percent improvement in productivity could add $399 billion into the economy with another $310 billion flowing in from improved worker health.[16]

Some countries are seriously tackling these issues. Brazil developed a psychosocial care network to help improve access to needed services. Ethiopia has invested in training and provision of mental health care across the country to make sure patients are accurately diagnosed and appropriately treated. South Africa has recently reengineered its primary health care system to make mental health care a primary component. Yet more needs to be done: the WHO estimates that government spending on mental health initiatives average about three percent of overall health budgets, which is clearly inadequate.[17]

RESPONSE TO THE BURNOUT EPIDEMIC

The transition from an artisan economy to the industrial scientific management that we covered in Chapter 1 is still a source of stress for workers. As workers become commodities, the context for Marx's theory of alienated labor becomes clear. Research shows that a whopping 70 percent of the American workforce is disengaged, and it's no wonder.

The conversation between people and profits is two-sided, however, and the world of management has been responding. In a *Fast Company* article entitled "How the Most Successful People Conquer Burnout," high-profile leaders weighed in with advice on how to achieve work "comebacks." The majority of their advice was rooted in the idea of work-life balance— resting and recharging, stepping away regularly, understanding that every opportunity has an opportunity cost. There is a maturing school of thought in the new self-help/self-management literary category that supports this concept—take, for example, the *New Republic*'s "How 2014 became the year of mindfulness."[18] Business reporter David Gelles's book *Mindful Work: How Meditation is Changing Business from the Inside Out* documents corporate America's efforts to institutionalize mindfulness.[19] Reducing stress, increasing compassion, and becoming better corporate citizens are all cited as the benefits of this approach, but so are the engagement and sense of meaning that ultimately drive productivity.

But the entrepreneurial dream of finding happiness through hustling lives on, as seen in a telling article in *Fast Company* by Wizeline CEO Bismarck Lepe. "If you're plugged in—and are fully committed to, and believe, in the mission of your work, you'll never truly experience burnout," he writes. "It's the difference between work-life balance and work-life integration."[20] This represents the other side of the coin—an approach to dealing with the reality of burnout that seeks "meaning" as the ultimate motivator. This philosophy is well represented in self-help literature. Tim Leberecht's *Business Romantic* urges us to "Expect more. Give more of yourself. Fall back in love with business and your life."[21] In other words, find the meaning that can drive you to keep up and as always, do more. Work-life integration isn't about dividing work and life into two equal components, Wharton professor Stewart Friedman argues in his best-selling book *Leading the Life You Want,* but understanding that certain areas of your life will require at times more of your attention and effort than others.[22]

Work-life is a useful model to help us take a holistic, macro view, and hopefully achieve an alignment between our work, our communities, and our private selves. A big risk, of course, is that in a work-obsessed culture, work-life integration becomes a way of rationalizing behavior without addressing the underlying beliefs that led us there in the first place. So much of the literature we've been reading offers tips to managers like "Have programs and systems in place so that whenever an employee feels overworked or spent, they can fall back on the idea that at least their company appreciates them for their extra time and hard work." Is this really going to address burnout?

We have outlined two distinct responses to burnout: stepping back and leaning all the way in. But in both there appears to be a strong sense of denial, as though the fix to this real and quantifiable problem is as simple as a shift in mindset or developing a meditation practice. There's still an implied stigma that goes along with admitting that you are struggling to keep up with job descriptions and tasks that are no longer anchored in any semblance of a balanced workday. We turn the lens back on the individual: what do YOU need to do to cope? We ask them to take responsibility for economic, organizational, and cultural systems that they have zero control over, and we ask them to be happy about the whole thing, to boot.

Ultimately, all of these articles dance around the issue, addressing the symptoms and not the root cause. When we look at how we have created a "constantly connected" culture that is focused on intense performance, we see that burnout is not just a risk but an inevitability.

PRODUCTIVE CREATIVES AND BURNOUT

The problem comes into even sharper focus when we consider the implications of a burnout epidemic for the creative industries. After all, as we've mentioned before, one of the fundamental struggles of our modern work life is our attempts to wrangle the unpredictable nature of creativity into a standardized productivity-oriented model. Let's not forget what we learned earlier—that productivity as an economic metric has one goal: to standardize tasks in a bid to lower costs and improve efficiency. Efficiency is a particularly interesting word, because it captures the unspoken promise of every how-to book about getting things done. We know how to get things done, we just want to get more done faster. We have carried productivity's obsession with quantity into the frameworks we use to evaluate our quality of life. So the real issue is that we're not focusing on doing better work, we're focusing on doing more—because we believe (thanks to the rituals of Work Devotion and our cultural narrative around work ethic) that success means outperforming each other. Our rush to adopt the latest system that will allow us to do more with less stems from our desire to achieve competitive advantage.

This would be fine and good if we were actually performing standardized tasks, but the creative industries are dependent on highly unpredictable things: coming up with ideas, solutions, campaigns, etc.—tasks that are the opposite of the type of work that was done when productivity measures were a good idea. This is important because as a species, we have developed a very specific set of skills to help us cope with uncertainty and stress—evolutionary responses that help ensure our survival. These stress responses were meant to be used in bursts, to escape a predator, to coordinate a hunt, to problem-solve by creating a tool—not to carry us through our 24/7 jobs. Our quest for more efficiency is harming our health and our creativity.

Throughout the history of technological progress, we've used automation to reduce the amount of predictable, certain, or repetitive tasks we have to do, so we can further develop our creativity and interpersonal skills. In many ways, this is the narrative around a utopian future of work, where we no longer have to toil at menial or meaningless tasks. But the reality of burnout teaches us that uncertainty is a key driver of stress. If too much overly mindless work is stressful, then too much overly mindful work will be too. The common denominator: too much work.

We're so focused on efficiency that we're missing a key point: humans (and the market) are adaptable. Once a new tool for efficiency (typewriters, computers, mobile phones, driverless cars) makes its way along the adoption curve, the expectation for minimum productivity increases. Let's take, for example, a virtual assistant powered by AI. If you were to use a product like this, perhaps you could save two or three hours a week scheduling meetings and managing your calendar, gaining ten to fifteen hours a month compared to everyone else. But once everyone else is using a virtual assistant, the market has been level-set again and everyone adapts—effectively diminishing your gains. (Remember that "gains" in economic terms are only gains if they help you move up relative to your position in society.) So instead of working less, we're working the same but doing more stressful work that is rooted in uncertainty and unpredictability.

BURNOUT AND THE FUTURE OF WORK

Gallup's 2017 State of the American Workplace report states that only 33 percent percent of the American workforce is fully engaged by their jobs, meaning an overwhelming majority of the American workforce is not engaged.[23]

When we consider that companies with engaged employees (defined as "those that were involved in, enthusiastic about and committed to their work and workplace") generate 147 percent higher earnings per share—*and* that those employees tend not to be motivated by pay and hours—management science's quest for a way to engage employees makes a lot of sense. Each year, Gallup recognizes organizations that engage their workforce with their "Gallup Great Workplace Award." These are the organizations that "understand that employee engagement is a force that drives real business outcomes" or, in other words, bigger outcomes with little cost.

There is an old adage that most of us are familiar with: "work expands to fill the time available for its completion." This is known as Parkinson's Law, after Cyril Northcote Parkinson, who formulated it as a reflection on the growing bureaucratization of the British Civil Service in a humorous article in *The Economist* in 1955. Parkinson's Law and the science behind make-work have been studied and riffed on by scientists and the life-hacking community alike. When work expands so does stress.

Let's do some productivity math. If Parkinson's Law tells us that work will take up the amount of time one has to complete it, and research shows us the diminishing returns on over-working, it seems obvious that to be effective and healthy at work, we should take a serious look at our frame of reference for what is (and is not) appropriate working hours. Until we start to drive home the connection between these two realities, we're bound to keep chasing our tails in search of a better solution.

The goal isn't to be critical of these engagement initiatives, which can legitimately create better workplaces. Instead, it is to try to understand why it is that we are driven to produce relent-lessly in the first place.

Organizations and social structures can create the perfect environment for burnout. Despite the abundance of books and articles on how to overcome it, the responsibility for diagnosing it and seeking treatment for it rests squarely on the individual. We are supposed to raise our hands and admit that we can't do what we have been conditioned to want to do—a task that can have Everest-like proportions when you consider the context that likely led to our burnout to begin with.

While absenteeism has been a long-standing issue (with stress being a lead cause for long-term sick leave in the United Kingdom), now presenteeism has become one, too. A recent study by the Chartered Institute of Personal Development (CIPD) cites job insecurity as one of the reasons that fewer sick days are being taken in the United Kingdom and more people are coming to work while ill.[24]

Back in Japan, where workers sleep less on work nights than in most other countries, employees are encouraged not to sleep more but to nap on the job to improve their performance, a proverbial Band-Aid over the deadliest of wounds.[25] It's almost like Stockholm syndrome—we are abused by but grateful to our captors. We understand we are being overworked but are so happy for the opportunity to do so that we convince ourselves that it is a good thing—a reflection of our moral standing and character, a demonstration of our ability to be accountable for our own success, despite the costs. We have become used to this unforgiving work environment, and instead of addressing its root causes, we have formalized a discipline that focuses on managing the symptoms.

This is most evident in the reemerging optimism in the American workplace. In the Gallup research study we mentioned earlier, 42 percent of respondents in 2016 said that it was a good time to find a quality job, compared to only 19 percent in 2012. To us, this reflects the normalization of burnout as the status quo. We have become so used to this new reality that we're no longer as bothered by it, despite the devastating consequences. This is the danger of the hidden forces impacting our culture: they can make us believe something is good when it isn't.

Summary of Big Ideas

- ➡ Burnout is a real condition with real physical and psychological side effects that can severely impact your health and mental well-being.
- ➡ Burnout, as a result of overwork, is costing global economies hundreds of millions of dollars due to employee illness, absenteeism, and mistakes made on the job.
- ➡ It is ok to rest. It is ok to take a break. The obsession with measuring our productivity has created a powerful intrinsic motivator that makes us feel guilty when we're not working.

12.

THE FORCES UNMASKED

IN DOERS WE TRUST

Fiverr, an online marketplace for freelance talent, launched its new ad campaign by boldly dividing the world into two groups of people: dreamers and doers. "Dreamers kindly step aside," one poster proclaimed. "You could have finished that project by now," another insisted. The tagline for the campaign left no doubt about who it supported: In Doers We Trust. Not stopping there, Fiverr decided to be even more explicit about what makes someone a doer; a poster featuring a frazzled-looking woman provided the following helpful guidelines: "You eat coffee for lunch. You follow through on your follow through. Sleep deprivation is your drug of choice. You might be a doer."

That's right, skipping meals is a badge of honor, and depriving yourself of rest is a high you willingly chase because you are a DOER. Once upon a time, we might have looked at this poster and felt inspired to nod our heads in solidarity. Now, we see something far different.

We hope that by this point you'll recognize the same tropes: celebrating Work Devotion as a way to validate your own worth. The ad is nakedly honest. The model isn't the usual glossy and filtered image of success (oversaturated pictures of minimalist desks and shiny Apple products accompanied by a perfect cappuccino; you know the aesthetic); instead she looks exhausted. She certainly doesn't look happy. The image comes off as a bizarre mugshot, which makes a depressing kind of sense when you realize how much this type of thinking has entrapped us. It's not even the image that is depressing but the fact that companies and ad agencies see value in this kind of rallying cry—that we continue to push these distorted values, making the idea of skipping food and sleep an *aspirational goal*.

In this chapter, we'll take a final look at the three forces that have formed the belief system that ads like Fiverr's play into. We'll explore how to identify and extirpate those unhelpful core beliefs and how to start making the changes to our work culture that are so desperately needed.

UNMASKING THE FORCES

We started this book with the hope of better understanding our relationship with work. One of our most profound realizations was the extent to which our behaviors, beliefs, and attitudes can be influenced without our conscious awareness.

We might feel guilty for not staying as late as the office workhorse without ever recognizing the role the Puritans played in linking suffering, work, and morality. We might feel discouraged after reading yet another magazine article about an entrepreneur who wakes up at 5:00 a.m. and "hustles" nonstop without ever thinking about the media ecosystem that has created and proliferated a very specific vision of success, repackaging sacrifice and work ethic into a how-to guide that assures us that we can do it too. We might try yet another methodology for managing our insane inboxes without ever stopping to consider how many of our ideas about productivity come from a twentieth-century mechanical engineer who envisioned a world where "first class men" proved their worth through efficient, standardized, and repetitive tasks. Finally, we might see an image on social media of someone who seems to endlessly love what they do, or fail to follow through with yet another digital detox, without understanding how modern-day apps have hijacked our cognitive processes—pings and dings acting as stimuli to release pleasure chemicals into our brain, while social networks effortlessly manipulate ancient survival instincts of status and social cohesion.

It wasn't until we finished writing the very different first draft of this book that we were able to stand back and actually see how the forces of Systems, Stories, and Self have combined to form our work culture. We had read about each of these forces individually but had never mapped out their interconnections before. Unmasking and naming them was an act of liberation. Suddenly, we saw signs of Work Devotion everywhere, their intent transparent and obvious. The sheer insanity of trying to force our creative productivity within a system designed to stifle it became unflinchingly clear.

It's especially important to recognize the human-centric aspect of work, now and in the future, when artificial intelligence and automation will play larger and larger roles. There are deep-seated issues that we need to sort out within our hearts and minds right now, even before the robots come to steal our jobs (a subject we will discuss in the next chapter). The first step is to understand where these forces come from and why they've manifested in our lives in this way. Guess what? By reading this book, you've already done that. Congratulations.

To summarize, this is how our current work culture is hurting us:

- **Overwork is hurting us mentally and physically.** Beyond chronic fatigue and chronic sleep deprivation, working too much is also linked to anxiety, higher risk of substance abuse, and a variety of physical ailments, including heart disease.

- **Overwork doesn't result in more ideas.** Not giving yourself the time to "float" will only hurt your ability to come up with the creative solutions you need. If you want to be a better Productive Creative, work less, not more.

- **Overwork results in lowered performance.** Even if you are one of the rare exceptions who manages to come up with endless ideas regardless of lack of sleep or food or rest, guess what? Pushing yourself will have an influence on your ability to execute. Your performance will suffer.

BELIEFS

After we wrote the above paragraphs we looked at each other in disbelief. Do we really need to spell out these conditions? Don't we all (regardless of grand ambitions) want to be healthy, creative, and able to perform to the best of our ability? Why, then, is it so damn hard to change these behaviors?

At its root, this isn't a knowledge problem or a policy problem. This is something that goes beyond fact, beyond objective truth, and dives into the heart of the subjective. The potent mix of Systems, Self, and Stories have merged to create something far more powerful: a belief system. The reason we act in ways that are often contrary to our professional and personal self-interest is because, despite evidence to the contrary, we believe that what we are doing is right. We believe in the

American Dream, we believe in the myth of the self-made man. We believe in the fundamental truth that effort is proportionally related to wealth and success. This goes beyond intellect and into emotional and psychological systems that are impossible to defuse with reason and research.

This explains why otherwise sane people ignore reasonable advice that would improve their lives in favor of systems that only reduce our ability to do the type of work we really want to do. While you might agree with us on a logical, rational level about some of the incompatibilities of productivity and creativity systems, nodding your head as you recognize the problematic nature of a system of values that promotes overwork, you'll still have a hard time making changes in your own behavior unless you tackle your belief systems.

We found this to be true in our own lives. Even after learning everything that we did, we would still catch ourselves falling back into old habits: overworking or pushing through when we knew a rest would be more beneficial, socially signaling Work Devotion by using busyness or lack of sleep as a sign of corporate athletic prowess. Feeling guilty at taking an afternoon off.

Why is it, Riwa texted me, *that you're feeling bad about needing an afternoon off when we are literally making a case for why it's the necessary thing to do?*

I don't know, I replied. *I just know I feel bad about it.*

Yes, even after three years of research, it was difficult to ignore the persistent guilt that comes from the influence of a work culture that still links continuous output with increased productivity.

That's when it struck us. Our belief systems have given rise to a complicated economic model, so any changes to that model need to be reflected in the philosophy that is informing it.

HOW BELIEFS ARE BORN

At its most basic level, a belief is simply a conditioned perspective that is formed from our previous encounters with pain and pleasure stimuli. Over time, these multitudes of perspectives combine to form a complex and comprehensive framework that influence the assumptions that we make about ourselves and inform the expectations we have about the people around us and the world we inhabit. Beliefs apply a layer of order into an otherwise chaotic and unpredictable world, translating everything we experience into a context which we can understand. They make us feel both secure and in control, two things we as humans have craved since the beginning of time. However, by highly valuing this sense of certainty, we engage in two dangerous behaviors: first, we hold on tightly to our belief systems even when it is against our best interests, and two, we believe so strongly that we turn our perception of the world into fact, even when that's absolutely not the case.

Dr. Michael Shermer, author of the *The Believing Brain*, summed up the link between rationality and beliefs best. "We form our beliefs for a variety of subjective, personal, emotional, and psychological reasons in the context of environments created by family, friends, colleagues, culture, and society at large," he writes. "After forming our beliefs we then defend, justify, and rationalize them with a host of intellectual reasons, cogent arguments, and rational explanations. Beliefs come first, explanations for beliefs follow."[1]

Dr. Shermer describes the brain as a "belief engine," explaining that we use a two-step process to create meaning. The first, patternicity, is our natural tendency to find and spot patterns in the world around us. The second part, agenticity, is our tendency to then apply meaning, intention, and agency to those patterns. Those meaningful patterns eventually form the building blocks of our beliefs. Once created, we search out evidence that confirms that those beliefs are true, forming a continuous self-reinforcing positive loop.[2]

Lionel Tiger, an evolutionary biologist and anthropologist at Rutgers University and author of *God's Brain*, provides further support for Shermer's model, drawing on neurobiology. When a person has their beliefs confirmed, their brain releases a specific neurotransmitter that we've talked about before: serotonin, which floods the central nervous system, making the person experience feelings of happiness and well-being.[3] This creates a pretty strong evolutionary imperative to seek out religious experiences that make us feel good while increasing our sense of security and comfort. Tiger believes that this neurochemical response is an important biological need for humans and that it explains our drive as a species to seek out spiritual experiences and participate in various religions (at current count there are more than 4,200 religions in the world).[4]

Think about how this plays out within the context of contemporary work culture. We have created a self-reinforcing system in which we see our overwork, Work Devotion, and "hustling" as confirmation of our status as upstanding, moral, "hard workers." Even though you might not be aware of it, every time you drown yourself in busyness, a part of your subconscious is reinforcing your beliefs about what it takes to be successful and the acceptable behaviors of those who are entitled to that success. Beliefs override logic, or, to be more precise, they twist logic through rationalizations that explain our behavior in more positive terms, even when we know or are presented with research or information to the contrary.

Core Beliefs and Identity

Our susceptibility to work-related beliefs lies in the shift we've made from a work culture that used to be more group-focused, to one that centers around the individual. As we've written earlier, much of our obsession with productivity and success is concentrated on our own selves, our own behaviors, and our own abilities to fulfill the notion of the American Dream. Unlike an assembly line worker whose success (the successful creation of a final product, such as a car) is directly dependent on the cooperation of all of his counterparts on the factory floor, creatives are often directly responsible for their own performance: their idea, report, presentation, project. Even within organizations that stress collaborative efforts, many performance reviews are still focused toward the individual.

In addition to the belief systems that we have absorbed as a society on a cultural level, we must also contend with the beliefs that we have built that make up a core portion of our identity. So if we relate success to cultural archetypes like Steve Jobs or Elon Musk or Mark Zuckerberg, then it would make sense that we would want to unconsciously mirror their behaviors and begin to believe that these behaviors are the essential trademarks of a successful entrepreneur.

Such behaviors fuse into our "core beliefs" that directly link to how we view ourselves. If the definition of success includes displaying a relentless work ethic and cultivating a societally approved obsession about our work, then we will inadvertently replicate those behaviors in our own lives as we try to ensure that our own actions are aligned with this agreed-upon version of success.

Our work is so much more than what we do—it has become a complex reflection of who we are, including our beliefs about love, security, self-worth, and fulfillment.

Take love, for example. The Puritans believed that outward signs of success were a direct reflection of a person's goodness, proof that God had chosen them to be saved and live on in eternal happiness in heaven. Brené Brown wrote extensively about using the shield of being busy in order to numb the unhappiness and deep shame that stems from our unconsciously held belief that we are not worthy of love. Work becomes a sort of salvation, a way to prove to yourself that you matter, an opinion often amplified by how we treat people who are traditionally successful versus people who are unemployed or poor.

Security is an easy one. We read about this in Chapter 3, where we saw that more and more workers are willing to accept subpar working conditions in exchange for job security. Despite the looming threat of burnout, a part of you still receives enough positive reinforcement from overwork that it overrides its physical toll.

If you believe your job determines your worth, then that belief could lead to a whole set of behaviors in which you prioritize your job over other things. Recall in Chapter 10 where we saw how the brain linked changes in social status at work with a flight or fight response.

Finally, the trickiest one of all: fulfillment. The idea that your work should be linked to some higher spiritual calling is the latest iteration of the American Dream, wrapped up in glossy motivational sayings about "doing what you love" and "finding your spiritual work calling." We're combining achievement with fulfillment, pushing ourselves to continuously strive for more in a futile effort to touch the horizon—a point we know we'll never reach.

Call of Duty

Our sense of worth and our identity have become wrapped up in our jobs and further incorporated into our core beliefs. The risk of not addressing core beliefs can take us down some very misleading paths. A great example of this is the generally valid career advice in Alain de Botton's *The Book of Life*. De Botton points out the sense of duty that is instilled in us as children and that replaces the otherwise hedonistic, pleasure-seeking wiring that we have before we start serious schooling.

This sense of duty is drilled into us in the form of responsibility, delayed gratification, and sacrifice and runs so deeply because it is inherently connected to our desire for future security in the "adult world." As we grow up, our sense of duty subtly governs our beliefs about how to reasonably spend the majority of our time.

But duty isn't enough to succeed anymore. Instead, The School of Life argues, we must bring "extraordinary dedication and imagination to [our] labors" in order to succeed in the modern economy and truly differentiate ourselves from others who merely work out of duty.[5]

Let's think about that for a moment. While it is absolutely reasonable to encourage finding pleasure and fun at work, don't you get the sense that we're not quite addressing the root of the issue? Hacking our way to fun at work is a surface level rewiring, but why does the modern economy require "the very high levels of energy and brainpower necessary to stand out from the competition?" What is driving us to believe in the premise that good work and true success demand the utmost love and devotion when, in fact, so much of our modern work lives have been shaped by an industrial era and economy that couldn't be farther from where we are today?

The School of Life advises us to take the perspective of the deathbed as a way to drill down to what we might truly want to do with our lives. Again, while this can be a useful tool to question the sense of duty that is instilled into us at a young age and to keep sight of the bigger picture, isn't it fair to say that if we perhaps dig in with the right framework to understand what is driving our deepest beliefs, modern work might not be part of that picture at all?

Can we rewire our beliefs?

The short answer is yes, we can. But the hardest part of the process is identifying them in the first place. In his now-famous commencement speech at Kenyon College in 2005, David Foster Wallace told the story of two young fish who pass an older fish along the way. "Morning boys," the older fish says. "How's the water?" The two fish continue on their way before one turns to the other, bewildered, and asks, "What the hell is water?" Our beliefs are like that, swirling around the reality we move through, and without a conscious effort on our part, we might never notice them.

THE PRESENT NOW

After a long journey through genetics, behaviors, culture, and history, here we are. We hope you have a deeper understanding of why our contemporary work culture is the way that it is and the challenges that we are facing. You might be asking yourself, now what?

There is both good news and bad news.

We'll start with the bad news: There isn't one clear cut solution that can fix all of this. No ten-step program or handy framework with a cool acronym. This reality can't be ignored in favor of a daily hour of meditation or a gratitude practice. It's not as simple as implementing a new work policy or starting yet another life-hack program. It's complicated and messy, so addressing some of these issues is going to be uncomfortable.

The good news is this: if you're not scared off by uncomfortable and messy, then there is a lot that you can do. There are a few steps we can suggest to get you started, but the length of the journey is up to you. We can help guide you, but only you can decide how far to go.

IDENTIFYING THE FORCES & CORE BELIEFS IN YOUR OWN LIFE: THE 3S DISCUSSION GUIDE

After understanding where the forces came from and why they are present in all of our lives, the second step is to take an honest look at how they manifest within your own life.

Ask yourself the following questions and pay close attention to your response. Your mind might try to trick you by making it seem like everything is fine, but trust your gut on this one, and don't be afraid to probe deeper.

- How do my friends and I talk about our work?
- How does working make me feel?
- What roles do fear and competition play in my standards of working? (Hint: technology is often a proxy for an underlying fear that if you take a break, you won't keep up.)
- What meaning, if any, do I truly derive from the work that I do? (Hint: no right or wrong answer.)
- Going back to the age when I chose my career, what drove my choice? What did I imagine doing, wanting, achieving? How does that differ from where I am today?
- How do I represent my professional identity to the outside world? How does this serve me?
- How do I define success?
- In what ways do I communicate or signal my work ethic? Where did I learn this?
- What behaviors are rewarded or well-regarded in my workplace?

This will sound very obvious, but we've found this process to be unsettling. In truly searching for some of these signs, we were forced to confront our own egos and vanity, our need for status and recognition amongst our peers, and the pressure to conform to societal definitions of success distorted by the hyper-curated and staged nature of social media.

Here's the main thing: it's ok for you to feel the way you feel and for you (for all of us, really) to want recognition, validation, and financial prosperity. We are the product of our history and environment, so it's completely natural for our desires, ambitions, and dreams to reflect this rich and complicated history. The trick is in realizing that we have the option to choose something else—that we can challenge ourselves to examine our professional objectives and figure out if we are pursuing them because we actually want them or only because we think we do.

If you decide you do want to continue in the same path that you've been on all along, then more power to you. The point is that you are actively choosing instead of being led by forces that you have no idea are influencing your decisions. But if you're ready to disrupt widely held beliefs and attitudes about work and see if there's a different way forward, then read on.

Identifying Core Beliefs & Self-Limiting Beliefs

Once you've started seeing the presence of Systems, Stories, and Self as powerful forces, it's time to examine your own core beliefs and how they relate to your identity. Again, there is no right or wrong answer here—we all have core beliefs that might put us in conflict with the type of life we want to live. These are called self-limiting beliefs. We all have our own baggage—it's the price of admission for being alive.

A gap between what we want for ourselves and our core beliefs about what we should want is why programs that focus on behavioral modifications alone so often fail. It's not about having enough inner strength to meditate every day, write regular morning pages, or the willpower to disconnect from social media on the weekends, but about examining the core beliefs we have about ourselves in relation to these tasks.

Programs that emphasize the importance of automating good behavior through habits are fine and good, but if your core beliefs don't align with what you're trying to accomplish, you'll have an endless uphill battle. If your core belief about your self-worth is negative, then no promises to work less or take better care of your health can be successful until you modify that belief from *I am not worthy* to *I am enough, and I value my health.*

In short, your core beliefs will dictate your long-term actions. You might be able to force yourself through sheer willpower to make some short-term changes, but in the end, without an underlying shift in core identity beliefs, you'll revert back to what you truly think to be true.

Identifying core beliefs is an exercise in listening to the voice inside your head that chatters in the background as you go about your day. Beliefs usually reveal themselves through the repetitive thoughts you have, so pay attention to them, especially if they feel objectively true to you.

Here are some examples of self-limiting beliefs that we collected from our family, friends, and clients during our workshops, research, and keynotes:

- If I rest, I'll fall behind at work.
- I have to work nonstop to make money.
- Success is for people who never stop hustling.
- My job is the most important thing about me.
- I'm no good at managing money.
- I'm too old to change careers.
- Work is difficult and full of stress.
- My colleagues don't appreciate me.

- I'm the only one who cares about this project.
- I'd never be able to make enough money doing what I love.
- Working long hours is the only way that my performance will be recognized.
- Only morning people get things done.
- I'll be happy once I'm rich.

Could you see why someone who believes that if they rest they will fall behind at work could have some trouble picking up Arianna Huffington's book, *Thrive*, that encourages maintaining a healthy and regular sleep cycle? That's exactly our point—the models that are designed to address some of the ways modern work culture is failing don't take into account the three forces of Systems, Self, and Stories, nor do they account for the core beliefs that arise because of them. I might read that book, nod to myself that, yes, sleep is important, but if my core belief contradicts that view, then I'm never going to stick with that program long enough to make a meaningful change.

Another approach is to ask yourself what you believe to be true about:

- Money
- Success
- Happiness
- Achievement
- Work
- Career

We don't want to get sidetracked by deep diving into the psychology of self-limiting beliefs, but there are many other books that do a brilliant job of it. (One of our favorites is *The Big Leap* by Gay Hendricks. Head over to www.hustleandfloat .com to see the graphic summary we did of it.)

What we will say is that unravelling these beliefs takes time and effort. You can make the process a little bit easier for yourself by just being aware of this. Commit to be open to change and be willing to challenge your own assumptions.

Once you've identified your core beliefs, you can start changing them by creating an alternative belief and supporting that belief with small actions that reinforce it. *I believe rest is an essential part of improving my performance.* Saying that, coupled with deliberate actions like turning off your phone over the weekend, will eventually create a new belief system that will lead to deeper and longer-lasting changes in your life.

HAVING CONVERSATIONS WITH THOSE AROUND YOU: UNDERSTANDING EXPLANATORY COHERENCE

Once you've spent some time uncovering your own beliefs, we hope you'll want to talk about them with friends, family, and colleagues, too. After all, change takes place one conversation at a time.

In discussing our findings with our friends and within our community of fellow creatives, we were heartened and encouraged to hear how much our message resonated. We were also shocked by some of the pushback: aggressive defensiveness, as well as people accusing us of not "having what it takes" to be successful, and of trying to "rationalize our own failures into a model of distorted success." Yikes.

Apparently, we touched a nerve for daring to suggest that our hyper-obsession with productivity has less to do with an outward desire for success and more to do with heaps of internal beliefs and signals that originate from our cultural, historical, and personal experiences. Some people will interpret any challenge to widely held norms as a personal attack—as a criticism of the way they are living their lives—and they will respond in an overly emotional manner.

Generally, we found that discomfort usually means there are some truths that we might not want to face. And yet, facing them is exactly what we need to move beyond these limitations. We're telling you this so that you can be prepared—an unexpected reaction is a clue that you're asking the right types of questions. This is especially important if you're having these discussions with colleagues or friends.

We conducted one *Hustle & Float* workshop with a client of ours and saw this reaction play out in a group dynamic. There were about eight of us sitting in a circle discussing some of the signals of Work Devotion that were a part of the organizational culture. Most of the people in the room felt relieved to know that they weren't the only ones feeling the pressure of being constantly connected and productive. They liked their teams, they liked their boss, they were simply beginning to feel a little drained by the constant pace. Then one woman raised her hand and said "I don't understand what the big deal about answering emails at all hours is. I love my job, and I don't mind being constantly connected. I'm proud to be on the fast track to senior management."

One of her colleagues sat up, his expression hesitant. "It sounds like you're signaling Work Devotion," he said hesitantly.

"No, it's not," she argued. "I just want it badly enough."

This makes us think of "crab mentality," a term used to describe the behavior of crabs trapped within a bucket. Instead of escaping the bucket (as each of them is capable of doing as an individual) they combine their forces to pull any crab who is trying to escape back down, ensuring that none of them can get free. We see this same self-defeating behavior in social networks. If one member tries to challenge the status quo or question the group's collective beliefs, the others try to prevent that member from straying.

Some people just won't be ready to address some of these questions, and that's ok, too. The important thing is to ensure that your own personal well-being is prioritized. You're not trying to convince anyone to do anything, just increasing your own awareness. Unfortunately, this can have some long-lasting implications for some of your relationships, so proceed with caution. If some people are uncomfortable with the changes you are making, that has nothing to do with you.

Remember, it's nearly impossible to change someone's mind by presenting them with facts and research, especially if you're going against a hardwired core belief. Most people will discount research if it doesn't mesh with their personal ideologies. This phenomenon, which was first identified by the cognitive scientist Paul Thagard, author of *Coherence in Thought and Action,* is called "explanatory coherence."[6]

Let's say we've been telling you that overwork actually hinders your performance (as we've been doing now over the course of this entire book). But, when you look around you, you see the media rewarding entrepreneurs who work nonstop. Your colleague gets promoted because of his endless late nights at the office, and you remember feeling especially good in the past when you hustled hard to complete a project on time. You have formed a belief that working nonstop is an essential component of success, and no research or book is going to nudge you out of that position. If you do want to change people's minds, it will take more than statistics. Keep your dialogues open and nonjudgmental, and expect there to be multiple rounds. You're not going to shake someone's deeply held beliefs about work and self-worth over one coffee. But hopefully this book has armed you with a powerful piece of knowledge and understanding of how and why we got here, and that will help in these conversations, as well.

Organizational Beliefs vs. Organizational Culture

It's especially important to have these conversations within organizations. Most conversations about the "softer" side of a company fall under the cultural umbrella. We talk a lot about values and mission statements, but not so much about the actual underlying belief systems that drive an organization. Organizations tend to believe that their cultural environment exists in a vacuum and is somehow immune to the social and historical context we all must grapple with. That's an enormous oversight. There can be big gaps between a culture and its beliefs.

We noticed this during one of our workshops at a multinational corporation.

Our client was a vice president named Mark who managed a team of fifteen people. He had brought us in talk about our *Hustle & Float* research. This company prided itself on having work-life balance as a core cultural value—it was written into its mission statement. But when the company culture was being discussed, we felt a strange tension in the room. We asked Mark to step out of the room briefly and told the team they could speak freely and anonymously.

It turned out that the reality of working in the company day to day was much different than you might have supposed. Mark sent emails at all hours of the day, including weekends. The unspoken expectation was that they were to be answered promptly.

We brought Mark back in and asked him why he was sending emails at night and on the weekends. He was stunned. Evenings and weekends were the only times he could catch up on his inbox, he explained. But he never expected his team to respond on their time off, he said.

Seeing the looks of surprise on his team's faces, we asked a simple follow-up question: "Did you ever clearly communicate that you didn't expect your emails to be answered immediately?"

It turned out he had never verbalized this to his team, and so they had picked up on his behavior as a signal of what he wanted. Following that discussion, Mark drafted a memo with very clear instructions: no team member was to answer emails on their time off, in the evenings, or on the weekend. In the event of an emergency situation, the protocol would be to call the person on the phone and to speak directly. Any email an employee received from Mark while they weren't on the clock could be ignored until the next working day. Mark also announced that he would be making changes in his own behavior and delegating more to the team, so that he would be able to enjoy his own downtime as well.

Mark booked an executive coaching session with us afterwards. Interestingly, he told us that he struggled with downtime because the man who had mentored him had been a workaholic. Mark had internalized the belief that a successful vice president had to work all the time in order to achieve a level of excellence.

Acknowledging that came as a revelation to him. Before, when he had tried to turn off his phone's email functionality in the evening, he felt waves of discomfort and guilt. Through our conversation he recognized that that was a sign of his ego at play: constantly receiving emails from colleagues reinforced his belief that he was an essential part of the organization. His constant availability was a sign of Work Devotion, a way for him to signal his indispensability to his boss. Mark decided to create a new set of expectations and beliefs moving forward. By facing his ego, he started deliberately delegating work to team members and ensuring that Floats, as they started calling their downtime, were considered sacred within their team.

We checked in with Mark and his team a few months later, and they reported a big change in performance and mood. The team was happier and more productive, even during crunches, knowing that they would have ample time to recover. In addition, they had started experimenting with Float afternoons, when they would bucket off chunks of time where no meetings were allowed to take place, giving people the opportunity to sit and reflect, which unsurprisingly (to us, and we hope at this point to you) resulted in an increase of creative ideas and a further rise in productivity.

Even if you work in an organization that has a laid back culture, spelling out expectations clearly can have a big effect on highlighting any hidden or underlying individual, team, or corporate beliefs that could be at odds with the culture you're trying to build.

Former Vice President Joe Biden offers a wonderful example of a leader who understands the importance of spelling out these expectations. The following quote is from a memo he sent out to his team in 2014:[7]

> To My Wonderful Staff,
>
> I would like to take a moment and make something clear to everyone. I do not expect nor do I want any of you to miss or sacrifice important family obligations for work. Family obligations include but are not limited to family birthdays, anniversaries, weddings, any religious ceremonies such as first communions and bar mitzvahs, graduations, and times of need such as illness or a loss in the family. This is very important to me. In fact, I will go so far to say that if I find out that you are working with me while missing important family responsibilities, it will disappoint me greatly. This has been an unwritten rule since my days in the Senate.
>
> Thank you for all the hard work.

This is a great example of ensuring alignment between corporate beliefs and corporate culture. Remember, many organizations think they are creating their organizational culture in a vacuum, but we are all susceptible to the influence of the three hidden forces: Systems, Stories, and Self. No amount of "fun policies" can counteract our most deeply held beliefs.

DARE TO FLOAT

It might seem trite to suggest something as simple as having a conversation, but the truth is that these discussions are already taking place—in coffee shops, over email, on chat—and the real message is being lost in the subtext.

Yes, we as a species are marching toward an automated, AI-driven future. But many of us still have to grapple with the now. Until the robots come in, we are working in ways that are hurting our performance and our well-being. We need more than better work-life policies, more than free food in the break room, more than a productivity research paper being circulated at a meeting. We need to act, as individuals and as leaders, and the time to act is now.

Carol Dweck, professor of psychology at Stanford University and the author of *Mindset*, famously outlined the differences between fixed mindsets and growth mindsets. "In a fixed mindset students believe their basic abilities, their intelligence, their talents, are just fixed traits. They have a certain amount and that's that, and then their goal becomes to look smart all the time, and never look dumb," she writes. "In a growth mindset students understand that their talents and abilities can be developed through effort, good teaching and persistence. They don't necessarily think everyone's the same or anyone can be Einstein, but they believe everyone can get smarter if they work at it."

The problem is, we're looking at our modern work culture with a fixed mindset—we take it for granted, as an irrefutable fact, but, if we only pushed ourselves to have more of these uncomfortable conversations, then we could change it into something better and more humane.

Our beliefs around work are incredibly powerful. They are inextricably woven into the fabric of our modern society. One only needs to look at the deification of Elon Musk (who is awesome, by the way), who gets covered in the media as though he is fulfilling some great professional destiny. The overlap between work and spirituality, with all of the accompanying neurological baggage, is getting stronger. The concept of professional destiny, of "being chosen," is intoxicating. Tying our personal accomplishments to our connection with a higher divine purpose is a perfect storm of ego, serotonin, and cultural adoration. We're moving beyond simple attitudes about work and shifting into a new era of corporate pseudospirituality.

As we dig into the next chapter about the radically changing economy, stripping away the beliefs that point us toward a divine professional destiny might be our best way forward.

Summary of Big Ideas

➡ The influence of the forces (Systems, Stories, Self) are powerful and often hidden. Recognizing their presence is the first step in changing our behavior.

➡ The forces act as foundations for our beliefs about work, and these beliefs can become self-limiting, resulting in behavior that hinders our progress and creative prosperity.

➡ Challenging our beliefs is possible but requires hard, uncomfortable work.

13.

MAN AND MACHINE

THE FACE OF AMAZON

In 2018, Amazon, the global all-in-one e-tailer (not to mention cloud computing, fulfillment and logistics, entertainment, and OEM giant) won the right to patent an "ultra-sonic bracelet and receiver for detecting position in 2D plane," or, in layperson's terms, a wristband that continually monitors warehouse workers' hands as they pick-and-pack.[1] Should their pace slacken, it sends them "haptic feedback" in the form of a tap on the wrist, reminding them that they aren't working fast enough to meet their quota. This is what happens when Taylorism meets the cutting edge of technology.

Over the course of this book, we've focused on the economic and cultural ecosystems that have forged our current-day belief systems around work and on the pressure that we have put on ourselves as we've internalized a production-based approach to knowledge work. As we've seen, the relentless push to work faster, harder, and better is harming not just our mental and physical health but our ability to produce creative work. We believe it is essential for us to recognize and be more actively involved in shaping and responding to these trends, and not just as individuals but as employers and governments.

It would have been easy to end this book after the last chapter, with its lists of accessible and practical questions to help you assess and begin to deal with the impact of all these forces within your own life. But the implications of our societal belief systems are so much greater than our own individual struggles as Productive Creatives. We are on the brink of a truly seismic transformation that will cause us to question our very identities, not just as workers but as human beings, and we are not remotely prepared for it.

Yes, we're in the midst of a technological revolution, but it's our outdated beliefs that are driving us forward. To fully appreciate the extent to which our Stories, Systems, and Self are not just shaping our present but actively influencing our future, let's take a closer look at Amazon, a living case study of all three of these forces in action. One of the biggest and most valuable technology brands in the world, it ticks nearly every box we've talked about in this book so far.

To put things in context, as of 2018, Amazon has 566,000 employees worldwide (a sharp incline due to its acquisition of the grocery retailer Whole Foods in 2017—we'll have more to say about Whole Foods later). Amazon's net sales totalled $178 billion USD in 2017, and it was rated as the United States' most popular online store.

Even before it dreamed up those electronic wristbands, Amazon has been monitoring its workforce in pursuit of greater efficiency, creating working conditions that rival those of the "Satanic Mills" that William Blake wrote about at the dawn of the Industrial Revolution. A 2013 Channel 4 News report revealed that employees in its Rugeley, England warehouse were being tracked at work using GPS tags that recorded their movements and packing rates during their shifts.[2] Workers who failed to meet their rates were sent text messages admonishing them to pick up the pace, and those who failed to do so were fired. Other machines determined whether employees were packing boxes in the "best way" (like "first class men").

It gets worse: talking to colleagues while on the job, calling in sick, or spending too much time in the washroom also warranted warnings, and the rules against those infractions were enforced with a "three strikes and you're out" policy. The investigation also revealed that working conditions in the warehouse were so grim that locals from a recently closed coal mine refused to work there, forcing Amazon to use out-of-town temp agencies to find its workers.

The issue of targets was a regular theme, according to a survey conducted by Organise, an online workers' rights platform that surveyed 241 UK warehouse workers in 2018.[3] "The thing that came up again and again was the impact of high (and ever increasing) targets," the report stated. "Unreasonable targets meant that people are constantly working in fear with the threat of being fired if they fall behind." 74 percent of respondents avoided using the toilet for fear of being reprimanded for not working fast enough, the survey found (indeed, James Bloodworth, the author of *Hired: Six Months Undercover in Low-Wage Britain,* witnessed workers regularly urinating in bottles so as not to miss their rising quotas), and more than half indicated suffering from depression.[4] One worker described his quotas rising from 60 to 70 units to 110 to 120 units per hour. Another recalled a doubling of their packages, from 250 to 500.[5] These findings were echoed by the *Sunday Mirror*'s Alan Selby, who spent five weeks working in Amazon's Essex warehouse, where he witnessed workers falling asleep on their feet and collapsing during their shifts.[6] We were saddened to read the recommendations of the survey, which included telling a twenty-first century corporation to "give workers the ability to pause targets while they visit the bathroom."

In a separate 2016 report by the BBC, Amazon drivers in the United Kingdom stated that the only way for them to meet their delivery targets was to drive above the speed limit, as the assigned quotas don't take into account things like traffic jams or, you know, the time people need to use the restroom and eat.[7] We think you can recognize the echoes of the speed-up and stretch-out from Chapter 3, as well as the underlying philosophy that reduces each individual to a single microtask.

Over in the United States, a 2011 investigation by *The Morning Call*, a newspaper in Allentown, Pennsylvania, revealed that Amazon kept ambulances on standby outside one of their warehouses as workers collapsed from the heat—the unair-conditioned buildings recorded temperatures of 100 degrees Fahrenheit (almost 38 degrees Celsius). Vickie Mortimer, the general manager of the warehouse, insisted Amazon cared for the well-being of its workers and shared that the company had bought "2,000 cooling bandannas which were given to every employee, and those in the dock/trailer yard received cooling vests."

To underline the point that these horrific conditions were created *because* of Amazon's culture, and not in spite of it, we'll briefly mention the Whole Foods acquisition, where reports are emerging of similar practices being introduced to the five hundred grocery stores that Amazon just added to its portfolio. All of them received a new inventory management system, designed, you guessed it, to make stores more productive and efficient. In a 2018 *Business Insider* article, nearly thirty current and former Whole Foods employees described conditions that you might now find familiar: score cards that rate an employee's ability to keep every product in its exact place on the shelves, keep track of the scores they receive on the pop quizzes they are given about store sales statistics, and the penalty points they accrue for failing to meet the company standards. "I wake up in the middle of the night from nightmares about maps and inventory, and when regional leadership is going to come in and see one thing wrong, and fail the team," one supervisor said. "The stress has created such a tense working environment. Seeing someone cry at work is becoming normal."[8]

In his 2014 book *Mindless: Why Smarter Machines are Making Dumber Humans*, Simon Head recounts a confrontation between Amazon and German Work Councils, who were advocating for increased wages and better protections for temporary workers, Amazon said no. "Management refused on the grounds that employees should be 'thinking about their customers' and not about their own selfish interests."[9] (The divine professional destiny should be motivation enough for people to come to work instead of fair compensation, natch.)

If you think these kinds of conditions are unique to warehouse workers, then you'd be mistaken. According to FACE, a website created by former and current employees of Amazon, the same focus on hyperproductivity is evident within its corporate headquarters as well, where the culture is abrasive, abusive, and often toxic.[10] This was also documented in the *New York Times* in 2015, in a harsh 7,000 word expose of the tech-giant's culture of overwork.[11]

The article, which contained interviews with over one hundred current and former Amazon employees, included all the classic elements of a good soul-crushing work story: extreme hours, unrelenting expectations, unachievable objectives, hypercritical management, high-churn, and competitive relationships—the list goes on and on. "This is a company that strives to do really big, innovative, groundbreaking things, and those things aren't easy," the article quoted Amazon's top recruiter, Susan Harker, as saying. "When you're shooting for the moon, the nature of the work is really challenging. For some people, it doesn't work."

Ah yes, it's about time someone mentioned the Shadow Dream, a reminder of the unconscious belief that your failure to attain a desired state (in this case, "the moon,") is a direct reflection of your inability to perform and not, say, management's unrealistic expectations combined with the steep psychological and physiological toll exacted by prolonged overwork. The *New York Times* article captured the contradictory feelings employees had about their difficult working conditions, stating that many "tried to reconcile the sometimes punishing aspects of their workplace with what many called its thrilling power to create."

We were also unsurprised to learn that Amazon refers to their employees as "athletes," a nod to the new Work Warriors who are expected to treat their jobs like an endurance sport. One former employee, Dina Vaccari, stated that she was addicted to the feeling of being successful. "For those of us who went to work there, it was like a drug that we could get self-worth from."

The *New York Times* article wasn't particularly surprising, given all those other reports, but it was the first major media account of the impact of Amazon's punishing work culture on white-collar professionals and knowledge workers, who, if they're not being forced to wear tracking gear, are being pressured to produce 24/7.

We should point out that the article wasn't uncontested; in a somewhat misguided *Medium* post, Amazonian Nick Ciubotariu attempted to rebut many of its claims (the gist of his argument was that he personally had never witnessed such misconduct, and therefore it must not exist within the company).[12]

Revealingly, Ciubotariu references Amazon's employee engagement initiatives, writing that "aside from our yearly survey, which asks very precise questions hitting at the core of employee happiness, our organization conducts our own polls, which get actioned by my group's Leadership Team, of which I am a part of." No pressure there. A case study in Work Devotion, Ciubotariu defends practices that saw colleagues fired for failing to maintain their performance metrics because of a serious illness, a family crisis, or having a baby. Ciubotariu attests that no one from Amazon asked him to write a response nor reviewed the content, save for his wife who "was upset that I was spending a perfectly good Saturday in front of my computer." You can safely bet that he's spent a lot of Sundays and weeknights in front of his computer, too.

In a leaked memo, Amazon CEO Jeff Bezos, one of the most idolized and admired CEOs in the world, flatly denied the allegations. "The article doesn't describe the Amazon I know or the caring Amazonians I work with every day," he wrote. He goes on to say "I strongly believe that anyone working in a company that is really like the one described in the NYT would be crazy to stay. I know I would leave such a company." The final touch you might recognize from Chapter 9, in which we discussed happiness: "But hopefully, you don't recognize the company described. Hopefully, you're having fun working with a bunch of brilliant teammates, helping invent the future, and laughing along the way."[13]

Look, we get that it's not always black and white, and we're sure there are many people who have wonderful and rewarding work experiences at Amazon. But there are enough stories about those who do not to raise a bright red flag—and some really important issues about how one of the biggest and most highly valued companies on the planet uses its power to amplify some truly shameful and destructive policies. We all need to be aware of it.

In the rest of this chapter, we'll take a closer look at the technology revolution that is being driven by megacorporations like Amazon and its implications for the evolving relationships between people and machines. We'll delve into the heart of the robotics economy but also into the cultural reach of the companies who are creating it, driving a new social narrative of machine/human collaboration.

AI AND WHITE-COLLAR TECH: THE CHAOTIC NOW

The innovative disruptions that are shaking up industries and countries are taking place at breakneck speeds. Technology is remaking the world of work, and we are being swept along for the ride. Some of the biggest disruptions include the rise of automation, the development of sophisticated predictive algorithms, and the increasing capabilities of artificial intelligence. These tools aren't just changing the way we work but are forcing us to challenge the very notion of work itself.

What do they mean for Productive Creatives?

For one thing, we should be aware that these technological changes are going to shake up virtually all of the creative industries. When we raise the subject of robotics and AI and big data in our conversations with Productive Creatives, everyone mentions self-driving cars and robots on assembly lines. They foresee the consequences for manufacturing, logistics, and retail, but most consider this revolution to be firmly blue-collar. They regret that long haul truckers, Uber drivers, and cash register operators may soon be out of work, but they see that as an unfortunate but necessary step forward in the names of efficiency and progress.

This sense of security is false. While creative automation is not as advanced as its manufacturing counterpart, it is being developed and deployed in decidedly creative jobs: from lawyers and doctors, to writers and artists. And this is happening today. Right now. While you're reading this chapter. For all of our horrified fascination with the dystopian hellscapes that are on display in the latest season of *Black Mirror*, we are missing the fundamental changes that are happening in the present, or what we call the Chaotic Now, where disruption has become the norm.

To be clear, at the time of this writing (and most likely the near future), artificial intelligence still doesn't have the capacity to fully replace humans. But, considering the exponential pace at which developments in the field are progressing, we clearly can't presume that this will always be the case. Sophisticated software is already changing jobs that were once considered invulnerable to technological displacement.

Our point isn't to scare you, but to thoughtfully explore how the addition of disruptive technology is influencing our already complicated relationship with work, especially creative work, which, as we've seen over the course of this book, is so much more than just a job; it's a source of our identity, social standing, and sense of purpose.

Consider the legal profession, where an AI algorithm can generate new contracts by analyzing and comparing what's needed to a database of similar types of contracts and extracting the relevant language, all in the span of seconds. Reviewing piles and piles of documents for discovery can also now be done by machines that can scan documents for relevant dates and keywords. And, higher legal analysis isn't immune. In 2015, a collaboration between Michigan State University and South Texas College of Law researchers yielded a statistical model that was able to accurately predict the outcomes of 71 percent of US Supreme Court cases. These skills, which involve understanding which legal arguments are going to be the most effective, establishing the legal context of past precedents and rulings, and even recognizing the preferences of the presiding judge, all fall under the domain of lawyers but can now be done by software.

The same analytical skill sets can be used in other industries where people require access to large amounts of information. Financial analysts and advisors are competing with algorithms that use big data and predictive analytics to analyze and stock performance and spot good investment opportunities. Consider the start-up SigFig, which learns about an investor's profile, including their risk tolerance and goals, and creates a unique investment strategy to suggest and manage a portfolio for them.

The field of medicine is also feeling the impacts of new technologies as sophisticated machines and algorithms provide new ways to provide more accurate diagnostic services to patients. The huge influx of data makes it very hard for doctors to keep up with the latest research and breakthroughs. IBM's Watson, for example, can review in seconds what it would take a normal physician 160 hours of reading per week to keep up with.

What about a field like journalism? Reuters' News Tracer program monitors hundreds of millions of social media posts, especially on Twitter, to identify potential breaking news stories. When clusters of unrelated users are suddenly tweeting about the same event at the same time, the system is alerted that a new story might be developing. The algorithm considers the profiles of the people who are posting (for example, whether they are police or political officials), the structure of the tweets, the numbers of retweets, and whether or not other users are corroborating the information, in order to generate a "newsworthy" score. The information is then reviewed and verified by human reporters before being released. Reuters has successfully used this technology to break news stories, including the shooting in San Bernardino, California, the 2016 earthquake in Guayaquil, Ecuador, and bombings in both New York and Brussels.[14] Today, Reuters uses these types of automation software to publish around 8,000 articles *a day* in various languages. In the race to break the top stories first, the *Columbia Journalism Review* estimated that News Tracer gives Reuters anywhere from an eight minute to a full hour's head start over its corporate rivals.[15]

Narrative Science, a Chicago-based AI firm that specializes in natural language, created a platform called Quill, which, according to the website's description, "analyzes data from disparate sources, understands what is important, then automatically generates perfectly written narratives to convey meaning from the data for any intended consumer or business audience, at unlimited scale." Whether it's a news article or a summary of a company's published financial documents, Quill can research, collate, and generate findings in a fraction of the time it would take humans to do the same tasks.[16]

In 2016, a novel called *The Day A Computer Writes a Novel*, which was actually written by an AI software package (with the collaboration of a human team of programmers) passed the first round of judging for a prestigious national Japanese literary prize. In the first round, the judges use a "blind reading" policy that anonymizes the submissions, so the judges can focus purely on the materials, preventing any biases about authorship. Despite not taking home the big prize, the AI's creator, Hitoshi Matsubara from the Future University Hakodate, saw this as a tremendous early step. "So far, AI programs have been used to solve problems that have answers, such as [games like] Go and shogi," he said during a press conference. "I'd like to expand AI's potential so that [it] resembles human creativity."[17]

Matsubara is not alone. At the time of this writing, we've come across AI algorithms that are producing original works of art, composing music, writing poetry, and even creating new recipes for food. There are AI programs that can argue in traffic court to have your speeding ticket dismissed, some that are challenging mathematical theorems, and others that create new consumer products.

Yes, for now the outputs are mostly rudimentary, but what makes this technological revolution different from its predecessors is the speed and scalability at which progress is taking place. Especially when you consider that we are training algorithms to program and improve themselves. Once a computer can tweak and improve its own code, we'll see an explosion of innovation take place that's like nothing that's come before.

This isn't a book about AI, so we don't want to dive too deep into the technical aspects of the tools. We just wanted to make the point that with the advances of AI, creativity is no longer the sole domain of humans.

THE GIG ECONOMY:
THE AMERICAN DREAM, PIECEMEAL

All of these disruptions are making a mockery out of many traditional career paths. Having a career path or even a job in the same way that our parents and grandparents did is no longer an option for most Productive Creatives. Professional uncertainty has become the norm as technology shakes up whole industries across the board.

Reid Hoffman, the former CEO of LinkedIn, has a solution. His book *The Start-up of You* encourages individuals to treat their careers as their own microbusinesses. "The key is to manage your career as if it were a start-up business: a living, breathing, growing start-up of you," he writes. "The strategies in this book will help you survive and thrive and achieve your boldest professional ambitions...[empowering] you to become the CEO of your career and take control of your future."[18]

You should be able to recognize many of the themes we have isolated interwoven here: the myth of the self-made man, the idealization of entrepreneurs, the pursuit of higher career purpose, and of course, the pressure on the individual to measure their professional performance against that of a business. It's fascinating, isn't it? Once you become aware of the forces, you start to see their influence everywhere. Interestingly, Hoffman refers to our constant focus on hyper-competition as "permanent beta," a technology term for a product that is not yet finalized now applied to us as human beings. We don't want to read too much into this, as we're sure he was just searching for a catchy phrase rather than making a philosophical statement about our role as Productive Creatives within an increasingly technological context, but it is something to ponder.

This shift toward the "CEO of Me" or the "CEO of One" is further promoted as an answer to the anxiety of unemployability, but the sense of control it gives us, of being able to escape the rigid confines of full-time employment and achieve financial freedom by writing our own rules, is an illusion. Nowhere is this more evident than in the rise of the real-life Gig Economy. The promises it offered—to be your own boss, set your own schedule, choose your own clients, and in general, break free of the drudgery—were seductive but unrealistic.

We have now entered a new, more dangerous phase in our work culture, the merging of technological platforms with the microeconomy itself. The Gig Economy has been largely powered by scalable technological infrastructure. Companies like Airbnb, TaskRabbit, Uber, Deliveroo, Etsy, and others, have made it possible for individuals to run their own microbusinesses, to actually be a CEO of One. And they are selling us this vision of the future, the premise of earning as much as you want, or translation, as much as you're willing to work for (there's that American Dream popping up again). It *is* a compelling vision, often wrapped up in a slick interface and clever branding.

But the truth is a little less shiny. Consider a now deleted blog post from the ride-sharing app Lyft from late 2016, praising one of its female drivers who, though nine months pregnant and with a delivery date just a few days away, continued to take passengers, even after she started having contractions. The post read:

> After a few rides, Mary started having contractions. Since she was still a week away from her due date, she assumed they were simply a false alarm and continued driving. But as the night went on, they didn't stop, so Mary decided to drive herself to the hospital. Since she didn't believe she was going into labor yet, she stayed in driver mode, and sure enough—ping!—she received a ride request en route to the hospital.
>
> Luckily, the ride was a short one. Mary drove herself straight to the hospital after she dropped off the passenger. When she

arrived at the hospital, the doctors informed her that she was indeed in labor!

Mary welcomed Maven Mia into the world on July 22, 2016 at 7:23 a.m.

Reported on by the technology blog Gizmodo, aptly filed under the rubric "Our dogshit future," Bryan Menegus, the post's author, highlighted what was so troubling about Lyft's treatment of this event as an inspiring example of work ethic and go get 'em spirit.[19]

"What a trooper, that Mary, who almost certainly wanted to be working while nine months pregnant at a job that does not provide its nonemployee drivers with basic amenities like health care or maternity leave," he said sarcastically. "Ignoring birthing contractions to make an extra buck is not cute—it points to how fundamentally lopsided contract jobs are in the euphemistically-named sharing economy."

Because, you see, Mary wasn't an employee of Lyft, but a self-starting entrepreneur. Lyft therefore didn't owe her anything like health care benefits or maternity leave. Those responsibilities, along with managing one's own employability of course, have been passed on to us to deal with. Companies like Uber and Lyft get to benefit from having a large multinational global network without having to provide anyone with things like sick days, or holidays, or pay into government employee benefit schemes.

In fact, many of these companies go to great efforts to ensure that no one who works on their platforms mistakenly gets the notion that they are, in fact, employees. Deliveroo, a UK start-up that uses bike couriers to deliver restaurant take-out to people, recently received some bad press over a leaked memo that outlined a strict vocabulary that employees of the company were required to use when referring to their deliverers. Couriers are to be called "independent suppliers," it specified. The company even stopped providing training to new couriers because it would give the impression that Deliveroo was managing employees and not contractors. Like Uber, Deliveroo riders get paid per delivery and must purchase and maintain their own bikes. They get assigned specific zones, which according to a 2018 *Guardian* article are "constantly expanded in size, meaning it takes longer to make deliveries, meaning less money."[20] (The great stretch-out is alive and well.)

The promise of the entrepreneurial lifestyle is alluring. As we've seen in previous chapters, entrepreneurs are the current "Gods" of our work culture, larger-than-life figures whose rags to riches origin stories cement our society's belief in earning material wealth as a direct result of one's moral perseverance and drive. However, this myth also has a shadow, which is that the creation of a workforce of micro-CEOs erodes their ability to collectively bargain for better working conditions and often operates outside of traditional business government structures, depriving them of access to health care insurance and other resources (this isn't as strongly felt in countries like Canada and France, where health care is considered a basic right).

In our desire to believe in this myth of glorious autonomy, we ignore the fact that we're creating a new set of jobs that don't pay a living wage. While Uber is currently valued at $62 billion USD, with its founder and former-CEO Travis Kalanick worth $4.8 billion USD, its average driver isn't so lucky.[21] As a mini-CEO, Uber drivers are responsible for maintaining their vehicle, paying for tolls, their license, permit fees, repairs, gas, insurance, a data-heavy phone plan, and other associated expenses including taxes, all of which come after Uber takes its 25-30 percent cut of their revenues. When looking at their net incomes, what drivers can expect to take home after all of those expenses (which doesn't even factor in the initial investment of buying a car), a recent report concluded that most Uber and Lyft drivers barely make minimum wage.[22] Another study by the MIT's Center for Energy and Environmental Policy Research calculated a median hourly pay for Uber drivers of $8.55 an hour, with 41 percent of respondents making less than their state's minimum wage, and 4 percent actually losing money while on the job.[23]

Deliveroo's tactics take advantage of another feature of our work mythology. The company offers the best shifts to the riders who make the highest number of deliveries, which at first sounds like a great incentive. "You sell it to the riders in this really macho way, that if you're really speedy and committed to the company, you'll make loads of money," said one driver in an interview. "But the reality is there are so many variables out of your control: restaurants taking too long, customers not being in, bike tire punctures." (*Work Devotion, Work Warrior, the Shadow Dream*—those who are drawn by the American Dream's promise of the great equalizer of hard work are especially vulnerable to this come-on.)

UNIONIZATION AND THE INNOVATION PUSHBACK

In response to the reality of these business models, it shouldn't be surprising that some workers, realizing they're getting the raw end of the deal, are pushing back by demanding the same protections that their industrial-era ancestors struggled to obtain back in the day. It's been a fierce battle, as technology has enabled organizations to harness the benefits of a workforce without considering them as such. Plus, companies like Uber and Deliveroo are flush with venture capital, giving them deep pockets to sustain prolonged legal battles—and to craft their one-sided contracts.

In 2017, the Central Arbitration Committee in the United Kingdom, a tribunal which is responsible for handling worker disputes, ruled that Deliveroo riders were self-employed contractors because the company allows them to have someone of their choice (say a friend) step in to cover a shift, which is something that you couldn't do at a normal job.[24] During the tribunal proceedings, it was revealed that Deliveroo had made a series of changes to its contracts, including the right to substitution, specifically so that it could categorize its riders as independent contractors.[25] This distinction makes all Deliveroo riders exempt from minimum wage, holiday pay, and collective bargaining.

However, this issue is still unfolding as the Independent Workers Union of Great Britain (which brought the original claim against Deliveroo) was given the right to challenge the previous ruling on the grounds that the court should reassess the rights of riders to collectively bargain, moving the issue away from the minutiae of job classifications and into the territory of human rights, as collective bargaining is a fundamental right according to the European Convention on Human Rights. As of this writing, the issue is still undecided, but governments are beginning to take notice.[26]

Frank Field, an MP and the chairman of the Work and Pensions Committee, has launched a parliamentary inquiry into the hiring and compensation practices of companies in the Gig Economy, including Uber, Parcelforce, and Deliveroo. "The weight of the evidence I've seen shows that bogus self-employment is being peddled by those who benefit so handsomely from the gig economy, to avoid the obligations they have to their workforce," Field said.[27] The UK government also announced some planned labor market reforms that will take into account the emergence of the Gig Economy.

In the United States, the Bureau of Labor Statistics released its first report assessing the "gig economy," defined as the reliance on temporary work, freelancing, and on-demand apps.[28] It found that 16.5 million Americans relied on these "alternative work arrangements" to make a living. The challenge in accurately mapping out this market is that the technology has created a high level of ambiguity that makes it difficult to classify these new types of work (on call, contingent, alternate arrangement, small business owner, independent contractor, etc.), which makes applying any type of regulatory protections nearly impossible. Workers and employers must hash out their differences in court, which of course the companies can much more easily afford to do.

The rulings have been mixed thus far, but the big companies are fighting hard to keep the classification of their "workers" as independent contractors. Handy, an online marketplace connecting consumers looking for help with handymen who can handle routine household tasks like cleaning, unclogging toilets, or assembling furniture, has put forward bills in eight different states seeking to permanently define gig workers as independent contractors, strengthening their defense against future legal action.[29] If these bills get signed into laws, then any company that so brands their workers will be able to set wage rates and monitor and fire their workers without having to worry about Workers' Compensation, unemployment taxes, or adhering to anti-discrimination laws. States like Colorado, Arizona, Kentucky, and Indiana have all adopted similar legislation.[30] Uber and Lyft have been known to send text messages to their customers, urging them to support similar legislation, with Uber spending close to two million dollars in lobbying fees and Lyft offering passengers free rides to voting locations.[31]

Their argument is that labor regulations are too burdensome, impacting the pace of innovation and the ability for a company to succeed. Instead, they'd rather pass on all of the risks and costs to the worker in order to pocket billions of dollars of profit. And they're not just passing on the risks, they are packaging those risks into a highly seductive lure that promises participation in the American Dream: flexibility, autonomy, and financial security. Who wouldn't want to be a part of that? And

then, reality strikes: this isn't innovation at all, this is industrial slavery delivered via a slick dot com interface.

We get it, we hear the siren's call because the other world
of work, let's call it traditional work, wasn't that great either,
especially after the 2008 financial crisis. We've been told that
there is a new alternative, a better way to thrive in these unpredictable times, a way to take control of our finances and time,
but the numbers simply don't add up. Instead, we see the rise of
new tech brands that enable us to participate in some capacity
in one of the most powerful contemporary myths: entrepreneur.

THE CREATIVE TECH

As we mentioned earlier, while technology-enabled business
models are disrupting hospitality, transportation, and cleaning
services industries, the platforms already exist that will do the
same things to writing, consulting, drawing, composing music,
researching, marketing, and more. These ratings-driven mar-
ketplaces enable me to engage in microtransactions for any creative service that I can imagine, from hiring a freelance writer
or marketer to a photographer, chef, or editor. And that's not
even accounting for the apps that are being used to help you
do everything from hire people to process your accounting and
expenses.

We've tried to go beyond the tech to focus on two key issues.
The first is that creativity is not immune to technological disruption. Though most of these technologies are in their infancy,
they will keep evolving and have a big impact on the way creatives work and on the work that creatives can do in the future.

The second point is that many of the biggest companies that
are thriving in this new economy pretend to be creating a new
future while firmly entrenching the systems, stories, and self
forces into their DNA—and worse still, setting back the clock

on labor rights a century and more. We cannot become dazzled by the new opportunities they offer that seem too good to be true. They are. Artificial intelligence, automation, and algorithms are just lines of code. It is us, the humans who are programming these codes, who are creating the context for their roles in our lives.

The technology that held so much potential for freedom turned into a different kind of shackle: the birth of the Gig Economy has created a workforce that undercuts each other's prices in an effort to line up freelance assignments that come with no job security or benefits. We've become our own slave drivers. Technologies have enabled us to create alternative systems of work, but the work philosophies that we live by are backwards-looking and self-destructive. Furthermore, many of the companies that provide this type of technological infrastructure for freelance work deliberately play into that fact: they know they're selling you a corrupted version of the American Dream, but they wrap it up in a package of self-starting, go-getting, work-warrior archetypes that they know is hard for you to resist. We get lured by the idea of working less and instead get roped into working far more than we did before. As we gain more transparency into how these technologies work, we will realize that the innovation that comes with this new digital infrastructure does so at a price: destabilization of labor for the millions of people who must now fend for themselves.

It's funny that these companies make up the "Sharing Economy" because they don't share any of the risks—or their profits.

Summary of Big Ideas

➡ Technology disruption will impact every industry from journalism and accounting, to law and consumer package goods.

➡ Large multinational technology giants are creating global digital infrastructures that are scaling our ideologies around work at an unprecedented level.

➡ Futuristic technologies are still being embedded with outdated work baggage.

➡ The Gig Economy is exploiting attitudes about work (the American Dream, rags to riches) to profit by creating an unsustainable economic model where workers struggle to earn a livable wage.

14.

A WORLD OF WORKERS WITHOUT WORK

Three years of researching, writing, questioning, doubting, and fighting our own biases has brought us to this critical point: we are standing on the brink of a technological revolution that *will* transform our world, whether we are ready for it or not. And we don't think anyone is ready for what's coming.

Work used to be about survival; it was what you had to do to make enough money to eat and put a roof over your head. As knowledge industries evolved and grew, buoyed by scalable technologies and new business models, we looked to work for things that are more nuanced but just as important to us as food and shelter: our identities, our values, our very worth. Work has morphed into a search for self-actualization. Our struggles in the workplace are a modern-day rite of passage, heralding our entry into adulthood as mature contributing members of society. The value of work is so intertwined with our other social and cultural ideals that we must recognize that they will persist, even as our economic conditions grow too turbulent to support them, even after our crumbling institutions can no longer provide us with the promise of a stable and financially secure future.

The financial blow is easy enough to understand. It's the psychological and emotional repercussions that pose the most danger—especially in the world of knowledge work, which has productivized creativity as an economic metric while offering up an iteration of the American Dream in which our sense of well-being, happiness, and even spirituality is closely linked to our jobs.

But never mind our personal unhappiness and disappointment. How will our consumption-based society continue to function as larger and larger groups can no longer find the work they need to survive, never mind shop? The solutions on the table include a universal basic income, taxation for artificial intelligence, steeper regulations on job-killing technologies, job sharing, and simply trying to compete with robots. As we've shown over the course of this book, all of these solutions address the symptoms and not the underlying cause.

The cause is two-fold: one, that technological advances beyond our control are on the way, and two, that our beliefs and values surrounding work, that we've accumulated over the course of the Fourth Industrial Revolution, will make it even harder for us to adjust to the new technological advances that we are sure to encounter in our lifetime. Given the importance of that cultural baggage, it's beyond ironic that we are talking about it as little as we are.

We *can* tell you this much: the solution to this conundrum is not going to be more jobs or to work harder. While economists might wonder what will happen to an economic system (capitalism) that's lost its central unifying tenet (everybody works), we're asking a different question: who will be without work? What will happen to us when our chosen path for self-actualization is taken over by robots? The reckoning that's coming will challenge the very core of who we are. Asking ourselves the questions that we outlined in Chapter 13, explicitly identifying and naming the hidden forces of Systems, Self, and

Stories that have given us this false identity, is a beginning; certainly, it will give us a stronger foundation to stand on when the rest of our world is under siege. But it's only a start.

THE CULTURAL AND SOCIAL IMPORTANCE OF WORK: START UP YOU

The pillars of our self-worth, our identity, and our purpose, all of which we've built upon the idea of work, have begun to crumble. Forget the future—our current reality is that there aren't enough stable, steady jobs for everyone. The great promise of the New Deal, a job and a house for all, once considered an inalienable right, has now become an uncertainty, a relic of a bygone era. Consider this: as people fail to maintain steady employment, many of them will blame themselves. The Shadow Dream is hard to shake. If you're not succeeding, then you simply must not be working hard enough.

Universities are scrambling to update ancient pedagogies that won't help us outsmart robots. A 2017 special feature in the *Financial Times* assured anxious parents that they could "robot-proof" their children's future careers. One of their suggestions? Be more creative. "Artificial intelligence tends to solve problems methodically but the human brain is far better at making logical leaps of imagination." This might be true now, but as we know, AI is making huge headway into all sorts of tasks that were previously considered firmly in the domain of the human brain. What if we started teaching kids that there's more to who they are than what they do?

A growing subset of the self-help industry is devoted to helping people find gainful employment as quickly as possible. One of the main strategies involves personal branding, differentiating oneself in order to stand out from the competition, and optimizing one's value in the labor market. Those without jobs are encouraged to spend time learning new skills, networking for new opportunities, pursuing entrepreneurship avenues and part-time work (the Gig Economy), and a myriad of other activities. In short, we've turned the state of being unemployed into, well, a job.

Much as we've internalized the responsibility for our own productivity, we also take accountability for our employability, even if it's not about how hard we've worked, or the skills that we have, but about the fact that the jobs (as we've grown to expect them) just aren't there anymore. Trying to compete with robots is a short-term solution that underscores these big challenges and completely misses the point. It's deeply unsettling to realize that, after idolizing work as an essential indicator of moral virtue and status, the system itself is now failing us.

Instead of addressing our own participation in co-creating this narrative, we focus on surface level solutions and policies to give us the illusion of control. Much of the discussion about the future of work is framed around the technology itself, the tools and the business models that will make these types of commerce feasible. We talk about GDP and the decreasing availability of full-time, steady jobs. We know you can probably guess what we're going to say next: what's missing from our conversation is how our deeply held belief systems are failing to keep up with the speed of the new technology. However forward-thinking about work we believe we are, most of us are still carrying subconscious expectations of what having a job means as both a measure of security and identity. What's happening is not simply a phase of disruption but a permanent rupture in our model of the world.

The other thing we'd like to point out is the time frame for these changes. Many theorists talk about the future of work with a long view in mind. They prefer to envision scenarios where these changes have already taken place, in order to try and imagine the models and philosophies that would govern this new society. However, between then and now, there will be a severe period of intense transition, a phase in which we will experiment with different models, almost certainly making mistakes and failing as we learn. We are already at the beginning of this transition, and it's not hard to imagine how much worse things are going to get—and the indelible consequences if we, as a society, don't wake up and face the facts soon. But myths are hard to walk away from.

THE MYTH OF FULFILLMENT

Industriousness, as we've shown in this book, has been the de facto religion of choice for generations of "hard workers" who believe their efforts will pay off in spades. In the past, work has offered us salvation, moral high standing, distraction, status, and now, as if the list of promises wasn't already long enough, fulfillment. Yes, work will now also provide you with pseudo-spiritual benefits in the guise of a higher calling or finding a creative purpose. Just like the professional destiny we wrote about in the last chapter, the idea that work can provide any of these things within the boundaries of current economic reality is laughable. And yet, we have beliefs, and so we maintain the faith: against all odds, in despite of facts, rationality, and logic, we cannot help but trust that the suffering and sacrifice we are inflicting on ourselves will one day make us worthy of some promised land, or, worse still, simply worthy.

The question of fulfillment has been a cornerstone of philosophic debate for millennia, with everyone from Socrates and the Buddha to Bill Gates and Oprah weighing in on what it means. It's true that work offers many people an easy out: it takes up the majority of our adult lives and comes with status, dogma, and suffering, all rolled up in a shiny promise of potential. There is something romantic about the notion of your "life's work" that conveys a sense of status and prestige. Entrepreneur and lifestyle guru Marie Forleo, founder of MarieTV and B-School, an online business school geared at women, has managed to pack all that into an oft repeated motto: "The world needs that special gift that only *you* have." It's a very compelling message that, while lovely in its sentiment, is rooted in a consumption-based empowerment that requires the purchase of digital products to help people "discover their true calling."

It's a heady promise but also adds to the pressure of work-centered fulfillment, insinuating that not only are we doing a disservice to ourselves if we somehow don't find this calling but we are depriving the world of an essential resource. It's a double-edged sword and very indicative of the current state of contemporary work culture. To be clear, Forleo is not in the wrong here. We are avid fans of her content and much of her messaging is very aligned with *Hustle & Float* ideology—for example, she often recommends self-care and periods of rest and creative recovery. We were delighted to note that she—and her entire team—take off several weeks during the summer in order to unwind and recharge. But her message does reflect the cultural context we exist in today while providing the seductive pull of job-based spiritual fulfillment with a strong new narrative that is driven by social media.

Creative jobs are being sold as a path toward self-actualization, with graphics that overlay motivational quotes like "Do What You Love" and "Find your purpose" onto pictures of nature, usually a beach or a forest (the irony notwithstanding that we now work long hours at jobs that are decidedly not near any of these things—unless you're really lucky—and yet we're still motivated by an image of a waterfall snapped by a trust fund kid).

We focus on spiritual fulfillment because it's normal to be fulfilled at your job, to take personal satisfaction and pride in your work. But there is a line between skill-based achievement and the premise of a sacrosanct duty that is tied to the idea of a benevolent universal plan. Creative production is not just an economic metric, which is bad enough; it has become idealized as a blessed and holy pursuit. Additionally, we focus on fulfillment at work because, as we've seen earlier in the book, the cognitive demands on knowledge workers are severe, and the hours we work are so long that many people find themselves completely drained when they come home, with no energy to devote to anything else. So linking jobs with a higher purpose does make a kind of sense; it takes the edge off a reality where most of us just get home after work, maybe squeeze in a workout, and settle in to watch some Netflix.

But while we've updated our cultural offerings to bundle "destiny" with efficiency and productivity, we're ignoring the fact that the very thing we've hinged all of this meaning on is in the process of disappearing. As David Frayne, author of *The Refusal of Work,* so eloquently put it, "we are becoming a society of workers without work."[1]

We desperately need to update our beliefs about work, creativity, and fulfillment. It all goes back to self-actualization—the more we cling to work as a means of validating our self-worth through achievement, the more we will hurt ourselves as its role in our lives erodes, whether we want it to or not.

We're not saying we've reached the end of human creativity—far from it. We simply don't think that the future of human creativity will happen within the context of work.

BULLSHIT JOBS AND THE RISE OF THE USELESS CLASS

In 2015, mysterious posters popped up on the London Tube. In bold black text against a neon yellow background, there was one simple phrase: *It's as if someone were out there making up* *pointless jobs just for the sake of keeping us all working.*² There was a hashtag underneath: #bullshitjobs. The quotes turned out to be excerpts from a 2013 essay anthropologist David Graeber had written for *STRIKE!*, a radical magazine. Entitled "On the Phenomenon of Bullshit Jobs: A Work Rant," Graeber's essay went viral; its scathing condemnation of what he termed to be pointless busy work to keep people occupied clearly hit a nerve.³ "The ruling class has figured out that a happy and productive population with free time on their hands is a mortal danger (think of what started to happen when this event began to be approximated in the '60s)," he wrote. "And, on the other hand, the feeling that work is a moral value in itself, and that anyone not willing to submit themselves to some kind of intense work discipline for most of their waking hours deserves nothing, is extraordinarily convenient for them." These bullshit jobs keep the money that powers the economy flowing but at the cost of the core ideal of having purposeful, meaningful work.

While we understand and relate to Graeber's anger at capitalism and the ruling class, what caught our attention was the role that we, as individuals and workers within this ecosystem, play in our own oppression. We are motivated by intrinsic drivers that we don't question. We as a society have decided that work for the sake of work as its own reward. Graeber notes that this view crosses the whole political spectrum, writing that "more jobs is the one political slogan both the left and right can always agree on."

It is this pressure, driven by the three forces of Systems, Self, and Stories, that will be the cause of many of the pain points we will encounter as the job market continues to dwindle. It's a pain point that Yuval Noah Harari, author of the best-selling *Sapiens: A Brief History of Humankind,* covers in his follow-up book, *Homo Deus: A Brief History of Tomorrow.* Harari explores several different scenarios of what a technology-focused future could look like. On the positive end, technology helps us overcome the limits that disease, aging, and climate change could impose, turning us into god-like creatures. On the downside, well, we place our fate in the control of intelligent algorithms that will eventually make us economically redundant, giving rise to what Harari calls the "useless class."

As more and more people get eliminated from the job market and long-standing institutions like universities have trouble adapting, billions of people will find themselves unsuitable for paying jobs, a scenario that Harari categorizes as one of the most catastrophic threats to our species. His deliberate choice of the world "useless" is a reflection of our current value system and not a person's actual worth. "I choose this very upsetting term...to highlight the fact that we are talking about useless from the viewpoint of the economic and political system, not from a moral viewpoint," he explained.[4] If a person's value is measured solely by their economic contribution to the system, what happens when there are no longer any avenues for them to participate in it?

Currently, we're seeing people trying to stave off the rise of the useless class with the creation of endless useless jobs, but that's like putting a Band-Aid on a bullet wound. It's not going to do much, especially in the face of exponential technological advances.

For Graeber, the first step is clear. "We need to change what we value," he said in an interview with *Vox*. Graeber suggests that we need to challenge the assumption that a job is the only way to provide tangible value to society. "What if we just accepted that technology can perform a lot of the essential tasks and just worked less," he asks. "What if we just spent more time doing what we actually want rather than sitting in an office pretending to work for 40 hours a week?" He points to the many ways people contribute to society but aren't economically rewarded for it—people like volunteers, caregivers, and stay-at-home parents who have labor intensive responsibilities that aren't reflected in the GDP, making their efforts invisible to those trying to quantify the worth of things.

In their paper, "The Crisis of Social Reproduction and the End of Work," the social theorists Helen Hester and Nick Srnicek put such tasks under the rubric of "reproductive labor," which they defined as "the activities that nurture future workers, regenerate the current workforce, and maintain those who cannot work—that is, the set of tasks that together maintain and reproduce life, both daily and generationally."[5]

LEISURE: INDUSTRY AND EXPLOIT

As we've seen in this chapter, we've morphed our view of work beyond simple productivity and now enjoy work for its own sake, or rather for the sake of the status it imparts. In today's cult of busyness, having too much leisure is frowned upon as it is a visible sign of one's unimportance.

When researching the concept of leisure and how it's tied in to our ideas about work and status, we started with the granddaddy of leisure theory: the American economist Thorstein Veblen's classic *The Theory of the Leisure Class: An Economic Study of Institutions,* which was published in 1899. Veblen argued that leisure was "a badge of honor" afforded by those who could pay others to do the mundane, repetitive, and boring tasks (Veblen called these types of tasks "industry"), thus freeing themselves up to use their time in pursuit of "exploit," far more rewarding and prominent callings such as investing, philanthropy, debating, magistracy, and writing.[6] Wealthy women of this time were esteemed hostesses, managed large households, championed notable causes, and devoted time to community service.

If the above isn't the first thing that leaps to your mind when you think of leisure, then you're not alone. In their excellent paper "Post-Industrious Society: Why Work Time Will Not

Disappear for our Grandchildren," Jonathan Gershuny and Kimberly Fisher noted that Veblen's definition of leisure sounds a lot like, well, work.[7]

"These members of the 19th century leisure class were, in sum, active in sports, arts, justice and law, scientific research, charitable and caring activities, administration of large enterprises," they wrote. "These people might sensibly be considered as *working*, in the modern third person criterion sense, and indeed they are often doing things that are entirely familiar to us as the *paid* work of the various parts of the dominant class in the 21st century: precisely, sports, arts, law and justice, scientific research, charitable activities and the administration of large enterprises!"[8]

As we made the shift to a postindustrial economy, wealth generation shifted from the ownership of assets capable of producing material goods (land, factories, ships) to the application of knowledge and creativity in the production of services. As we wrote in Chapters 2 and 3, as the nature of work changed, our activities more closely resembled the "badge of honor" label that Veblen applied to leisure, which explains why some people are choosing to work more even when they don't have to.

Those of us lucky enough to enjoy more creative and gratifying work can enjoy the same type of "exploit" afforded only to the wealthy in Veblen's day, including the status and prestige that come with it. Additionally, research shows that people who enjoy intellectually satisfying jobs tend to prefer them to their home life.[9]

As we've mentioned in earlier chapters, our judgmental attitudes toward the unemployed reflect some of the most pervasive and harmful beliefs in our society. We are far too quick to label those without jobs as lazy, immoral, or unindustrious. Now that literally billions of people must confront the prospect of their own redundancy due to circumstances that are completely out of their control, this must change. Psychologists consider unemployment, particularly for high achievers, as a "traumatic mind state."[10]

It is a trauma that will soon become all-too-familiar. "What to do about mass unemployment," wondered Elon Musk at the 2017 World Government Summit in Dubai. "This is going to be a massive social challenge. There will be fewer and fewer jobs that a robot cannot do better than a human. These are not things that I wish will happen. These are simply things that I think will probably happen."

POST-WORK SOCIETY/ANTI-WORK

There is no clearer indication of the power of work as a pseudo religion than our resistance to admitting that it's failing. It's no longer a guarantee of prosperity, nor stability, nor socioeconomic mobility. Instead we're moving toward a work reality that is chaotic, erratic, and unpredictable for many people—be they a part of the Gig Economy at the mercy of algorithms and technocracy, full-timers who must survive the next wave of restructuring, or part-timers who grapple with short-term contracts (or zero-hour contracts) where they get none of the benefits of being employed.

As it exists today, the state of work for many Productive Creatives is leaving us exhausted and anxious with no viable solution in sight. We've been told that to work is one of our defining characteristics as humans. Hard work has been made synonymous with virtue. We've since coupled hard work with consumerism and looked to consumerism as a means to happiness. Is it time for a new ideology?

The Post-Work movement researches and explores what could possibly replace this failing system. We have been documenting the power of human creativity over the course of this entire book, and it seems that it is coming up against its biggest challenge yet: the need for us to imagine an alternative future.

As David Frayne, the author of *The Refusal of Work*, one of the most convincing and thoughtful works of post-work philosophy, wrote, "So are we the utopians? Or are the utopians the people who think work is going to carry on as it is?"

What might a post-work society look like?

Well, there is a mix of ideas. Some post-workists advocate for universal basic income, a controversial idea that is supported by both left-leaning (as a method to reduce inequality) and right-leaning (as a more streamlined welfare system) politicians.

The premise is that legal residents of a country would receive a standard monthly amount of money unrelated to any employment or the requirement to seek employment. Not only would it provide a social safety net for everyone, it would add stability to the lives of people who must often change jobs or deal with unsteady hours and do so without limiting their choices about how to utilize their benefits. On the flip side, left-wing detractors fear that UBI will be used to justify paying lower wages and removing existing social support programs, while their right-wing counterparts worry about who will foot the bill—and whether having a steady income will demotivate people from working and contributing to society at all. In a nutshell, there are a million reasons to be for and against this type of initiative.

We've read accounts of UBI experiments in Finland, Canada, Spain, India, Kenya, the Netherlands, and Uganda. In all of these cases, the experiment was temporary and carried out with a small sample of citizens, making it difficult to assess the feasibility of this type of model in a large-scale format.

Many of the arguments about UBI strike us as wrongheaded, as they are measuring an idea that is meant to address a very different future against suppositions that are drawn from the past. UBI doesn't appear to be feasible under current financial structures that estimate the cost of such programs for most countries to be anywhere between 5 to 35 percent of a nation's

GDP, but that doesn't mean it won't ever be possible in the future with different sources of revenue.

But even something as anti-work as UBI can get bogged down in work dogma. In Finland, a proposed experiment outlined a program whereby a sample of 2,000 Finnish citizens received a monthly amount of $675 USD (560 euros) for a period of two years. The proposal was adjusted by the country's conservative government to include only *unemployed* citizens who were receiving unemployment benefits. Completely missing the point of UBI, which is funding that is given with no strings attached, the Finnish government announced that "the primary goal of the basic income experiment is related to promoting employment." They wanted to see if participants in the program would be motivated to find low-paying work if they knew that they wouldn't lose their benefits. In other words, a post-work mechanism designed to free people from dependence on low-paying jobs was transformed into an initiative designed with one goal in mind: getting people to work more low-paying jobs. Cool.

Unsurprisingly, the Finnish government recently announced they would terminate the experiment by the end of 2018, a move applauded by (once again) both sides of Finland's political spectrum. Right-wing politicians declared that "work is the best social security," while the leader of the Social Democratic Party was quoted as saying, "I don't need any basic income. I have a good salary, and if I happen to lose my job, I'd have unemployment benefits." As Antti Jauhiainen and Joona-Hermanni Mäkinen, co-founders of a Finnish think tank focused on participatory democracy, wrote in the *New York Times*, "Universal Income Didn't Fail in Finland. Finland Failed it."[11]

Stephen Hawking advocated for wealth redistribution as the only way to tackle the inequality that is driven by emerging technologies. "If machines produce everything we need, the outcome will depend on how things are distributed," he wrote on Reddit in 2016, during one of the site's famous Ask Me

Anything segments.[12] "Everyone can enjoy a life of luxurious leisure if the machine-produced wealth is shared, or most people can end up miserably poor if the machine-owners successfully lobby against wealth distribution. So far, the trend seems to be toward the second option, with technology driving ever-increasing inequality." Bill Gates has argued that governments should tax robot workers in the same way they do human workers in order to make up for the income tax that will be lost as a result of automation.[13] He, along with Elon Musk, believes that UBI can also provide a much-needed buffer during this turbulent period of disruption, giving society the time to adjust, adapt, and figure out a way to move forward.

Supporters of UBI say it will give people the freedom to spend our time doing something that makes us feel good and gives us a sense of purpose. Detractors insist it will be a calamity to the economy, "a utopian fiction that wastes public money on the rich," and a form of corporate totalitarianism.[14] We're not going to get sidetracked by all of these arguments. At this stage it's far too early to draw any hard and fast conclusions. Fortunately, more and more governments are experimenting with the idea every year. We think it's an important idea to consider, though it will probably bring its own set of unexpected consequences and challenges. We will say that at the heart of many of the arguments against it is a deep and visceral fear. Fear of what it will mean to decouple our work from our finances and of the trauma of being without any work at all.

EMPTY PROMISES OF ENDLESS GROWTH

There are futurists who will tell you that our doom and gloom warnings are needlessly dire—that the new boom of technology will also create brand new jobs and opportunities for employment that we can't imagine right now. Consider all the jobs in IT, cybersecurity, programming, and other fields that didn't exist a few decades ago.

And yes, obviously they do have a point, there will be new in-demand skill sets and fantastical sounding job titles. Some of the more interesting ones we've already come across are Algorithm Ethicist, a position to ensure that the programmed behavior of our technology is free of unintentional (or intentional) biases, and Artificial Intelligence Psychologist, to help the increasingly sophisticated computers navigate our complex, and as it turns out, often nonsensical world. (We can just imagine a poor psychologist trying to explain meme culture to a very confused robot.)

The economic expansion into new industries has always been one way that we've mitigated the costs of rendering large swaths of working skills obsolete (though jobs are disappearing at a faster rate than new sectors are emerging). The other approach has been to double down on productivity gains and to start increasing output in order to justify the need for more labor. Both of these strategies rely on one of the biggest and most fundamental flaws of modern economic theory: the idea of unlimited resources and unlimited growth. While resources and opportunities might have seemed endless during the early days of the Industrial Revolution, it has been made very clear to us now that we are in fact working within hard parameters of space, natural resources, and yes, even human capital. We are already beginning to brush up against some of these limits, as witnessed by the dire warnings about climate change, deforestation, desertification, increased pollution rates, and the alarming endangerment of the bird, fish, and mammal species with whom we share this planet. The idea that we could power through this societal shift simply by continuing to endlessly expand, either with more output or new industries, is also unlikely when you consider the number of people who are going to be out of work. Who is going to buy all this stuff?

Even if we do create new categories of jobs, very few of the displaced workers will qualify for them. What are the odds that a truck driver who was replaced by an autonomous vehicle will be capable of becoming an algorithm specialist? While new opportunities will exist, they will be available to those with the socioeconomic privileges that allow them to adapt, learn, and evolve with the technology. Or to put it another way, a redundant secretary, bank teller, or analyst can drive an Uber or sign up for a microplatform doing ad-hoc tasks. By definition, these are new jobs being provided in this new digital economy, but are they the jobs that we want?

Summary of Big Ideas

➡ We must start thinking about a post-work society as technology disruptions have made it clear that many people will lose their jobs as a result of automation in the coming years.

➡ Experiments around universal basic income are flawed because they do not address "no strings attached" policies and try to fund the programs through current financial means (instead of implementing automation taxation schemes).

➡ We have been conditioned to expect endless growth and will hit hard limits in the near future (population growth and environmental damage). We must plan for alternatives to measure the economy instead of relentless upward growth.

15.

DREAM A NEW DREAM

THE ROAD LESS TRAVELED

Our search for answers about the genesis of our work beliefs has finally come to an end, though the next phase of our
journey, in which we apply all that we've learned to our lives, is
just beginning.

Writing this book was one of the most personally and professionally challenging experiences of my life. As Riwa and I
traced the origins of our work beliefs, I had to confront my own
emotional resistance. Translating our research into a truth that
my own heart would acknowledge was a real struggle for me. I
rarely succeeded on my first (or second, or third) attempts, and
the doubts and sense of failure I felt at every false start would
set me back weeks in delays and procrastination as deadlines
came and went. The shame of not creating was a sickening mix
of guilt and chronic anxiety, and I couldn't shake the stress no
matter how many Buzzfeed quizzes, Netflix binges, or YouTube
rabbit holes I tried to distract myself with.

My progress was slow and uneven, but it was real. What I
didn't realize in the moment but only much later was that my

research wasn't driven by mere curiosity; it was a survival imperative. I *had* to find a better way of creating, of navigating the modern realities of the Productive Creative economy because I simply could not go on as I had before. It's clear to me now that my strong work ethic had betrayed me, that my unending pursuit of higher output and all of the metrics of outward success that go along with it were inflicting more harm on me than good.

The more I chased after productivity, the further I fell behind. I was making myself sick, and because I didn't heed my body's warnings, I landed in a mess of my own making. I was angry at my own weakness and terrified I had done irreparable damage to my core self.

You see, I had tolerated the fatigue and insomnia. I even learned to deal with the hair loss. The one thing I couldn't cope with was my inability to write. At my lowest point, a simple sentence was beyond my capabilities. Worse yet, that engine inside my head, the one that was always buzzing with a million ideas, went completely silent. Losing that part of myself was a devastating blow that knocked me into such a deep depression I questioned whether I had the will (or the strength) to carry on.

What do you do as a writer who can't write?

I blamed myself a lot. Researching this book was cathartic because it helped me understand that it wasn't all my fault, that there were powerful cultural forces that were coloring my perspective, framing the issue in a specific way. Learning that gave me the strength to challenge some of my worst insecurities and gave me the courage to move past them.

As I mentioned in Chapter 13, this awakening comes in two phases. First, we must uncover the hidden causes of our attitudes and behaviors. And then we must apply those lessons in a way that makes sense to us as an individual.

It is my hope that *Hustle & Float*'s holistic approach, spanning a wide cross section of fields such as psychology, anthropology, history, sociology, philosophy, theology, media theory, art history, and more, has made the first part of your journey easier, as you've sought to better understand your own unique, complicated history with work. The questions included in this book are just a starting point. The second half of the work is something you must do for yourself.

It's not a tidy process, and it can't be neatly summed up in a framework. It will be messy and complicated and aggravating. You might have to do it in stages as I did, taking time to absorb and process different ideas. You'll have to find your own path, but it might help if I share a little bit about mine.

I've made a lot of changes in the past year, some small, some big—all helpful.

Breaking free of a continuous output model is the most significant and healthy change I've made in my life so far. We are not machines that can produce the same thing in the same way every single day. We are creatures that are ruled by cycles: seasons, even the moon. Witnessing just how far the quest for productivity had pushed us away from those natural rhythms made me want to become attuned to them once more. I started small: eating seasonally and locally from our local vegetable producers. I tracked my energy during the course of the day and found that I was at my most creative between around four in the afternoon and 1 am, so I learned to structure my day around what worked for me and started ignoring all those paeans to early-rising that I read online. Early risers may crow about how productive they are, but over the course of history there have been just as many geniuses that were night owls. I dug into the research and discovered that there is no one better way. Everyone is wired with specific preferences, so if you're not a morning person, don't let anyone tell you that it will hurt your creative productivity.

The longer I tracked myself, the more patterns I found. I had energy cycles that repeated daily, monthly, and even yearly. Respecting those cycles, I started to plan with them, instead of ignoring them, choosing specific weeks to focus on writing versus other projects. To be clear, there were times when clients, deadlines, and travel interfered, but that's ok—life is unpredictable. I just tried my best to align my work schedule with my natural energy flow whenever possible.

And funnily enough, even though I had all of this research that made the case for why this was a good idea, I still felt surprised when it actually worked. I noticed an improvement in my satisfaction at work, my mood, my energy, and my output. In tracking my energy, I learned about a different side of myself that I never knew before; for the first time, I felt like I was working with my body instead of against it.

Once you become aware of the cycles all around you, your time horizon naturally expands. Technology has imbued us with a false sense of urgency, where everyone wants everything immediately. I've learned to be ok with things taking a little longer.

With my newfound knowledge of my own energy cycles, I started planning things on a yearly scale instead of a daily or weekly one. I used to beat myself up because I wasn't putting in a few hours of fiction writing every day after my work was done. Now, I just set aside a few weekends every quarter to power through word count. It works for me, and it doesn't leave me feeling exhausted or guilty. I set aside time during the summer months to work on side projects like my podcast or to take some extra courses, knowing that in the winter I'll want to stay inside and write more.

So what if my progress isn't even?

You have to find the rhythms and the time horizons that work best for you. What's the point of rushing to a destination if you get sick, and, most importantly of all, don't enjoy the ride?

These changes might sound superficial, but for me, it had never been about not knowing what to do to take better care of myself. It was the frustration of knowing better and not doing it anyway. Researching and writing *Hustle & Float* gave me the perspective and the courage I needed to confront and address some of my deepest issues (my ego, my self-worth, my identity). Once I'd done that, I didn't have to depend on sheer willpower. Understanding the roots of my resistance helped me overcome it.

Once you learn to recognize the narratives that we're sold as Productive Creatives, the narratives lose their power over you. One of the first things I did was to purge my social media feeds of unnecessarily hyper-motivating quotes. "Nobody cares. Work Harder."—unsubscribe. "Hard work. Hustle. Grind." Nope. I blocked people who made me feel like I wasn't doing enough. I stopped reading articles that showed people getting up at ungodly hours to squeeze in more work.

I stopped saying that I was busy and started paying attention to my own displays of Work Devotion. For example, I used to post pictures of how many unread emails I had in my inbox. (Look how busy I am! Look how many people want to reach me!) I don't do that anymore. When we were researching the ego chapter, I was brought up against my own tendency to compare myself to other people (hello, Beyoncé!). Instead, I've started competing with myself, identifying ways that I can keep learning and improving and not worrying so much about what other people are up to. It's made me significantly happier.

I try to be kinder to myself and more realistic about what I can reasonably accomplish in a day. I rest when I need to, even if it's, gasp, during business hours. I have become fanatical about disconnecting during vacations. Breaking free of work and productivity dogma also means reinvesting the time you used to put in overwork in other places. You'd be surprised how much time you free up; it's a great opportunity to spend quality time with family and friends, pick up a new hobby, or do some volunteer work.

In diving into our long history as a species, I was reminded of how recent many of the attitudes we have about work are. The Protestant work ethic that is so entrenched in our lives was created in the sixteenth century, a mere blink in the timeline of our species' existence. That is to say, the ideologies we've built around work are not so old that they can't be challenged, nor are they, despite what we've been brought up to believe, a fundamental part of human nature. But if we don't question these ideas, we'll never break free of them.

I believe this self-reflection is an essential process that all Productive Creatives must go through. Questioning your own reality is never a pleasant experience, though it's an essential one for cultivating a growth-mindset and adaptability, two qualities that our community is going to need more than ever.

IT STARTS WITH YOU

Armed with this knowledge, I hope you'll think about your own behavior, as an individual, but especially if you lead creative teams. Beliefs are collaboratively created, and changes in organizational culture are the first steps in creating better workplaces. Those changes can start out small. Review your policies through the lens of what you've learned about creativity and the brain to see if you're creating optimal conditions for your people to thrive.

Talk to your teams. Talk to your colleagues. Talk to your bosses. Simply acknowledging the presence of the three forces of Systems, Self, and Stories is a great step forward. Making these hidden influences visible reduces their hold on us. We've included some resources for you online to help navigate some of these challenges within an organization, including workshop templates and a list of discussion questions. You'll also find additional material online.

Ultimately, I don't know what is going to happen to our jobs. I don't think anyone truly does. I believe the future will fall (hopefully) somewhere right in the middle of a spectrum between a utopian paradise and a dystopian nightmare. To that end, instead of scaring myself or setting myself up for disappointment by dreaming up future scenarios, I try to ground myself in the present and what we can do today. It starts with getting involved and being informed about the issues at hand.

As citizens, we have a responsibility to consume ethically—and that extends to new technological platforms. We must demand fair compensation and humane working conditions. We have the power to influence companies through our purchasing decisions, and we should support companies that have a vision of the future that includes shared prosperity for all—not just their shareholders. And we should avoid supporting those that don't.

I'm not an idealist. On the contrary, I'm highly pragmatic when it comes to my worldview. I'm pushing for shared prosperity models because, if the events we're seeing unfold are an indication, many of our current business models will be unsustainable over the long-term. Pillaging the Earth with abandon, decimating socioeconomic classes, and creating uncontrollable technology might yield short-term profits, but these practices will certainly bring about a catastrophe in time.

Innovation can no longer come at the cost of livable wages and workplace protections for all labor classes. Our work history is repeating itself, only this time, it's knowledge workers that will have to advocate for these rights, much like our industrial-era predecessors did. The atomization of the labor market into microsegments has succeeded in dividing us into units of one—individual workers who are disconnected from each other, united only in our service to tech conglomerates. We'll need to collaborate to ensure that businesses and politicians are creating policies that protect our interests. No one person can win this fight. There is an African proverb that aptly states: If you want to go fast, go alone. If you want to go far, go together. Our efforts will determine the state of the labor market for generations to come.

DARE TO DREAM

My hair has grown back. A few months after a period of prolonged rest, that still small voice in my brain returned; once again, my creativity began to flow. There was no miracle, no magical ten-step program. There was reflection and a lot of deliberate efforts to create the space I needed to be defined by more than what I could produce. It was a long and often painful journey, but I'm grateful for the lessons that it's taught me about the resilience of the creative spirit.

Remember, the future doesn't happen in a flash—it is gradually shaped by every decision we make in the here and now. Our current crisis of work is also, in a sense, a crisis of imagination. It's up to us, the Creative Productives, the daydreamers, the nap takers, the art makers, to do what we do best: dream up a better future. Now, before it's too late.

I know we're up to the challenge.

ACKNOWLEDGEMENTS

I have been very lucky in my life to find communities of people who have been incredibly generous in donating their time, opinions, expertise, and feedback. This was such a challenging project and I could not have done it without you. Thank you.

First, to my sister, Riwa. This book was shaped by your brilliant vision, ideas, research, and writing. Thank you for walking through Beyoncé's shadow with me and helping me to find the light.

To Arthur Goldwag, my editor. You helped me find my voice. This project wouldn't exist without you. Thank you.

To Cosimo Turroturro, my Yoda, who taught me to think bigger. Thank you.

My agent, Jim Levine, who believed in this project and who tirelessly reviewed proposals, chapter drafts, and endless emails. Thank you.

My editor at Diversion Books, Lia Ottaviano, who fought for *Hustle & Float*. Your sense of humor and support during this process was invaluable. Thank you.

To David Lavin, Charles Yao, Gord Mazur, and the Lavin Team, for helping me bring the message of *Hustle & Float* to life. Thank you.

The Red Thread Team, Heather Moffatt & Antoinette Schatz, for making sure my life stayed on track while I was in my writing cave. Thank you.

My mentor Don Tapscott, who always made time for me when I had questions. Thank you.

To Jay Goldman and Leerom Segal who offered me banter, advice, and fast Wi-Fi at Klick. Thank you.

To David Sarfati, my Krav coach, who understood sometimes the only solution is to punch the crap out of something. Merci.

My mother, Hanan Harfoush, who printed out the whole manuscript and carried it around in an envelope because she wanted to better understand what I was doing. Thank you.

My father, Nabil Harfoush, who calmly talked me off ledges during low points of the creative process. Thank you.

My older sister Rania, who never wavered in her belief that I could do this. Arigato!

My Kingmakers, Dan Dzombak, Kane Sarhan, Niamh Hughes, Kalsoom Lakhani, Fabian Pfortmuller, & DJ Saul. You were there from the beginning. Thank you.

To Richard & Ilse Straub, your guidance, friendship, and support have been wonderful gifts. Danke.

To my coaches, Michelle Saul, Willow O'Brien, & Mary Jane Braide, your patience, guidance, and wisdom gave me the courage to finish what I started. Thank you.

The Parisian cafes that I made my second home: Loustic's Channa & Virginie who celebrated each milestone with me. Kodama's Vincent & Martin, who cheered me up when I had writer's block. Merci.

To Sylvain Debonnet, my self-defense coach, thank you for helping me regain my confidence, fight through fear, and find my zen.

My dear friends: Mitch Joel, Erica Dhawan, Erin Bowser and Gerry, Erin Dahl & PC, Joel Halpern, Lindsay Tramuta, Nate Nicols, John Egan, Sarah Roocroft, Nalini Singh, Amber Mac, Enrique Vessuri, & Dan Ariely.

To everyone who commented on social media with suggestions, feedback, stories, and opinions. Thank you.

NOTES

Introduction

1. http://hackthesystem.com/blog/why-i-hired-a-girl-on-craigslist-to-slap-me-in-the-face-and-why-it-quadrupled-my-productivity/
2. http://www.nytimes.com/2015/05/25/technology/in-busy-silicon-valley-protein-powder-is-in-demand.html?_r=0
3. https://hbr.org/2014/03/should-you-automate-your-life-so-that-you-can-work-harder/?utm_source=Socialflow&utm_medium=Tweet&utm_campaign=Socialflow
4. http://www.lifehack.org/articles/productivity/16-everyday-habits-highly-productive-people.html;
5. http://www.forbes.com/technology/; http://it-jobs.fins.com/Articles/SBB0001424052702303404704577309493661513690/How-Googles-Marissa-Mayer-Manages-Burnout
6. http://allthingsd.com/20110601/jack-dorsey-of-square-and-twitter-live-at-d9/
7. Lyrics, from Six Inch Heels, Beyoncé, Lemonade
8. https://www.theguardian.com/music/musicblog/2010/feb/01/Beyoncé-hardest-working-woman-showbusiness
9. http://www.glamourmagazine.co.uk/article/solange-knowles-asos-magazine-talking-about-Beyoncé
10. From the musical, "Hamilton", Non-Stop, written by Lin Manuel Miranda.
11. http://www.glassdoor.com/blog/average-employee-takes-earned-vacation-time-glassdoor-employment-confidence-survey-q1-2014/
12. http://familiesandwork.org/site/research/reports/OverWorkIn America.pdf
13. http://www.rand.org/pubs/research_reports/RR1791.html
14. http://now.strategiccoach.com/timemanagement
15. See Hustleandfloat.com/resources for a list of additional books.

Chapter 1

1. https://en.wikipedia.org/wiki/Merlin_Mann
2. Observations on some points of seamanship, with practical hints on naval economy. Anslem john Griffiths. Page 107. Second Edition.

3. http://www.cmqr.rmit.edu.au/publications/jdtaylordeming.pdf
4. http://www.cmqr.rmit.edu.au/publications/jdtaylordeming.pdf
5. http://www.bls.gov/TUS/CHARTS/HOUSEHOLD.HTM
6. http://www.forbes.com/sites/learnvest/2013/06/14/why-men-dont-take-paternity-leave/
7. http://www.independent.co.uk/life-style/health-and-families/health-news/half-of-all-mothers-will-not-take-full-maternity-leave-because-they-are-scared-of-losing-their-jobs-9468452.html
8. https://media.netflix.com/en/company-blog/starting-now-at-netflix-unlimited-maternity-and-paternity-leave; Unlimited Vacation is a perk at approximately 1% of companies according to: https://www.washingtonpost.com/news/on-leadership/wp/2015/10/08/what-your-company-gains-when-it-gives-you-unlimited-vacation/; http://www.fastcompany.com/3051537/fast-feed/kickstarter-nixes-unlimited-vacation-time-for-employees?partner=superfeed
9. http://www.bloombergview.com/articles/2015-09-30/-unlimited-vacation-is-code-for-no-vacation-
10. http://thenextweb.com/opinion/2015/08/05/true-life-im-a-workaholic/
11. Michele Lamont, Money, Manners (chapter 2, pg 33)
12. Time Without Work: People who are not working tell their stories, how they feel, what they do, how they survive. By Walli F. Leff and Marilyn G. Haft (South End Press, 1983, page 27)
13. https://hbr.org/2013/05/why-men-work-so-many-hours/
14. Based on the hilarious Louis CK sketch about beliefs and our refusal to give them up.
15. http://people.hmdc.harvard.edu/~akozaryn/myweb/docs/final_work_to_live.pdf

Chapter 2

1. http://business.time.com/2013/04/26/the-time-creativity-poll/
2. Plato in The Republic (Resp. 597 D.)
3. https://www.theatlantic.com/entertainment/archive/2014/10/humanitys-earliest-art-was-spray-painted-graffiti/381259/
4. http://www.slate.com/blogs/quora/2015/01/09/what_s_the_difference_between_the_renaissance_and_the_enlightenment.html
5. Morner, Kathleen and Ralph Rausch. NTC's Dictionary of Literary Terms. Chicago: NTC Publishing Group, 1997.
6. Morner, Kathleen and Ralph Rausch. NTC's Dictionary of Literary Terms. Chicago: NTC Publishing Group, 1997.
7. http://openaccess.city.ac.uk/2955/5/Managing_Creativity_in_the_Cultural_Industries.pdf

8. Explaining Creativity https://books.google.co.uk/books?id= by7KBNosWVcC&pg=PA16&lpg=PA16&dq=rational+vs+romantic+ creativity&source=bl&ots=2S-cPCqJJw&sig=c3QZfIHt_Jg4LT69 EfZ89OAmYm4&hl=en&sa=X&ved=0ahUKEwjp3Iva2u3LAhW HaxQKHUo-BVEQ6AEIQzAH#v=onepage&q=rational%20vs%20 romantic%20creativity&f=false
9. History of 6 Ideas http://www.scribd.com/doc/225918776/ Wladyslaw-Tatarkiewicz-A-History-of-Six-Ideas-an-Essay-in-Aesthetics#scribd
10. http://members.optusnet.com.au/charles57/Creative/Brain/wallis.htm
11. http://arts.gov.au/sites/default/files/creative-industries/sdip/ strategic-digital-industry-plan.pdf
12. http://mayflybooks.org/?page_id=74
13. Elizabeth Wilson, Bohemians: The Glamorous Outcasts
14. http://www.adobe.com/aboutadobe/pressroom/pdfs/Adobe_State_of_ Create_Global_Benchmark_Study.pdf
15. http://www.newyorker.com/books/joshua-rothman/creativity-creep
16. https://wciw.org/about/history/

Chapter 3

1. https://en.wikipedia.org/wiki/Kar%C5%8Dshi
2. http://www.japantimes.co.jp/opinion/2014/11/15/editorials/getting-a-grip-on-karoshi/#.Vs8MXJMrKu7
3. http://www.economywatch.com/features/Government-moves-to-end-Japans-culture-of-death-by-overwork.03-05-15.html
4. http://nypost.com/2015/02/06/japans-plan-to-stop-employees-from-working-themselves-to-death/
5. http://www.economist.com/node/10329261
6. http://www.irishtimes.com/news/world/asia-pacific/overwork-remains-a-fatal-flaw-in-japanese-society-1.1815617
7. http://www.theguardian.com/world/2016/jan/07/kensuke-miyazaki-to-become-first-ever-japanese-mp-to-take-paternity-leave
8. https://www.cesifo-group.de/ifoHome/facts/DICE/Social-Policy/ Family/Work-Family-Balance/parental-leave-entitlements-historical-perspective/fileBinary/parental-leave-entitlements-historical-perspective.pdf; Initially, not all employees were eligible, but today nearly 100% of Japanese companies comply with these regulations.
9. http://www.theguardian.com/world/2016/jan/07/kensuke-miyazaki-to-become-first-ever-japanese-mp-to-take-paternity-leave
10. http://themarketmogul.com/core-features-traditional-japanese-corporations/
11. http://nypost.com/2015/02/06/japans-plan-to-stop-employees-from-working-themselves-to-death/

12. http://www.news.com.au/technology/dying-at-their-desks-the-countries-where-people-die-of-overwork/story-e6frfrnr-1226972701500
13. http://stats.oecd.org/Index.aspx?DataSetCode=ANHRS
14. It should be noted that while American hours have declined as well, most experts agree that the actual amount of hours worked is higher, due to undeclared overtime and the general overwork by white collar workers.; http://stats.oecd.org/Index.aspx?DataSetCode=ANHRS
15. http://www.theguardian.com/world/2015/feb/22/japan-long-hours-work-culture-overwork-paid-holiday-law
16. http://www.onlinepsychologydegree.net/2013/04/25/workaholism-in-a-21st-century-context/
17. http://delong.typepad.com/sdj/2011/01/the-end-of-procyclical-labor-productivity.html
18. http://www.motherjones.com/politics/2011/06/speed-up-american-workers-long-hours
19. Investigation of concentration of economic power. Final report and recommendation. By the United States Temporary National Economic Committee, page 105, chapter 5.
20. Aspirations and Anxieties: New England Workers and the Mechanized Factory, by Madison David A Zonderman. Pg. 33.
21. Aspirations and Anxieties: New England Workers and the Mechanized Factory Pg. 33
22. History of Pennsylvania, Philip S. Klein, pg. 221
23. South Carolina: A History, by Walter B. Edgar, pg 88.
24. South Carolina: A History, by Walter B. Edgar, pg 88.
25. https://en.wikisource.org/wiki/1911_Encyclop%C3%A6dia_Britannica/Owen,_Robert
26. http://psychclassics.yorku.ca/Munster/Industrial/chap17.htm
27. http://www.salon.com/2012/03/14/bring_back_the_40_hour_work_week/
28. http://www.hcgexperts.com/scheduled-overtime-effect-on-construction-projects.php
29. Sydney chapman, 1909 research paper, "Hours of Labor," published in the Economic Journal.
30. https://ccskills.org.uk/supporters/blog/freelancing-and-the-future-of-creative-jobs
31. https://www.brookings.edu/bpea-articles/mortality-and-morbidity-in-the-21st-century/
32. http://www.adobe.com/content/dam/acom/en/max/pdfs/AdobeStateofCreate_2016_Report_Final.pdf

Chapter 4

1. https://www.vanityfair.com/news/2016/09/elizabeth-holmes-theranos-exclusive

2. Key Concepts of Puritanism and the shaping of the American Cultural Identity, Andreea Mingiuc, Iasi University, Romania. (Pg. 210)

3. "A town built upon a hill cannot be hidden." (John 8:12)

4. https://en.wikisource.org/wiki/Address_of_President-Elect_John_F._Kennedy_Delivered_to_a_Joint_Convention_of_the_General_Court_of_the_Commonwealth_of_Massachusetts; Ronald Regan's 1980 Election Eve Address, "A vision for America"; Commencement Address by Senator Barack Obama June 2, 2006, University of Massachusetts Boston.

5. Key Concepts of Puritanism and the shaping of the American Cultural Identity, Andreea Mingiuc, Iasi University, Romania. (Pg. 213)

6. Worldly Saints: the Puritans as They Really Were, Leland Ryken (Pg.3, 30)

7. Richard Nixon, Address to the Nation on Labor Day, September 6, 1971 (http://www.presidency.ucsb.edu/ws/?pid=3138)

8. Self-Made Men. Seymour, C. B. Charles. 1858 Harpers press. Pg 428.

9. H.W. Brands, The age of gold: the California Gold Rush and the new American Dream (2003) pg 442

10. http://www.city-journal.org/html/whatever-happened-work-ethic-13209.html

11. We know. It's a horrible title.

12. Scharnhorst, Gary; Bales, Jack (1981). Horatio Alger Jr.: An Annotated Bibliography of Comment and Criticism. Scarecrow Press

13. https://horatioalger.org/about-us/

14. https://www.huduser.gov/periodicals/ushmc/summer94/summer94.html

15. Historical Dictionary of the 1950s, James Stuart Olson, pg 4.

16. Second Rate Nation: From the American Dream to the American Myth, Sam D. Seiber

17. The Progress Paradox: How Life Gets Better While People Feel Worse, George Easterbrook.

18. "What teens really think," Morin, Richard. Washington Post, Oct 23, 2005 https://www.washingtonpost.com/archive/lifestyle/magazine/2005/10/23/what-teens-really-think/9ffff170-b5e5-4c19-a1d5-c480c9fb00dc/

19. http://www.teenvogue.com/story/celebrity-fame-obsession

20. Celebrity Culture and the American Dream: Stardom and Social Mobility. Sternheimer, Karen. Pg 249

21. https://www.nytimes.com/2015/08/02/opinion/sunday/were-making-life-too-hard-for-millennials.html?smid=pl-share

22. https://www.nytimes.com/2015/08/02/opinion/sunday/were-making-life-too-hard-for-millennials.html?smid=pl-share
23. https://en.wikipedia.org/wiki/Twitter

Chapter 5

1. http://www.theatlantic.com/business/archive/2015/06/millennials-housing-purchase-money/396293/
2. http://www.vanityfair.com/news/2016/02/bill-gates-admits-he-was-a-nightmare-boss
3. https://www.quora.com/How-many-hours-a-week-does-Mark-Zuckerberg-actually-work-at-the-Facebook-office
4. https://www.entrepreneur.com/article/251020
5. http://gawker.com/5834158/tim-cook-apples-new-ceo-and-the-most-powerful-gay-man-in-america
6. http://www.businessinsider.com/the-truth-about-marissa-mayer-she-has-two-contrasting-reputations-2012-7?IR=T
7. http://upstart.bizjournals.com/executives/features/2008/06/16/Starbucks-CEO-Howard-Schultz-Profile.html?page=all
8. http://uk.businessinsider.com/most-popular-youtuber-stars-salaries-2017?r=US&IR=T/#no-1-pewdiepie-541-million-subscribers-18
9. http://www.brainyquote.com/quotes/quotes/c/confucius134717.html
10. https://news.stanford.edu/2005/06/14/jobs-061505/
11. http://www.indiebound.org/book/9781941393475
12. http://www.lrb.co.uk/v35/n01/paul-myerscough/short-cuts
13. http://www.independent.co.uk/voices/want-the-uk-to-leave-europe-youre-suffering-from-british-special-snowflake-syndrome-and-you-need-to-a6853141.html
14. http://www.artofmanliness.com/2010/05/24/finding-your-calling-part-i-what-is-a-vocation/
15. https://hbr.org/2012/09/solving-gen-ys-passion-problem
16. http://nypost.com/2010/05/10/the-worst-generation/
17. https://www.psychologytoday.com/blog/freedom-learn/201509/declining-student-resilience-serious-problem-colleges
18. http://www.forbes.com/sites/kathycaprino/2015/02/11/why-figuring-out-your-best-career-is-a-spiritual-endeavor/#6ed26d6d4998
19. https://www.amazon.co.uk/Buddha-Walks-into-Office-Livelihood/dp/1611800617
20. https://www.goodreads.com/author/quotes/29655.Rhonda_Byrne
21. http://www.chopra.com/the-seven-spiritual-laws-of-success
22. http://www.pewtrusts.org/en/research-and-analysis/reports/0001/01/01/pursuing-the-american-dream
23. http://www.nytimes.com/roomfordebate/2015/01/01/is-the-modern-american-dream-attainable/the-numbers-show-rags-to-riches-happens-only-in-movies

24. http://bigthink.com/think-tank/millennials-first-modern-generation-doing-worse-economically-than-their-parents
25. http://www.bloomberg.com/news/articles/2014-01-24/goldman-2013-corporate-profits-grew-five-times-faster-than-wages
26. http://fivethirtyeight.com/features/the-american-middle-class-hasnt-gotten-a-raise-in-15-years/

Chapter 6

1. http://www.abrahamlincolnassociation.org/Newsletters/5-3.pdf
2. http://www.merriam-webster.com/dictionary/hustle
3. http://www.whiteboardbusiness.com/always-be-hustling/
4. http://www.forbes.com/sites/85broads/2013/12/10/learning-how-to-hustle/#57c4271947f3
5. http://tommorkes.com/hustle/
6. https://www.youtube.com/watch?v=PIJElPStJpg
7. https://books.google.fr/books?id=3ETfBQAAQBAJ&pg=PA198&lpg=PA198&dq=work+ethic+depicted+in+film&source=bl&ots=kZCO7CsCTy&sig=B01iuy9TcRcblLDK9-NHFOa9yes&hl=en&sa=X&redir_esc=y#v=onepage&q=work%20ethic%20depicted%20in%20film&f=false
8. http://www.lifehack.org/articles/productivity/8-things-successful-people-sacrifice-for-their-success.html
9. https://www.opendemocracy.net/5050/ruth-rosen/who-said-%E2%80%9Cwe-could-have-it-all%E2%80%9D
10. The World Split Open, Ruth Rosen, pg. 12-13 https://play.google.com/books/reader?id=hdjNDvvlFbEC&printsec=frontcover&output=reader&hl=en&pg=GBS.PA2010.w.1.2.50
11. http://www.theatlantic.com/magazine/archive/2012/07/why-women-still-cant-have-it-all/309020/
12. http://christinehassler.com/2010/04/the-myth-of-having-it-all/
13. http://www.slate.com/articles/double_x/doublex/2014/04/arianna_huffington_s_thrive_reviewed.html
14. http://www.usatoday.com/story/money/columnist/kay/2013/08/31/at-work-self-esteem-depression/2736083/
15. Mike W Martin, Happiness and The Good life https://books.google.co.uk/books?id=xIxpAgAAQBAJ&pg=PA130&lpg=PA130&dq=joanne+ciulla+we+have+gone+beyond+work+ethic&source=bl&ots=3nByZNe8sn&sig=EviIavD8HTxMvGCuYr2BFz4JjzY&hl=en&sa=X&ved=0ahUKEwjowdzKwfXMAhUNL1IKHdC-BqkQ6AEIIjAB#v=onepage&q=joanne%20ciulla%20we%20have%20gone%20beyond%20work%20ethic&f=false
16. Joanne Ciulla, The Working Life https://books.google.co.uk/books?id=06jjhGFWkakC&printsec=frontcover&dq=the+working+life+the+promise+and+betrayal+of+modern+work&hl=en&sa=X&ved=

oahUKEwjUwem8xPXMAhVGeFIKHYJWAXsQ6AEIHTAA#v=
onepage&q&f=false

17. http://www.usatoday.com/story/money/columnist/kay/2013/08/31/
at-work-self-esteem-depression/2736083/

18. https://www.psychologytoday.com/articles/200310/self-esteem-work

19. https://hbr.org/2010/10/how-much-are-you-worth.html

20. http://mag.havasww.com/prosumer-report/the-modern-nomad/
(I downloaded and have the report)

21. http://www.adweek.com/news/technology/were-not-nearly-busy-we-
pretend-be-according-new-study-166785

22. http://www.bls.gov/news.release/empsit.t09.htm

23. http://www.thebookoflife.org/you-are-not-what-you-earn/

24. http://www.huffingtonpost.com/ellen-huerta/why-i-left-google_b_
3795140.html

Chapter 7

1. http://pps.sagepub.com/content/7/4/352

2. http://www.sciencedirect.com/science/article/pii/B97801237050
99001819

3. Kalina Christoff, Alan M. Gordon, Jonathan Smallwood, Rachelle
Smith, and Jonathan W. Schooler. Experience sampling during fMRI
reveals default network and executive system contributions to mind
wandering. *Proceedings of the National Academy of Sciences*, 2009

4. http://www.your-brain-at-work.com/files/NLJ_SCARFUS.pdf

5. http://www.your-brain-at-work.com/files/NLJ_SCARFUS.pdf

6. Schoenewolf, G., (1990). Emotional contagion: Behavioral induction
in individuals and groups.' 'Modern Psychoanalysis; 15, 49-61

7. The Willpower Instinct, Kelly McGonigal

8. http://www.pnas.org/content/111/24/8788.full

9. http://www.mysahana.org/2011/05/emotion-suppression-effects-on-
mental-and-physical-health/

10. https://www.psychologytoday.com/blog/changepower/201504/why-
saying-just-one-word-can-calm-runaway-emotions

11. http://lifehacker.com/5991392/calm-yourself-by-labeling-negative-
feelings

12. http://www.npr.org/templates/story/story.php?storyId=95256794

13. http://www.huffingtonpost.com/2015/01/31/multitasking-brain_n_
6564738.html

Chapter 8

1. Kuszewski, Andrea Marie, The Genetics of Creativity: A Serendipitous
Assemblage of Madness (March 1, 2009). METODO Working Papers,
No. 58. Available at SSRN: http://ssrn.com/abstract=1393603

2. The Genetics of Creativity research paper
3. Wallas, G (1926) The Art of Thought. New York: Harcourt Brace
4. Rossman, J (1931) The Psychology of the Inventor. Washington DC: Inventor's Publishing
5. Osborn, A (1953) Applied Imagination. New York: Charles Scribner
6. https://en.wikipedia.org/wiki/Torrance_Tests_of_Creative_Thinking; Runco, M. A., Millar, G., Acar, S., Cramond, B. (2010) Torrance Tests of Creative Thinking as Predictors of Personal and Public Achievement: A Fifty Year Follow-Up. Creativity Research Journal, 22 (4). DOI: 10.1080/10400419.2010.523393.
7. Phares, E.J.; Chaplin, W.F. (1997). *Introduction to personality* (Fourth ed.). New York: Longman. pp. 8–9. ISBN 0-673-99456-2.
8. Myers, Isabel Briggs with Peter B. Myers (1995) [1980]. *Gifts Differing: Understanding Personality Type*. Mountain View, CA: Davies-Black Publishing. ISBN 0-89106-074-X.
9. Skinner, B.F. (1938). *Behavior of Organisms*. New York: Appleton-Century-Crofts
10. Sobel, Dava (August 20, 1990). "B. F. Skinner, the Champion of Behaviorism, Is Dead at 86". *The New York Times*
11. A bobo doll is a five foot tall inflatable toy, that was bottom weighted so would pop up after being hit. It was normally painted to look like a clown, and the authors think that it is horrifying.
12. Lauridsen Kurt (ed) and Whyte, Cassandra B. (1985) An Integrated Counseling and Learning Assistance Center-Chapter for New Directions Sourcebook. Jossey-Bass, Inc
13. Phares, E.J.; Chaplin, W.F. (1997). *Introduction to personality* (Fourth ed.). New York: Longman. pp. 8–9. ISBN 0-673-99456-2.
14. Silvia, P. J., Nusbaum, E. C., Berg, C., Martin, C., & O'Conner, A. (in press). Openness to experience, plasticity, and creativity: Exploring lower-order, higher-order, and interactive effects. Journal of Research in Personality. Article in Press. doi:10.1016/j.jrp.2009.04.015
15. Toward an Integrative Model of Creativity and Personality: Theoretical Suggestions and Preliminary Empirical Testing. (Publication of the Creative Education Foundation) The Journal of Creative Behavior, Vol. 0, Iss. 0, pp. 1–24 © 2014 by the Creative Education Foundation, Inc. DOI: 10.1002/jocb.71
16. DeYoung, 2006 C.G. DeYoung, Higher-order factors of the Big Five in a multi-informant sample, Journal of Personality and Social Psychology 91 (2006), pp. 1138–1151.
17. We recognize the limitations of this paper due to the small sample size, but believe the extensive review of previous research coupled with the new model offer a comprehensive look at these interplaying factors.
18. Creative People Must Be Stopped: 6 Ways We Kill Innovation (Without Even Trying), David A Owens, Wiley and Sons, 2011.

19. http://lifehacker.com/the-seven-elements-of-a-creative-personality-480346063

20. Stafford, L., Ng, W., Moore, R., & Bard, K. (2010). Bolder, happier, smarter: The role of extraversion in positive mood and cognition. *Personality and Individual Differences*, 48(7), 827-832 DOI: 10.1016/j.paid.2010.02.005

21. https://en.wikipedia.org/wiki/Stephen_King

22. BROOKS WAS HERE.

23. https://en.wikipedia.org/wiki/Tabitha_King

24. https://en.wikipedia.org/wiki/Joe_Hill_(writer)

25. https://en.wikipedia.org/wiki/Owen_King

26. https://en.wikipedia.org/wiki/Kingsley_Amis

27. https://en.wikipedia.org/wiki/Bront%C3%AB_family

28. Maybe soon to be followed by the Harfoush Sisters? ;)

29. "Hereditary Genius," Richard Galton, 1869, Introductory Chapter, B

30. Kyaga, S., Lichtenstein, P., Boman, M., Hultman, C., Langstrom, N., & Landen, M. (2011). Creativity and mental disorder: family study of 300 000 people with severe mental disorder. *The British Journal of Psychiatry*, 199 (5), 373-379 DOI:10.1192/bjp.bp.110.085316

31. Tan YT, McPherson GE, Peretz I, Berkovic SF, & Wilson SJ (2014). The genetic basis of music ability. *Frontiers in psychology, 5*, PMID: 25018744; Genome-wide copy number variation analysis in extended families and unrelated individuals characterized for musical aptitude and creativity in music. Ukkola-Vuoti L, Kanduri C, Oikkonen J, Buck G, Blancher C, Raijas P, Karma K, Lähdesmäki H, Järvelä I. PLoS One. 2013;8(2):e56356. doi: 10.1371/journal.pone.0056356. Epub 2013 Feb 27.

32. Ukkola-Vuoti, L., Kanduri, C., Oikkonen, J., Buck, G., Blancher, C., Raijas, P., Karma, K., Lähdesmäki, H., & Järvelä, I. (2013). Genome-Wide Copy Number Variation Analysis in Extended Families and Unrelated Individuals Characterized for Musical Aptitude and Creativity in Music. *PLoS ONE*, 8 (2) DOI: 10.1371/journal.pone.0056356

33. http://www.ncbi.nlm.nih.gov/pubmed/23460800

34. Engelmann, Jan B.; Damaraju, Eswar; Padmala, Srikanth; Pessoa, Luiz (2009). "Combined Effects of Attention and Motivation on Visual Task Performance: Transient and Sustained Motivational Effects". *Frontiers in Human Neuroscience*. 3.

35. Heilbronner S, Platt M. Causal evidence of performance monitoring by neurons in posterior cingulate cortex during learning. *Neuron*. 2013.

36. Leech R, Sharp DJ (July 2013). "The role of the posterior cingulate cortex in cognition and disease". Brain.137 (Pt 1): 12−32.

37. Pearson, John M.; Heilbronner, Sarah R.; Barack, David L.; Hayden, Benjamin Y.; Platt, Michael L. (April 2011). "Posterior cingulate cortex: adapting behavior to a changing world". *Trends in Cognitive Sciences*. 15 (4): 143−151.

38. Kraus, C., Ganger, S., Losak, J., Hahn, A., Savli, M., Kranz, G., Baldinger, P., Windischberger, C., Kasper, S., & Lanzenberger, R. (2014). Gray matter and intrinsic network changes in the posterior cingulate cortex after selective serotonin reuptake inhibitor intake *NeuroImage*, 84, 236-244 DOI: 10.1016/j.neuroimage.2013.08.036

39. Mann JJ, Huang YY, Underwood MD, Kassir SA, Oppenheim S, Kelly TM, Dwork AJ, & Arango V (2000). A serotonin transporter gene promoter polymorphism (5-HTTLPR) and prefrontal cortical binding in major depression and suicide. Archives of general psychiatry, 57 (8), 729-38 PMID: 10920459

40. Jones BF, Barnes J, Uylings HBM, et al. Differential Regional Atrophy of the Cingulate Gyrus in Alzheimer Disease: A Volumetric MRI Study. *Neuroscience*. 2006.

41. Moore, D., Bhadelia, R., Billings, R., Fulwiler, C., Heilman, K., Rood, K., & Gansler, D. (2009). Hemispheric connectivity and the visual—spatial divergent-thinking component of creativityBrain and Cognition, 70 (3), 267-272 DOI: 10.1016/j.bandc.2009.02.011

42. https://med.stanford.edu/news/all-news/2015/05/researchers-tie-unexpected-brain-structures-to-creativity.html

43. Front. Hum. Neurosci., 08 July 2013 | http://dx.doi.org/10.3389/fnhum.2013.00330 The structure of creative cognition in the human brain. Rex E. Jung*, Brittany S. Mead, Jessica Carrasco and Ranee A. Flores

44. https://med.stanford.edu/news/all-news/2015/05/researchers-tie-unexpected-brain-structures-to-creativity.html

45. http://www.theatlantic.com/science/archive/2016/03/the-driving-principles-behind-creativity/474621/

Chapter 9

1. http://historynewsnetwork.org/article/46460

2. Study, Dr. Michael Argyle: https://personal.eur.nl/veenhoven/Pub1980s/89a-C9-full.pdf

3. Warr, Peter, (2009). The Joy of Work? Jobs, Happiness and You. 1st ed: Routledge

4. Morrow, I. J. (2011). "Review of 'the joy of work? jobs, happiness, and you'". *Personnel Psychology*. 64 (3): 808–811. doi:10.1111/j.1744-6570.2011.01226_3.x.

5. https://www.esquire.com/uk/life/fitness-wellbeing/news/a4915/matthieu-ricard-what-ive-learned/

6. https://www.ted.com/talks/chade_meng_tan_everyday_compassion_at_google/transcript#t-216173

7. https://www.versobooks.com/books/2162-the-happiness-industry

8. http://apps.nlrb.gov/link/document.aspx/09031d45820a5493

9. https://s3.amazonaws.com/ghc-2018/UAE/Global+Happiness+Policy+Report+-+Full.pdf

10. https://press.princeton.edu/titles/9269.html
11. https://www.medicalnewstoday.com/releases/225526.php
12. https://warwick.ac.uk/fac/soc/economics/staff/dsgroi/impact/hp_briefing.pdf
13. Study: Warwick Univserity http://www.futurity.org/work-better-happy/
14. https://hbr.org/2012/01/positive-intelligence
15. http://www.nytimes.com/2011/09/04/opinion/sunday/do-happier-people-work-harder.html?_r=1
16. http://sea-globe.com/workplace-stress-productivity/
17. https://hbr.org/2012/01/the-science-behind-the-smile
18. Eckersley, R. 2009. Progress, culture and young people's wellbeing. In A. Furlong (ed). Handbook of Youth and Young Adulthood: New perspectives and agendas. Routledge, London, pp. 353-360.
19. Organizational Behavior and Human Decision Processes, 2009, vol. 108, issue 1, 25-38
20. http://www.aom.pace.edu/News/Press-Releases/Good-moods-are-fine,-but-it-s-in-tandem-with-bad-ones-that-they-most-boost-workers--creativity,-study-suggests.aspx?terms=mood%20performance%20Rice
21. http://webwriterspotlight.com/happiness-can-make-you-less-creative-competitive
22. It's like rain, on your wedding day. It's a free ride, when you've already paid. It's good advice, you just can't take. Who would have thought, it figures?

Chapter 10

1. http://pages.teamexos.com
2. https://hbr.org/2001/01/the-making-of-a-corporate-athlete
3. https://hbr.org/2001/01/the-making-of-a-corporate-athlete
4. https://hbr.org/2001/01/the-making-of-a-corporate-athlete
5. https://hbr.org/2006/12/extreme-jobs-the-dangerous-allure-of-the-70-hour-workweek/ar/1
6. https://hbr.org/2006/12/extreme-jobs-the-dangerous-allure-of-the-70-hour-workweek/ar/1
7. http://www.workaholics-anonymous.org/pdf_files/wafamilyfriends.pdf
8. http://www.science20.com/news_articles/workaholics_the_socially_acceptable_addiction_of_the_21st_century-142577
9. https://hbr.org/2006/12/extreme-jobs-the-dangerous-allure-of-the-70-hour-workweek/ar/1
10. http://www.bloomberg.com/news/articles/2008-05-22/conditioning-the-corporate-athletebusinessweek-business-news-stock-market-and-financial-advice

11. Pronounced: Mee-high Chick-sent-me-high-ee - you're welcome.
12. Creativity: The Work and Lives of 91 Eminent People, by Mihaly Csikszentmihalyi, published by HarperCollins, 1996, retitled as: Creativity: Flow and the Psychology of Discovery and Invention.
13. Cantankerous creativity: Honest-Humility, Agreeableness, and the HEXACO structure of creative achievement. Paul J Silvia, James C. Kaufman, Roni Reiter-Palmon, Benjamin Wigert. Personality and Individual Differencs, Volume 51, Issue 5, October 2011, pages 687-689 http://dx.doi.org/10.1016/j.paid.2011.06.011
14. http://bodyodd.nbcnews.com/_news/2011/07/21/7114042-creative-types-are-full-of-themselves-study-confirms
15. http://insight.kellogg.northwestern.edu/article/losing_touch
16. "Overlooked but not untouched: How rudeness reduces onlookers' performance on routine and creative tasks" from Organizational Behavior and Human Decision Processes, Volume 109, Issue 1, May 2009, Pages 29-44
17. While the paper argues that both working hours have decreased (globally) and leisure time has increased, the research paper only looks at figures between 1965 and 2003, where as shown in our research in chapter 2 and 3, employees were enjoying more stability and power. This changed (along with working hours, during and after the 2008 crisis.;
18. http://www.bls.gov/tus/
19. http://qz.com/678208/the-inequality-that-matters-most-hint-its-not-income/; "Would you be happier if you were richer? A focusing illusion", by Daniel Kahneman et al, Science, 2006
20. "The expanding workweek? Understanding trends in long work hours among US men, 1979-2004", by Peter Kuhn and Fernando Lozano, National Bureau of Economic Research, 2008

Chapter 11

1. http://www.ncbi.nlm.nih.gov/pmc/articles/PMC3230825/
2. https://baptistnews.com/2014/11/19/author-cites-alarming-trends-in-pastor-burnout/
3. The Burnout Companion To Study and practice: a critical analysis. Wilmar Schaufell, D. Enzmann
4. Burnout: History of a Phenomenon, Flavio Muheim, 2012, Springer Press.
5. http://journals.plos.org/plosone/article?id=10.1371/journal.pone.0104550
6. http://www.ucl.ac.uk/news/news-articles/1005/10051205#sthash.58uU4Iyw.dpuf
7. http://businessjournal.gallup.com/content/162953/tackle-employees-stagnating-engagement.aspx

Notes

8. http://www.who.int/mental_health/media/en/712.pdf
9. http://www.independent.co.uk/life-style/health-and-families/health-news/depression-and-burn-out-at-work-afflict-one-third-of-employees-9294596.html
10. https://gigaom.com/2012/07/05/former-france-telecom-ceo-indicted-over-35-suicides/
11. http://www.dw.com/en/workplace-stress-is-costing-germany-time-money-health/a-16557927
12. http://neurosky.com/2015/04/stress-a-300-billion-cost-to-the-american-economy/
13. https://osha.europa.eu/en/tools-and-publications/publications/literature_reviews/calculating-the-cost-of-work-related-stress-and-psychosocial-risks
14. http://www.workplaceoptions.com/polls/analysis-of-global-eap-data-reveals-huge-rise-in-depression-stress-and-anxiety-over-past-three-years/
15. http://www.who.int/mental_health/management/depression/wfmh_paper_depression_wmhd_2012.pdf
16. http://www.who.int/mediacentre/news/releases/2016/depression-anxiety-treatment/en/
17. http://www.who.int/mediacentre/news/releases/2016/depression-anxiety-treatment/en/
18. https://newrepublic.com/article/120669/2014-year-mindfulness-religion-rich
19. https://www.amazon.com/Mindful-Work-Meditation-Changing-Business-ebook/dp/B00LZ7GPH4?ie=UTF8&btkr=1&ref_=dp-kindle-redirect
20. http://www.fastcompany.com/3030120/bottom-line/why-work-life-integration-trumps-work-life-balance
21. https://www.harpercollins.com/9780062302519/the-business-romantic
22. https://www.amazon.co.uk/Leading-Life-Want-Stewart-Friedman/dp/1422189414
23. https://news.gallup.com/reports/199961/7.aspx?utm_source=gbj&utm_campaign=StateofAmericanWorkplace-Launch&utm_medium=copy&utm_content=20170224; http://www.gallup.com/poll/181289/majority-employees-not-engaged-despite-gains-2014.aspx
24. http://www.hrzone.com/perform/people/a-ticking-time-bomb-the-workplace-stress-epidemic
25. http://www.theguardian.com/world/2014/aug/18/japanese-firms-encourage-workers-sleep-on-job